Enhancing Multilingual Development

This accessible volume presents an up-to-date overview of how young children, older youth, and adults develop multilingual proficiencies. Importantly, it highlights an assets view of multilingualism, offering clear recognition that multilingual competencies are both functional and highly valued in communities across the globe.

Dispelling common myths, it explores the benefits of multilingualism spanning interpersonal, academic, and professional settings. With these settings in mind, the book provides practical information on how professionals can promote effective communication with colleagues and clients from a variety of language backgrounds. Each chapter comes equipped with a series of true or false statements where you can record your predictions and learn as you read. Chapters cover topics including the economic and cognitive benefits of multilingualism, social influences, the age factor, family bilingualism and optimal teaching and learning conditions. Finally, the book concludes by providing various step-by-step resources for creating optimal conditions that further develop and support multilingualism in your professional field.

Containing suggestions for research-based practices in home, school, and professional settings to enhance multilingual development, this book is essential for professionals working with multilingual young children, older youth, and adults, as well as those who require a foundational understanding of multilingualism.

Nadeen T. Ruiz is Professor Emeritus in bilingual multicultural education at California State University Sacramento (CSU), Sacramento, USA. Formerly, Dr. Ruiz was Chair of Bilingual Multicultural Education at CSU. Dr. Ruiz is the author of over 40 articles and books on students' bilingualism and biliteracy, and on the preparation of bilingual teachers, regularly presenting on these topics at national and international conferences.

Andrea García is a principal research associate at Westat. Formerly, Dr. García was an associate professor in literacy studies at Hofstra University, New York, USA, teaching courses in literacy, biliteracy, literacy evaluation, and qualitative research. She continues to pursue her academic interests teaching a graduate course at Columbia University and serves in the executive board of Words of Words Center for Global Literacies and Literatures.

Applying Child and Adolescent Development in the Professions Series

Kimberly A. Gordon Biddle, *Emeritus Professor of Child and Adolescent Development, Sacramento State, California, USA*

The field of Child and Adolescent Development is being recognized and legitimized more and more as good preparation for a variety of careers in various fields, such as psychology, education, allied health, non-profits, and social work. As more theories are created and research is conducted, more attention and recognition are given to the field of Child and Adolescent Development.

This series will take the core and current topics in the field of Child and Adolescent Development, define these topics, describe these topics as they develop in children from infancy to age 25 or describe how the topic impacts children from infancy to age 25, and then apply them to careers in five main fields, psychology, education, allied health, non-profits, and social work. Various application strategies and techniques will be shared. The core topics addressed in this series of books are attachment, motivation, social and emotional competence, executive function, and multilingual and multicultural development. The current niche topics represented in the series are these; transformative frames for anti-racism, socio-cultural deprivation, and growth mindset for transformative thinking. The writing level is to be accessible and engaging for students in high school and the first or second year of college. However, the information may be useful for graduate students, too. These books are excellent for early, mid, and late career professionals, too. Employee training and professional development can be enriched with the books of this series.

It is the intention of the book authors that our books are helpful to all people who work with and care for children. Indeed, the 8 books of the Applying Child and Adolescent Development in the Professions Series move the field forward.

Dr. Kimberly A. Gordon Biddle spent over 30 years working full-time in the field of Child and Adolescent Development, with 2 years as a Research Analyst and 28 plus years as a College Professor. Currently, she is an Emeritus Professor of Child and Adolescent Development from Sacramento State in California. Her BA is in Psychology and Music from the University of Redlands. Her EdS is in Program Evaluation and her PhD is in Child and Adolescent Development. Both of her advanced degrees are from Stanford University.

Over her career she has been an American Psychological Association MFP fellow. She has authored or co-authored over 20 articles and some book chapters. She has presented or co-presented over 40 presentations. Before being the overall editor of this series she had co-authored or co-edited 4 textbooks. She has obtained approximately $1,000,000 in grants. Her research and teaching areas of expertise include motivation, academic resilience, social and emotional development, and the education and socialization of marginalized groups. She also has some expertise in field work placement and coordination and policies concerning children and families. Her career efforts have been rewarded. For example, she has received Outstanding Teaching and Service Awards from Sacramento State. She also won a Stanford Graduate School of Education Award for Excellence in Education in 2018 and a Career Award from the University of Redlands in 2019.

She is thrilled that Editor Helen Pritt at Routledge asked her to be the lead editor of this book series and she has enjoyed nurturing the series into life. She is happy to now be working with editor Molly Selby. This series is near and dear to her heart and she is honored to edit it and co-author one of the books. She firmly believes that this book series will move the field of Child and Adolescent Development forward. Core concepts of the field and current topics of the field are explored and applied in an engaging manner. Dr. Biddle firmly believes that knowledge of the field of Child and Adolescent Development can assist so many people, whether they are family members of children or are in careers working with children. This series aims to assist those in a wide range of careers who work with children. Those aims are met and surpassed in this series in the opinion of Dr. Biddle. It is her hope that this series is used with students in secondary, undergraduate, and graduate education settings in addition to adults in the fields of education, psychology, social work, allied health, and non-profit organizations. This series is the jewel in Dr. Biddle's career crown. She hopes it shines brightly.

Inspiring Motivation in Children and Youth
How to Nurture Environments for Learning
David A. Bergin

Promoting Regulation and Flexibility in Thinking
Development of Executive Function
Kristen M. Weede Alexander and Karen M. Davis O'Hara

From Cultural Deprivation to Cultural Security
Tackling Socio-Cultural Deprivation with Children and Young People
Dale Allender and Arya Allender-West

Social and Emotional Development in Children through Emerging Adults
A Guide for Professionals
Kimberly A. Gordon Biddle and Christi Bergin

Bringing Antiracism into Focus
Using Transformative Lenses to Reframe Professional Practice
Alicia Herrera, Kevin Ferreira van Leer and Samantha Blackburn

Enhancing Multilingual Development
A Guide for Professionals
Nadeen T. Ruiz and Andrea García

For more information about this series, please visit: www.routledge.com/Applying-Child-and-Adolescent-Development-in-the-Professions-Series/book-series/ACADP

Enhancing Multilingual Development

A Guide for Professionals

Nadeen T. Ruiz and Andrea García

NEW YORK AND LONDON

Designed cover image: © kali9 via Getty Images

First published 2026
by Routledge
605 Third Avenue, New York, NY 10158

and by Routledge
4 Park Square, Milton Park, Abingdon, Oxon, OX14 4RN

Routledge is an imprint of the Taylor & Francis Group, an informa business

© 2026 Nadeen T. Ruiz and Andrea García

The right of Nadeen T. Ruiz and Andrea García to be identified as authors of this work has been asserted in accordance with sections 77 and 78 of the Copyright, Designs and Patents Act 1988.

All rights reserved. No part of this book may be reprinted or reproduced or utilised in any form or by any electronic, mechanical, or other means, now known or hereafter invented, including photocopying and recording, or in any information storage or retrieval system, without permission in writing from the publishers.

Trademark notice: Product or corporate names may be trademarks or registered trademarks, and are used only for identification and explanation without intent to infringe.

Library of Congress Cataloging-in-Publication Data
Names: Ruiz, Nadeen T. author | García, Andrea, 1972- author
Title: Enhancing multilingual development :
a guide for professionals / Nadeen T. Ruiz and Andrea García.
Description: New York, NY : Routledge, 2025. |
Series: Applying child and adolescent development in the professions series | Includes bibliographical references and index.
Identifiers: LCCN 2024059893 (print) | LCCN 2024059894 (ebook) | ISBN 9781032106571 hardback | ISBN 9781032106540 paperback | ISBN 9781003216414 ebook Subjects: LCSH: Multilingualism
Classification: LCC P115 .R85 2025 (print) | LCC P115 (ebook) | DDC 306.44/6071–dc23/eng/20250408
LC record available at https://lccn.loc.gov/2024059893
LC ebook record available at https://lccn.loc.gov/2024059894

ISBN: 9781032106571 (hbk)
ISBN: 9781032106540 (pbk)
ISBN: 9781003216414 (ebk)

DOI: 10.4324/9781003216414

Typeset in Times New Roman
by Deanta Global Publishing Services, Chennai, India

In memory of my husband Bob who, though seriously ill, encouraged me to take on this project. Life did not offer him many opportunities to become multilingual until we met. But he then put his fledgling American Sign Language and Spanish to great effect, charming everyone around him, and reminding me of the heart-warming benefit of learning new languages.

Nadeen

To Jorge, Ana Lucia, and Mariana, who give me the strength and inspiration to pursue my dreams every day. I am so proud of our bilingual family and of the stories, songs, and memories that we share in both Spanish and English. Gracias por acompañarme en esta aventura, and for believing that it was possible.

Andrea

Contents

List of Figures xiii
List of Tables xiv
About the Authors xv
Series Editor Foreword xvi

PART I

Introduction 3
Overview 3
Note on Chapter Formatting: Accessing Background Knowledge and
 Setting a Purpose for Reading 4

PART II

1 **Exploring the Benefits of Multilingualism** 9
Overview 9
Multilingualism 10
Why Develop Multilingualism? 13
Economic Value of Bilingualism 14
  Higher Education Access by Bilinguals 14
  Higher Earning Power of Bilinguals 15
  Employer Preference for Bilinguals 17
Cognitive Benefits of Bilingualism 18
  Bilinguals' Linguistic Skills and Metalinguistic Knowledge 19
  Executive Functioning 20
Time to Think and Connect 32

2 The Development of Multilingualism 33
Overview 33
Bilinguals and Bilingualism 34
Active Multilingual Processing 35
   Code-Switching 36
   Code-Switching Functions in Children 40
Becoming Multilingual 43
   Simultaneous and Sequential Bilingualism 43
   Social Influences on Bilingualism 45
   Language Loss through Subtractive Bilingualism 48
Learning Multiple Languages: Patterns in the Processes 50
   Interaction in the Development of Multilingualism: The Need for Input and Output 50
   Creative Construction in Adding a New Language 51
   L2 Approximations Resembling Early First Language Learning 52
   Developmental Sequences while Moving Toward the Target Language 54
   The Interconnected Underlying Language Proficiency of Bilinguals 55
Individual Differences that Influence Becoming Bilingual 60
   The Age Factor: It's Complicated 60
   Becoming Multilingual along the Lifespan 61
   Personality Factors 62
   Motivation and Attitude in L2 Learning 64
   Aptitude for Learning Languages 64
   Identity Matters in L2 Learning 65
   Learning a Third (or Fourth!) Language after the L2 66
Time to Think and Connect 67

3 Increasing Multilingual Competence in the Home, Community, and Workplace: Applications of the Research on Multilingual Development 69
Overview 69
Two Highly Effective Ways of Developing Multilingualism 70
   Family Bilingualism 70
   Bilingual Education 71
Optimal Teaching and Learning Conditions for Becoming Bilingual 78
Optimal Condition #1: Learner-Centered Instruction and Support 80

Key Research 80
Examples of Instruction and Support for L2 Learners 81
Optimal Condition #2: Learner Choice 82
Key Research 83
Examples of Instruction and Support for L2 Learners 83
*Optimal Condition #3: Whole Texts for Maximum Comprehension
  and Explicit Teaching of Skills and Strategies 85*
Key Research 85
Examples of Instruction and Support for L2 Learners 86
Optimal Condition #4: Active Participation 88
Key Research 88
Examples of Instruction and Support for L2 Learners 90
Optimal Condition #5: Meaning First, Followed by Form 92
Key Research 92
Examples of Instruction and Support for L2 Learners 93
Optimal Condition #6: Authentic Purpose 95
Key Research 95
Examples of Instruction and Support for L2 Learners 95
*Continuing the Work in Optimizing Professional Settings
  for Multilingual Development 96*
Time to Think and Connect 97

4 Multilingualism and Intercultural Communication: Working toward Intercultural Citizenship — 99

Overview 99
Multilingualism and the Workforce 100
Language: What's Culture Got to Do With It? 102
Being an Intercultural Citizen in the Workplace 104
Intercultural Communication 106
  *Two Perspectives on a Single Intercultural Communicative
    Interaction 108*
  Intercultural Communicative Competence 110
*Approaches to Promoting Intercultural Communication Across the
  Professions 112*
  Informal Intercultural Communication Learning Experiences 113
  *Structured Professional Development Approaches to Promote
    Intercultural Communicative Competence 117*
Summing Up 125
Time to Think and Connect 126

Appendix A: True–False Answers to Chapter Anticipation Guides	*129*
Appendix B: Optimal Instructional and Professional Development Practices to Enhance Multilingual Development	*131*
Appendix B1: Anticipation Guides	*132*
Appendix B2: Cloze Passages: Focus on Language Forms	*134*
Appendix B3: Daily News (Primary Level)	*137*
Appendix B4: Graphic Organizer Example: Literary Analysis of Theme	*139*
Appendix B5: Home–Expert Groups ("Jigsaw")	*140*
Appendix B6: Interactive (Dialogue) Journals	*142*
Appendix B7: K-W-L Charts	*144*
Appendix B8: Quick Writes	*146*
Appendix B9: The Survey Text Method	*148*
Appendix B10: Think–Pair–Share *(Also known as "Turn and Talk")*	*150*
Appendix B11: The Writing Process (Writing Workshop)	*152*
References	*154*
Index	*164*

Figures

1.1	Two views of a grid—one blocked and one open—that children ("participants") used to either take the perspective of the adult ("director") or not during the task (Fan et al., 2015)	27
1.2	Panels of pictures presented to children in a classic false belief task (Peristeri et al., 2021)	30
2.1	Iceberg analogy of surface features and underlying, interdependent language proficiency (Cummins, 2021)	58
3.1	Academic achievement patterns of Grades 1–11 students learning English as their L2 and who participate in different types of program models designed to meet their needs as minority-language speakers (Collier and Thomas, 2017)	76
3.2	Mild positive effect of short-term (first three years of schooling) Transitional Bilingual Education in Grade 11 compared to English-only instruction (Collier and Thomas, 2017)	78
4.1	Components and aspects of intercultural communicative competence (Fantini, 2020, p. 55)	112
4.2	Linguistic profile	118

Tables

1.1	A beginning list of useful terms for exploring multilingualism	12
2.1	Switching languages for your friends in a bilingual special education classroom (Ruiz, 1988)	40
2.2	Trying to follow your friend's language choice (even though you don't know that language well) (Ruiz, 1988)	41
2.3	Choosing the language with the best chance of being understood when you know the word in both English and Spanish and you have articulation difficulties (Ruiz 1988)	42
2.4	Similarities in approximations (errors) between children acquiring English as their first language and children learning English as a second language (Ruiz, 1988)	53
3.1	Useful terms for understanding bilingual education	73
3.2	Optimal conditions for multilingual development #1–6	81
3.3	Optimal conditions for multilingual development #7–12	97
4.1	Pros and cons of intercultural training tools (Deardroff, 2020, p.8)	120

About the Authors

Nadeen T. Ruiz, Ph.D., obtained her M.A. and Ph.D. at Stanford University in bilingual education and linguistics. Formerly, Dr. Ruiz was Chair of Bilingual Multicultural Education at California State University Sacramento and Director of Elementary Education at Stanford University, receiving teaching awards at both institutions. In addition, Dr. Ruiz is the recipient of the *California Association of Bilingual Educators Teacher Preparation Program Award*, and the *University of California at Davis School of Education Outstanding Alumna Award*. Dr. Ruiz co-founded the *Optimal Learning Environment (OLE) Project*, a research and professional development program that focuses on effective literacy instruction for emergent bilingual students in both general and special education classrooms, and for migrant children. The OLE Project has provided professional development to several thousand special and general education teachers in the US and in Mexico. Dr. Ruiz is the author of over 40 articles and books on students' bilingualism and biliteracy, and on the preparation of bilingual teachers, regularly presenting on these topics at national and international conferences. She is Professor Emeritus in Bilingual Multicultural Education at CSU Sacramento.

Andrea García, Ph.D., holds a M.A. and a Ph.D. in language, reading, and culture from the University of Arizona. Her B.Sc. is in neurolinguistics and psychopedagogy, from the Colegio Superior de Neurolingüística y Psicopdadgogía in Mexico, where she did her thesis on implementing the OLE Project conditions with young readers identified with learning disabilities. Formerly, Dr. García was an Associate Professor in literacy studies at Hofstra University, teaching graduate and undergraduate courses in literacy, biliteracy, literacy evaluation, and qualitative research, among others. At Hofstra she served as Director of the Reading/Writing Learning Clinic, conducting research, building community partnerships, and securing funding for strength-based and culturally relevant out of school literacy programs and family literacy initiatives in underserved communities. Currently, Dr. García is a Principal Research Associate at Westat, where she directs projects and serves as a technical assistance lead. She continues to pursue her academic interests teaching one graduate course at Teachers College, Columbia University, and serving in the Executive Board of Words of Words Center for Global Literacies and Literatures at the University of Arizona.

Series Editor Foreword

The field of Child and Adolescent Development is in infant stages of development, but it is steadily maturing. It is time for it be recognized and legitimized. As the theorizing and conduction of research in the field become more solid, complex, and applicable to life; recognition comes that the field is for people in a variety of professions. The traditional education and psychology fields are enriched with the knowledge obtained from the field of Child and Adolescent Development. Additionally, allied health, social work, and non-profit fields are improved with knowledge of how to apply Child and Adolescent Development in the workplace setting. Everyone who works with or cares for children from birth to 25 years will benefit from reading and applying the information from the books in this series. Collectively, the authors have created books rich with foundational information and application techniques and strategies. Thematic boxes of interviews, case studies, and research and theory into practice run throughout all the books. These books help to answer some of the most important questions concerning children and their development. All who love and care about children should read every book in the series.

I am quite happy to welcome this pertinent textbook into the Applying Child and Adolescent Development in the Professions series. Multilingualism development is quite an important topic in Child and Adolescent Development today. Dr. Nadeen Ruiz and Dr. Andrea Garcia have done a wonderful job of presenting the importance and practical value of multilingualism for professionals. The title of their textbook truly exemplifies the contents, *Enhancing Multilingualism Development: A Guide for Professionals*. The textbook explains the positive benefits of multilingualism, including economic and cognitive benefits in an engaging manner. It also describes the complicated process of teaching children to be multilingual in homes, schools, communities, and workplaces; and it promotes the idea and possibility of Intercultural Citizenship. Most importantly, it dispels myths and presents research evidence and has an asset-based perspective. This book is an excellent addition to the literature and the bookshelves of many college students and professionals in a variety of fields.

Dr. Kimberly A. Gordon Biddle

Part I

Introduction

Overview

The introduction to the book presents authors' central goal of providing current and future working professionals with a foundational understanding of multilingualism. This initial section also establishes the connection between multilingual competence with positive interactions across different groups in professional settings. It also includes an explanation of the book's format, noting that each chapter begins by asking readers to access their current background knowledge about the topic and to set a purpose for reading.

Across a range of professional communities spanning the globe, linguistic and cultural diversity is the norm. Finding ways to positively and productively interact among diverse groups in a professional setting is a shared goal throughout these communities. An essential component of positive interaction within different cultures is the ability to communicate in each other's language. As one expert in intercultural interactions has stated:

> Understanding fully another culture is probably impossible for most people. Those fortunate and diligent enough to be brought up in more than one language or those who take the time and trouble to acquire additional languages probably have the best chance.
>
> (Coulby, 2006, p. 252)

In this way, and in many others that we will examine throughout this book, multilingual competence is a prized resource to be fostered, retained, and further developed.

As authors, we write this book with professionals foremost in our minds. Whether shared in work settings or studied as a supplemental textbook at universities, this book has as its central goal to provide current and future professionals with a foundational understanding of multilingualism. The overwhelming majority

DOI: 10.4324/9781003216414-2

of work settings—medicine, law, technology, business, allied health, engineering, construction, retail, manufacturing, entertainment, and so on—depend entirely on effective communication among colleagues to be successful. Increasingly, many of those colleagues will speak a variety of languages. Fortunately, productive communication among professional colleagues with multiple language backgrounds can be enhanced through a solid understanding of the benefits and processes of becoming multilingual.

In addition to knowing how multilingualism is developed and advanced, we need to dispel notions about multilingualism that are not scientific or valid. A few common examples of those unscientific comments are: "Speaking two languages doesn't pay off; English is the global language," "Speaking to your children in two languages delays their language development," and "Real (Americans/Brits) only speak (English)" (Grosjean, 2010). These statements can impede both access to skilled multilingualism and successful interactions in professional and other types of communities. As authors, we respond by providing in this book succinct, up-to-date reviews of current research on how young children, older youth, and adults acquire multilingualism. Importantly, we emphasize an *assets view* of linguistic diversity, that is, a clear recognition emanating from research that speaking more than one language is highly valued by many sectors of our communities (Chen & Padilla, 2019). As we will see, the benefits of multilingualism span academic, economic, and professional advantages. With these benefits in mind, we provide suggestions for research-based practices in home, school, and professional settings in order to enhance multilingual development.

Note on Chapter Formatting: Accessing Background Knowledge and Setting a Purpose for Reading

Readers will note that at the beginning of each chapter, there is a series of statements which prompt you to predict whether they are true or false. The statements are a version of an instructional approach called an *Anticipation Guide* (Catts, 2022). Anticipation Guides have been shown to enhance readers' comprehension of new material by first asking readers to speculate whether the statements are true or false *before* reading the information. To do this, readers use the knowledge they already have—their background knowledge and personal experience with the topic—to predict or make their best guess as to the accuracy of the statement. Tapping into background knowledge before reading new material improves comprehension of the information (Smith, Snow, Serryn, & Hammond, 2021). Furthermore, after making predictions before beginning to read the chapter, readers now have an additional purpose for continuing their reading, which is confirming or changing their original answers. The final step in the process is to revisit the statements after reading the chapter and to make sure that all answers reflect the chapter content. Given the usefulness of Anticipation Guides in enhancing comprehension, we provide in Appendix B a specific, step-by-step resource for creating your own Anticipation Guide in your professional field.

In this book, our Anticipation Guide takes the following format. Each chapter begins with five statements that we would like you to judge as true or false, using your best guess with the knowledge you bring to this book through prior study and/or your personal experiences. You can record those initial predictions in the Anticipation Guide that represent your thinking before beginning to read the chapter. When you finish the chapter, look once again at the statements listed there, and make any changes needed based on your reading. Remember that the goal of this type of activity is to facilitate your comprehension of the material by first acknowledging the information you already bring to the task, and second, setting a purpose for reading the chapter. For that reason, changing your answers based on new information through your reading is a positive, not negative, sign: it shows that you have processed the material in a deep way and have reached a new understanding. Our goal as writers of this book is precisely to increase those understandings about multilingualism and help you apply them in your current or future professional setting.

Part II

Chapter 1

Exploring the Benefits of Multilingualism

Overview

This chapter clarifies the terms *multilingualism* and *bilingualism* to readers. We then provide an up-to-date review of the research firmly establishing the sometimes surprising benefits of multilingualism, ranging from financial advantages to lifetime cognitive benefits. Economic benefits are at play in both macro contexts such as those at the national level, and more micro contexts such as categories of individual businesses and careers. Studies also converge in documenting that cognitive and linguistic gains from multilingualism that begin with infants extend to reach to those who are advanced in age.

Test yourself! (Tapping into your background knowledge): Before reading the chapter, read each statement and use your current knowledge and experiences to decide whether the statement is true or false.

True or False	Multilingualism
	1. Research has documented that bilingual people as a group have higher earning power.
	2. Employers of professions not requiring a college degree, such as construction, retail, and manufacturing, do not show any notable preference for bilinguals.
	3. Young bilingual children outperform monolingual children in being able to take another person's perspective that may be different from their own.
	4. Both monolinguals and bilinguals seem to experience the same level of cognitive decline as they reach advanced age.
	5. Parents of autistic children should keep to one language only in their homes so as not to further negatively impact their children's language and cognitive development.

DOI: 10.4324/9781003216414-4

Multilingualism

Throughout this book readers will see two core terms to refer to people who speak more than one language: *multilingual* and *bilingual*. In our book title we chose to foreground the term *multilingualism*, essentially a word that can encompass a reference to people who speak more than two languages. Our reasoning behind this initial emphasis lies with the fact that many of our world communities pragmatically use three languages in daily life, a number not captured by *bilingualism*, which denotes two languages. An example of such a community is the US Mexican indigenous population. In Pacific coastal California and the more northwestern US, there has been increased migration of families whose national origin is the country of Mexico, a primarily Spanish-speaking country, but one where they learned an indigenous language in their homes, such as Mixtec or Zapotec. In the context of their country of origin, these immigrant families have learned Spanish to function across Mexican institutions. Now, in the US as immigrants, their children are in schools where they are learning English, or, if they happen to be in an extremely rare bilingual education setting, English and Spanish (Ruiz & Barajas, 2012). But they are also keeping alive their home indigenous language to communicate with family and friends for a total of three life-relevant languages. In the same way, many families in Europe are multilingual, as in the case of people in the Basque region of Spain who speak Basque at home and with institutions that use Basque as part of impressive Basque language revitalization efforts, such as local television stations, certain government agencies, and schools. But Basque children also learn Spanish from living in Spain. Furthermore, various Basque regions are promoting the acquisition of English as a useful third language in a global context. Consequently, the term *multilingualism* often best represents the multiple language contexts of many areas of the world.

In this book, however, we will largely use the terms *bilingual/ism* and *multilingual/ism* interchangeably. It is the case that the majority of research on the acquisition and use of multiple languages focuses on the learning of two languages, and overwhelmingly uses the descriptor *bilingual* in those studies and articles. For our purposes in this book, then, we will often use the terms *bilingual* and *bilingualism* as they succinctly convey that we are referencing people who use more than one language. We will switch to *multilingual* when there is a specific reason in the research to call out the use of three languages, as in the case of Mexican indigenous children and families in the US. Readers will note that we also use the term *multilingual repertoire* in relation to people who know more than one language. We will use that term frequently when we reach the topic of how multilinguals can activate any or all of their collection (repertoire) of multiple languages when needed.

A final consideration in terminology relates to the degree of *proficiency*, or skills, in a bilingual's two languages. Is a person bilingual if they simply have beginning proficiency in one of their two languages? Or is a bilingual person one who has equal skills in both languages? In actuality, the research community is rather loose in its terminology linked to language skill. Throughout the research, *bilingual* can represent a range of dual language skills, from basic oral fluency (or sign language fluency, in the case of languages of the Deaf), all the way to native or native-like proficiency in both languages. When presenting research results we will attempt to clarify for readers the degree of language proficiency among the studies' participants. Furthermore, in our next chapter when we go into more depth about how people become multilingual, we will once again visit the question, "Who is bilingual?"

For now, there are a few more helpful terms that can guide the reader in the following sections, especially when making applications from research to real-world contexts. First, considering the macro level of a country (nation-state), *majority language* refers to the language expected to be employed by its citizens, especially when interacting with institutions such as government, major media, education, and so on. Languages other than the majority languages are labeled *minority languages*. At the individual level, *monolingual* is used to identify people who speak only one language. *Fluent bilinguals* and *balanced bilinguals* are two terms used to refer to people with highly developed language proficiency in two languages. *Biliterate* refers to bilinguals who speak two languages, but have the added skills of reading and writing both. Bilinguals in the US are often characterized as *English Learners*, shifting away from the previous, more deficit-focused term, *Limited English Proficient* to recognize the on-going process of adding on a second language. However, the term English Learners still emphasizes what people still need to learn instead of additional language skills they bring with them. In response, the term *Emergent Bilinguals* has recently begun to widely appear in journals. Many feel that the term Emergent Bilinguals better captures an asset view of bilinguals' linguistic possibilities. Emergent Bilinguals are people who through natural exposure and/or targeted study are adding on language skills to progress from a monolingual level of language use to the status of bilingual.

Throughout this book and almost all the related literature on bilingualism we will use a short-hand notation to refer to the language first learned by a person who is learning language sequentially—*L1*—and the second language—*L2*. But a heads up: We will also learn that some children learn their two languages simultaneously! We will look more closely at these young simultaneous bilinguals in Chapter 2.

Finally, readers will see references to *dialects* in addition to languages in the book. In general, when we refer to a dialect, such as the Piemontese dialect used by many people in mountainous northwest Italy, we are calling attention to a *variety* of the majority language of Italian. Sometimes dialects are region-specific, as is Piemontese. In some areas, dialects and their related majority languages are mutually intelligible, but sometimes they are not. In reality, the difference between a dialect and a language is often blurred and may have more to do with the history of who was in power when national languages were being decided upon among several varieties. These power dynamics led Yiddish scholar Max Weinreich to write "A language is a dialect with an army and navy." We may chuckle a bit

Table 1.1 A beginning list of useful terms for exploring multilingualism

Term	Definition
balanced or fluent bilingual	A general way of referring to people who have high levels of linguistic skills in two languages; their language proficiency in both languages is relatively similar
bilingual	A person who uses two languages or dialects in their everyday lives
bilingualism	A set of linguistic skills with two languages or dialects
dialect/language variety	A variety of a language that is not officially designated as a language, usually because of socio-political reasons; dialects range from mutually comprehensible by speakers of named languages and other dialects, to those which are not
dominant language	Among the languages in a person's multilingual repertoire, the language with which they have the most skill and, often, comfort level
Emergent Bilingual	A person who has any level of skill, even beginning, with using two languages; a term emphasizing the potential high levels of bilingualism possible given certain circumstances
English Learner	A common term for a person who is adding on the English language to their multilingual repertoire; a term characterizing the person in terms of their efforts in learning English without acknowledging the person's first language skills
home language/s	The language or languages that are usually first learned by people, often in the family or caretaking setting; equivalent to the term first language (L1)
L1	A language first learned by a person; the equivalent of "first language" and used to distinguish it from the second language (L2) which is added on sequentially
L2	The language a person adds sequentially after learning their first language; the equivalent of "second language" and used to distinguish the language first learned by a person (L1)
L2 learner	A person adding in a second language to their linguistic repertoire
language proficiency	The skill level in using a language, ranging from beginning to advanced and native-like
majority language	A language designated as official by socio-political entities, and often spoken by greater numbers of people than other languages or dialects; institutions expect that people will learn and operate in the majority language
minority language	Usually a language spoken by fewer people than a majority language; often a language with less social status
monolingual	A person who has learned one language to use in their everyday lives
multilingual repertoire	An individual's active language system that allows them to activate and use any and all languages in their everyday lives

(Continued)

Table 1.1 (Continued)

Term	Definition
multilingual	A person using two or more languages in their everyday lives
multilingualism	A set of linguistic skills with two or more languages
native language/s	The language/s learned by a person at a very young age, often at birth; the equivalent of a person's (L1)
native speaker	A person who has learned and used a particular language since birth or from a very young age, and has fluent proficiency and high-level skills in that language
non-native speaker	A person who has not had access to a particular language, and consequently must learn it through formal or informal means; the particular language is not their home or first language (L1)
primary language	Among a person's multilingual repertoire, the language with which they have the most skill and often a comfort level; in many cases, but not all, it is the first language learned (L1) by a bilingual person
sequential/successive bilingual	A person who first learns one language before beginning to learn a second language, usually after the first language is well established, e.g., around 7 or 8 years of age
simultaneous bilingual	A person who learns two languages at a very young age, usually well before ages 7 or 8; a person who is sometimes described as having two native languages
target language	The language that a person is attempting to acquire through formal education or informal means; the language that is the focus of teaching and learning for people still acquiring that language

at this saying, but there are real socio-political and historical patterns underlying Weinreich's quip.

Why Develop Multilingualism?

Current estimates of the percentage of people in the world who can speak more than one language puts the figure at around 60% (Gration, 2023). In the US, the number of people who speak a language other than English at home tripled from 1980 to 2018 (Zeigler & Camarota, 2019). What's more, the US ranked high in the world in terms of the range of living languages spoken in the country, in fifth place, only behind such countries as Indonesia and India (Hardach, 2018). Britain has also shown rapid growth of their multilingual population with over a third speaking another language. Significantly, it is a younger demographic group in Britain (ages 16–24) who are the most multilingual (Gration, 2023). Taking these data and other language demographics into account, the global future seems assuredly multilingual.

There is a disconnect, however, between high numbers of young multilinguals across the globe, and another data trend: rapid language loss among first and second generations as they stay in the host country, especially in countries where English is the national language. For example, though the US is currently on an upward trajectory to increased multilingual use, a paradox is evident: research shows that within about a generation and a half, immigrant families to the US tend to *lose* their native language and become English monolinguals (Portes & Rumbaut, 2005). Other statistics indicate that less than 1% of native-born US monolingual English-speakers attempt to add on another language to become bilingual (Friedman, 2015). Furthermore, enrollment in college foreign language classes in the US has steeply declined as measured by the Modern Language Association from 2013 through 2016, and suggests a continuing trend (Johnson, 2019). So, while the number of US multilingual homes continues to increase through immigration, refugee status, and global employment opportunities for foreign-born professionals, there is actually a relatively small pool of multilingual professionals who can mobilize languages other than English in meeting the needs of linguistically diverse populations in the US. Put another way, in the US and other countries where there is not an explicit stance or policy that promotes multilingualism, as in the contrasting cases of officially multilingual countries like Canada or Switzerland, it is a struggle to preserve multilingual competence among its current and future citizenry. In the case of our specific focus in this book, this same multilingual competence is at risk among a wide range of professionals.

Readers may ask at this point: Does the generational loss of multilingualism come at a cost? What do we give up when we accept—or even promote—monolingualism in place of bilingual competence? Framing the question more positively: *Why is it important or beneficial to develop bilingualism?* Fortunately, a look at recent research can help answer those questions. We will begin that discussion with a close look at a very tangible and observable benefit of multilingualism—economic value.

Economic Value of Bilingualism

We can explore the economic advantage of multilingualism by organizing our discussion into three interconnected categories: *Higher Education, Higher Earning Power,* and *Employer Preferences*.

Higher Education Access by Bilinguals

In order to understand the tie between bilingualism and higher education, let's look at the case of Latinos in the US. In general, Latinos are people who have ties to Latin America either through immigration, ancestry, or incorporation by the US of what once were territories claimed by Mexico. There is a substantial database showing that, as an ethnic group, Latino students are least likely to attain a college degree among other US ethnic groups (Gándara, 2018). Yet, when we dig further into Latino population data and look at their differing profiles of language proficiencies, something interesting happens in terms of the group's overall educational attainment: researchers have found that bilingual Latino students who have strong proficiency in both languages graduate college at a greater rate than Latinos who are English monolinguals. Furthermore, bilingualism counts for Latinos in other ways: fluent bilinguals have more options for careers and, as a group, secure higher salaries (Rumbaut, 2014).

Research has documented that the connection between bilingualism and higher education attainment occurs not only with US Latinos, but across a variety of ethnic groups. (We sometimes refer to these ethnic populations with multilingual skills as *ethno-linguistic* groups.) A series of studies combining two very large survey data sets from Southern California (6,135 respondents)—the *Immigration Intergenerational Mobility in Metropolitan Los Angeles Study* and the *Children of Immigrants Longitudinal Study in San Diego*—were conducted by Rubén Rumbaut and colleagues (Rumbaut, 2014; Portes & Rumbaut, 2005). Their investigation included participants from a wide variety of language backgrounds, e.g., Chinese, Vietnamese, Spanish, etc. The researchers found that balanced bilinguals, i.e., those retaining their home language to a high degree while adding on English, were more likely to stay in college than students who had lost proficiency in their home language. Other researchers reached the same conclusion, in their case, exclusively focusing on Latinos (Santibáñez & Zarate, 2014). Santibáñez and Zarate documented that Latino Spanish–English *bilinguals* were more likely to enroll in college than Latino English *monolinguals*. In addition, a research review by the *Bipartisan Policy Center* (2018) corroborated this very consistent finding: children of immigrants from various language backgrounds who developed strong bilingual and biliterate skills (they could read and write in both language) were less likely to drop out of high school, and more likely to proceed to college.

As a final look at the relationship between bilinguals and higher education, there is a classic US study often cited to draw the relationship between higher education and earning power. This research by Saiz and Zoido (2005) also confirmed that bilinguals obtained higher education degrees than monolinguals. Very relevant to our discussion of tangible economic benefits, all of the studies cited in this section, just as Saiz and Zoido (2005) did almost 20 years ago, have definitively connected bilingualism to higher education, and, in turn, to higher income. We look at that connection in more detail in the next section.

Higher Earning Power of Bilinguals

In exploring the research on bilinguals' higher earning power, it is useful to understand the big picture by first perusing data from the macro context—large-scale national levels—of the relationship between multilingualism and economics. For example, Hardach (2018), writing for the *World Economic Forum* in an article titled "Speaking More than One Language Can Boost Economic Growth," reports that Switzerland attributes 10% of its Gross Domestic Product (GDP) to its multilingualism. In contrast, Britain is considered to miss out on approximately 3.5% of its GDP because of its population's relative lower rate of bilingual skills (Ayres-Bennett, Hafner, Dufresme & Yerushumi, 2022). Hardach summarizes a key finding of this research: "Countries that actively nurture different languages reap a range of rewards, from more successful exports to a more innovative workforce" (2018, p. 2). A report sponsored by the RAND Corporation (Irving, 2022) makes a similarly forceful argument focused on the UK. The report acknowledges that nearly one in five people globally can speak English:

> But then again, if one in five people can speak English, that means the other four cannot. A new study from RAND Europe looked at how much the United Kingdom could gain if it spent a little more time learning other languages. If just 10 percent more students mastered Arabic, Mandarin, French, or Spanish, researchers found, the economic returns could be measured in billions of British pounds.
>
> (Irving, 2022, p. 2)

If we now turn from looking at national levels of bilingualism and earning power, to what happens within individual countries, we can probe further into understanding this relationship. At these more micro levels of research, studies consistently converge in their findings that bilinguals earn more. Returning to the immigration studies in Southern California that we referenced earlier (Rumbaut, 2014), bilingualism has direct and positive effects on earnings compared to the monolingual group. In 2018 dollars, Gándara estimated Rumbaut's figure on bilinguals' higher earnings to amount to $3,800 annually (2018). However, other studies have reported much higher annual incomes for bilinguals than these figures. For example, Agirdag (2014) examined a national sample of bilinguals and monolinguals (N = 3,553), and documented that the former group earned an average of more than $5,400 per year in 2015 dollars. For a conservative estimate of career-long earnings over 30 years, rounding down that figure to $5,000 annually, there is evidence that we can safely project around $150,000 more in total earnings at retirement age connected to bilingual language proficiency. Similar statistics to these we report here have been corroborated by financial institutions, e.g., *World Economic Forum* and *First National Bank of Dallas*; by think tanks, e.g., *New America*; and by bi-partisan political entities, e.g., *Bipartisan Policy Center*, just to name a few. Needless to say, a bilingual retirement nest egg of $150,000 would be welcome by many, not to mention the addition of accrued interest over time from the yearly income boost!

Thus far we have seen that studies have identified very tangible economic benefits of bilingualism. Digging even deeper, researchers have pondered whether the income benefit of bilinguals is due to an *indirect* connection, that is, whether, first, bilingualism leads to higher education, and then leads to higher salaries. They have also posited a *direct* effect, however: that bilingualism itself, with or without a college degree, accounts for increased income. The next section on employer preferences for bilingual employees may shed light on which theory—direct or indirect monetary benefit—best explains researchers' findings. Specifically, we can ask: Have researchers found the financial bilingual benefit only in companies or institutions that employ graduates with college educations? Or have they documented that companies primarily hiring high school graduates *also* prefer bilingual employees?

Employer Preference for Bilinguals

The US has produced a large number of studies looking into employer preferences and employees' language skills. For example, in California, the *Bay Area Council Economic Institute* (2022) documented that from 2010 to 2020, job postings in California requesting applicants with bilingual skills nearly quadrupled. In terms of the national picture, this same study reported that bilingual postings as a share of the total job postings increased at nearly a 2% faster rate than other postings.

Shedding further light on the question of preference for bilingual employees, researchers Porras, Ee, and Gándara (2014) conducted a nationwide survey of approximately 300 employers regarding the bilingualism of their employees. Each of the ten sectors represented in the study had at least 12 different employers who responded to the survey. Those sectors included: (a) Professional, Scientific Technical Services, and Information, (b) Public Administration and Utilities, (c) Health Care and Social Assistance, (d) Educational Services, (e) Arts, Entertainment, Recreation, Accomodation, and Food, (f) Finance, Insurance, Real Estate, and Rental/Leasing, (g) Manufacturing and Construction, (h) Retail Trade, (i) Management of Companies and Administrative Support, (j) Transportation and Warehousing. Results showed that the employer groups with the highest degree of preference for bilingual employees were, in order: Management and Administrative Support (100%); Retail Trade and Manufacturing and Construction (tied at 85%); Transportation and Warehousing and Arts, Entertainment, Recreation, Accommodation and Food Services (tied at 83%). Across all sectors, 2/3 of employers responded with a preference for bilinguals, all other things equal.

If we return to the question of whether bilingualism has an *indirect effect* on higher earnings (bilingualism leads to college education which in turn leads to employment benefits) or a *direct effect* (bilingualism itself leads to employment benefits), we believe the evidence points to a direct effect. Bilingual job applicants *without* a college degree get a leg up from prospective employers in the sectors of Administrative Support, Retail Trade, Manufacturing and Construction, Transportation and Warehousing, Arts, Entertainment, Recreation, and Accommodation and Food Services. In fact, in the list of the five sectors with the highest employer preference for bilingual employees, only Management likely necessitates a college degree. In sum, research strongly suggests that being bilingual directly opens career opportunity doors.

Digging a bit more into bilingual employment trends in a single US state, here, California, can add to the picture of bilingualism's economic value. We already summarized the large increase in demand for bilingual employees documented by the *Bay Area Council Economic Institute* (2022). This same body further examined the frequency of bilingual job postings vs. those who did not request bilingualism of the applicants. The results showed that in 2020, the healthcare industry asked for bilingual applicants over all other sectors, accounting for over 25% above other professions. The greatest subcategory of job postings in Healthcare was for registered nurses. Healthcare bilingual postings were followed in frequency by Software Developers, creating, as the authors of this report contend, a clear need for bilingual programs with a focus on sectors such as Healthcare and Software Development. These results create heightened impetus to plan for increasing bilingualism for workers in these professional areas. The report concludes:

> Many industry sectors and businesses are creating more and more job opportunities for bilingual individuals. What was once viewed as a deficiency is now seen as an *incredible asset* for interpersonal sectors engaging with local communities of non-English speakers, as well as businesses looking to interact with the global marketplace. Bilingual listings are not only keeping up with the growth rate of job postings overall but are exceeding them.
> (Kellerman & Raisz, 2022, p. 21, emphasis added)

Cognitive Benefits of Bilingualism

It may be hard to imagine, but in this section we proceed from the previous impressive research base on the economic advantages of bilingualism, to an even more extensively researched area: *cognitive benefits of bilingualism*. When we use the terms *cognitive* and *cognition*, we are referring to the mental processes we all mobilize to understand and learn about our world. Those processes include focusing our attention, perceiving, planning, reasoning, problem-solving, and many others. Active throughout many of these mental processes is language (Vygotsky, 1968). Language is a powerful vehicle and essential tool in our mental processes, making the study of language—*linguistics*—very relevant to and a significant part of the broader area of cognitive science.

For our discussion of the cognitive benefits of bilingualism, we begin with those enhanced skills most clearly connected to bilingualism, that is, the ability to communicate in multiple languages. We also consider the knowledge multilinguals have about their languages and their use referred to as *metalinguistic awareness*. We then delve into other cognitive benefits of bilingualism, including *executive functioning*, representative of the range of mental skills and strategies associated with being bilingual. The chapter concludes by discussing how bilingualism blooms even in people with severe disabilities or in the elderly. In fact, we will read how bilingualism can mitigate what some would view as negative aspects of disabilities such as autism (*autism mitigation*), or help us keep our cognitive skills into old age (*cognitive reserve*).

Bilinguals' Linguistic Skills and Metalinguistic Knowledge

In the next chapter we go into depth regarding the specifics of how we acquire multilingualism at different points along our lifespan. Before this extended explanation, however, we take a brief stop here to marvel at what seems to many adults as an almost impossible task, but one that infants and toddlers are able to accomplish seemingly without effort: attaining native-like fluency in multiple languages.

It is a well-established fact that all infants come equipped to learn the sounds and structures of any and all languages. Ramirez and Kuhl (2017) refer to these infants 6 months and younger as "citizens of the world." The authors selected this term based on brain science research showing that up to about 6 months of age, babies can discern sounds not only from the language/s in their environment, but also from foreign languages (Kuhl, Stevens, Hayashi, Deguchi, Kiritani, & Iverson, 2006). This same type of research has documented that, on the way to their first birthday, infants begin to lose that sensitivity to the sounds of languages outside their milieu. Consequently, they proceed from "citizens of the world" to becoming "native language specialists" in the language that surrounds them, or languages, in the case of infants hearing and interacting in multiple languages (Ramirez & Kuhl, 2017).

Young bilinguals' advantage in learning multiple languages extends beyond their use of the sound systems of multiple languages, and beyond their infancy. Research in early bilingualism has consistently identified a language benefit called *metalinguistic awareness*. In a nutshell, metalinguistic awareness is a set of skills with which people are able to think about and be strategic with their use of language. Another way to look at metalinguistic awareness is as the ability to treat language as an object and separate it from meaning. For example, a classic task to identify metalinguistic skills in young children is the *Wug Test* that asks children to apply their knowledge of grammatical rules (Berko, 1958). A sample question from that test is: *Here is a wug. Here is another wug. How many are there? There are two* ____. Though the sentence is nonsensical in that "wug" is not a real word, young children are able to use their knowledge of the way English works and supply the correct answer: "wugs." Metalinguistic knowledge comes into play with vocabulary, too, such as understanding that changes in word meanings result from adding prefixes and suffixes, or that a single word can have multiple meanings. Again, all these tasks, whether in the laboratory or in the classroom, require children to think and apply what they know about language as an object in itself. It is not surprising that research has demonstrated these metalinguistic skills are highly related to children's academic success, especially in the area of literacy.

When looking at bilingual children specifically, studies of metalinguistic awareness studies have shown that bilinguals consistently outperform monolingual children (Bialystok, Peets, & Moreno, 2014). To help understand how researchers identify metalinguistic skills in children, we can look at an example from a study comparing Grade 5 students in French–English bilingual classrooms with students in an English-only program (Bialystok et al., 2014). The children were asked to judge the grammaticality of two types of sentences. The first sentence type had grammatical errors such as *The horse <u>munch</u> on the grass* versus the correct grammar of *The horse <u>munches</u> on the grass*. After hearing each sentence, the children decided whether it was "the right way" (grammatically correct), or "not the right way" (grammatically incorrect). The second type of sentence contained similar patterns of errors and grammatical correctness, but had the added aspect of being "silly." In these sentences, "silly" meant that they did not make sense *semantically*, a term in linguistics for the study of meaning. An example of this type of sentence was *The horse sails the boat*. The sentence is grammatically correct, but not meaningful because of the nonsensical pairing of a horse with a boat. Again, for both types of sentences the children were asked if what they heard was "the right way," even if it was a silly sentence, such as a horse sailing a boat. Results showed that the bilingual students were better at homing in on the grammar in silly sentences as required by the task, and ignoring the strange semantic pairing. In contrast, the performance pattern of monolingual children was to reject that the "silly" sentence was "the right way," even though the grammar was actually correct.

The study described above and many others have converged in documenting that bilingual children outperform monolingual children on metalinguistic tasks, that is, when they are asked to treat language as an object. It seems that bilingual children's experience with more than one language gives them special skills in reflecting upon different language characteristics and systems. As we noted before, these metalinguistic skills have a strong connection to academic literacy, which in itself gives bilinguals a very useful advantage in schooling. Metalinguistic studies have been conducted across a wide range of languages, including Greek, Italian, Hebrew, Spanish, and many others, in addition to the study we just examined with French–English bilingual children. In short, the bilingual advantage is clear in terms of metalinguistic awareness.

Research has shown that the advantages of bilingualism extend from these overtly linguistic aspects of cognition, to other mental processes crucial to our daily functioning in the world. In the following sections we will return to the earlier-described study and see how bilingual children's metalinguistic skill pattern is linked to additional cognitive functions. Before proceeding, however, we want to highlight good news for monolingual children from this field of research. Once monolingual children enter a bilingual education program where they receive instruction in two languages, they, too, gain the metalinguistic advantage, even after only two to three years of dual language instruction (Nicolay & Poncelet, 2015; Trebits et al., 2021).

Executive Functioning

Executive functioning is a critically important set of higher-level cognitive skills that all humans need in order to control and manage other more impulsive ways of how we think and act. Diamond (2013) writes a very clear explanation for us in her extensive review of psychological research on executive functioning:

Executive functions (EFs; also called executive control or cognitive control) refer to a family of top-down mental processes needed when you have to concentrate and pay attention, when going on automatic or relying on instinct or intuition would be ill-advised, insufficient, or impossible ... Using EFs is effortful; it is easier to continue doing what you have been doing than to change, it is easier to give into temptation than to resist it, and it is easier to go on "automatic pilot" than to consider what to do next.

(Diamond, 2013)

This description steers us in the direction of one of the central types of executive functioning, *inhibitory control*, also more recently known as *attentional control* (Bialystok & Craik, 2022).

Inhibitory/Attentional Control

Inhibitory control refers to the ability to control our attention, behavior, thoughts and emotions, and do what is appropriate to the task or context (Diamond, 2013). Researchers concentrating on the core EF of inhibitory control have often identified a bilingual advantage. Specifically, several studies have found that bilingual children and adults outperform their monolingual peers on tasks of inhibitory control. In essence, these inhibitory control tasks are exercises where participants, even children, need to think something through before spontaneously acting. An example of this kind of activity is the *Bear/Dragon* task, a different version of the typical childhood game of *Simon Says*. Children in this kind of research are told that when the nice bear talks to them, they should do what he says. But, when the bad dragon tells them to do something, they should not do it. Bilingual children as young as 3 years old perform better on tasks of inhibitory or attentional control—in this task, paying attention to the bear and refraining from following directions from the dragon—than peers who are monolingual (Díaz & Ferrar, 2018). They seem to be able to manage their automatic or impulsive behaviors in favor of more effectively directing their attention to follow the instructions or solve the problem at hand. The emphasis on attention during tasks of inhibitory control is one of the reasons we frequently use the term *attentional control* in this section's discussion as a synonym for inhibitory control.

Here an interesting question arises: Why is it that knowing more than one language helps children in these studies show more attentional control than monolingual children? The theory that many researchers propose is that bilingual children, at any one time, are managing more than one language. In fact, studies have repeatedly documented that both languages are always active in the brain (Bialystok, 2017). The result is that when bilingual children need to speak primarily in one of their multiple languages due to their conversational partner's knowledge of only one language, bilingual children must "suppress" or "inhibit" the other language that is not useful at the moment. Researchers Díaz and Farrar (2018) describe the argument this way:

... bilinguals have enhanced EF inhibitory control abilities due to the need to hold and manage dual representations for linguistic information. This includes having to constantly inhibit one set of linguistic representations in favor of another set.

(Díaz & Ferrar, 2018, p. 384)

Consequently, on a daily basis, bilingual children actively manage their languages: they select the best language/s to use to fulfill their communicative intent in any given moment, and keep the other languages in the background, yet ready to activate when necessary. Bilingual children certainly have a lot of practice with inhibitory/attentional control of something so critical to human behavior: effective communication!

The tie between attentional control and metalinguistic awareness in the previous section is made clear if we recall the study asking Grade 5 monolingual and bilingual children to ignore the "silly" nature of the sentence and focus their attention on the "right way" (grammatically correct sentences). Grade 5 bilinguals could better inhibit or manage their first reaction that something was wrong with the sentence, that is, the semantic nonsense of a horse sailing a boat. Instead, they could be "effortful" (Diamond, 2013) during the task, and isolate the grammar aspect of the sentence.

Working Memory

Another core EF skill is *working memory*. Working memory refers to mentally being able to hold relevant information without observable clues, for example, remembering a code sent to your cell phone without writing it down, and then performing an action with the information, such as using the code stored in your memory to finish what you need to do. Our working memory is essentially a mental "storage" place that keeps a small amount of information for us, either to use immediately, or to go back to a bit later when we need to access it for cognitive tasks. Working memory is different from long-term memory where we keep a very large amount of information accrued over our lifetimes (Cowan, 2014). But the limited "space" for working memory is actually critical for many mental tasks. For example, we can use that information to make a plan of action, or to solve a problem, or accomplish many other mental activities. Your working memory must also tune out irrelevant information to be able to work with the information in some way (Diamond, 2013).

Readers can likely immediately detect the tight connection between working memory and—here it is again—inhibitory/attentional control. Being able to effectively work on the mental activity at hand is very much tied to screening out and controlling the interference from thoughts that are not productive. Indeed, cognitive science researchers are consistent in linking attentional control with working memory. They contend that working memory supports attentional control: "You need to hold your goal in mind to know what is relevant or appropriate and what to inhibit" (Diamond, 2013, p. 143). Furthermore, the reverse is also true: inhibitory/attentional control supports working memory:

> To relate multiple ideas or facts together you must be able to resist focusing exclusively on just one thing, and to recombine ideas and facts in new, creative ways ... To keep your mind focused on what you want to focus on you must inhibit internal and external distractions.
>
> (Diamond, 2013, p, 144)

At this point in your reading about working memory and its link to attentional control, we are confident that you are forming a prediction something along the lines of, "Given bilinguals' advantage in attentional control research, and the tie between attentional control and working memory, bilinguals probably perform better on working memory tasks than monolinguals." If you made that prediction, you are right. But for deeper understanding of this bilingual advantage, it is helpful to directly consider the research directly exploring this question.

As we weigh the evidence from research on whether bilinguals have an advantage in working memory as they do in attentional control, it is important to recognize that there are two central working memory components: *verbal* and *nonverbal*. Tasks involving verbal memory explicitly incorporate oral or written language. A representative verbal memory test may ask participants in the study to take a random series of animals—*mouse bee hippo dog*—and reorder the words according to smallest to largest—*bee mouse dog hippo*. In contrast to this verbal animal name activity requiring understanding and producing language, language is not key in *nonverbal* activities. Instead of remembering and working with verbal information, participants in nonverbal EF studies of working memory must hold on to what they have *observed* to work on the task required of them. Researchers often describe these nonverbal tests of working memory as visual-spatial in nature, that is, using one's vision to pay attention to where objects are located or moving in space. A representative test of nonverbal working memory is called the *Corsi Block Test* (Lezak, 1983). In this test, the examiner touches a series of blocks in different configurations and with an increasing amount of touches per turn, and the participants must repeat the sequence.

What does the overall body of research on bilinguals and working memory tell us currently about the existence of a cognitive advantage? It turns out that for this core EF, there is less consensus than for other components such as attentional control. Some researchers who have reviewed the evidence conclude that we do not yet have clear enough proof to state definitively that bilingualism confers a benefit in working memory (Papp, 2019). Others, including authors of a very careful and detailed review of seven studies that met a high level of scholarly standards (Liu & Liu, 2021), came down on the side of a bilingual advantage in working memory. Interestingly, however, these researchers identified evidence of the advantage in only nonverbal, not verbal tasks. One reason that there is less of a case for verbal working memory is that when researchers test bilinguals in only one language, say

English, as the societal dominant language in the US and England, bilinguals do not always demonstrate as high of level of working memory as monolinguals. In essence, limiting the bilinguals to one language in verbal working memory tasks does not take full advantage of their entire repertoire of multiple language skills. Of course, making up for these occasional lower working memory scores in one language, is the fact that bilinguals have an entire other language as a resource! Furthermore, people doing language and cognitive evaluations are now beginning to realize that, for example, to test the extent of a bilingual's vocabulary and metalinguistic knowledge, assessments should be given in both languages to fully assess the capabilities of multilinguals (Monsrud, Rydland, Geve, Thurmann-Moe & Lyster, 2019; Torregrossa, Eisenbeiss & Bongartz, 2023).).

At this point, researchers in bilingualism continue to explore the question of an advantage for bilinguals in verbal working memory. In contrast to a bit of the back-and-forth nature of the research on working memory and bilingual advantage, another core EF—*cognitive flexibility*—has a long history and a substantial body of research documenting bilingual benefits.

Cognitive Flexibility

Up until the last part of the twentieth century, the prevailing thought was that bilingualism was a negative factor related to children's schooling and would cause confusion. However, around 60 years ago, researchers Peal and Lambert (1962) found striking evidence to contradict that assumption. In their landmark study of Grade 5 students (around 10 years old), bilingual children with a high degree of dual language proficiency outperformed monolingual children on several cognitive tasks. Relevant to our present discussion, several of those tasks asked children to mentally organize objects one way, and then shift to another way of organizing them. Peal and Lambert called this enhanced ability among the bilingual children *symbolic/conceptual flexibility*.

The results emanating from the Peal and Lambert research was groundbreaking in at least two ways: (1) they caused a "swerve" away from the thinking at the time that bilingualism was a detriment, toward the possibility that bilingualism was actually a benefit (Bialystok et al., 2022); and, (2) they began to point out a path toward further investigation of any advantages or disadvantages associated with bilingualism. One of those branches in the path is another core EF which Peal and Lambert called conceptual flexibility, but is more commonly referred to now as *cognitive flexibility*.

In a nutshell, cognitive flexibility is a skill whereby people are able to *shift* their thinking and behavior when there are changes in circumstances and priorities. It also connects to *creativity*, that is, "thinking outside of the box." Another component of cognitive flexibility is *fluency*, that is, the quantity of a person's ideas within a certain context. The converse to cognitive flexibility would be to be stuck in the same way of thinking or solving problems despite important changes rendering the original strategies less effective. This *cognitive inflexibility* or rigidity would diminish a person's capacity to generate new ways of looking at or addressing problems.

It turns out that it is not alway easy to change our previous patterns of thinking or doing; scientists have referred to this challenge to adapt as our *inertial tendencies*. In contrast to inertial tendencies, cognitive flexibility can help us switch to more valuable and effective ideas and behaviors when the older ones have not been working. It is likely apparent that cognitive flexibility positively relates to academic performance, especially with regard to increasingly complex tasks. Whether it be a math problem, or chemistry project, or analytical essay about a historical event, being able to generate alternative paths or solutions in reaching the best outcome is certainly an asset.

How do researchers explore people's cognitive flexibility or inflexibility? Once again, over decades researchers have devised various tasks to observe and document these EF skills. For the "thinking outside the box" aspect of cognitive flexibility, a typical task may ask you to consider four words such as *cut*, *ball*, *do*, *pin*, and think about a way that they connect. (Answer: by putting the word *hair* at the beginning of each word, there is a familiar word combination such as *haircut*, *hairball*, etc.). For the fluency aspect of cognitive flexibility, you may be asked to generate as many items found in a kitchen as you can in 60 seconds, and then in the next 60 seconds, the names of animals. You may even be asked to alternate kitchen items with animal names. As Diamond writes in her overview of EF functions (2013), common answers come to mind first, but then you must use all of your mental resources to generate the less common items, and perhaps do so when switching categories.

The notion of switching brings up one more dimension of cognitive flexibility relevant to our discussion of bilingualism: *task-shifting*. When you are asked to suddenly change your behavior or thinking, and can do so seamlessly, then you are definitely showing your cognitive flexibility. A representative example of an activity tapping into task-shifting might be sorting cards depending on a changing set of criteria, such as shape, color, number, etc. Since the earliest research on cognitive flexibility, there is wide agreement that bilingual children and adults outperform monolinguals on tests of task-shifting. Here we look at three studies to further understand this strong relationship.

Hartanto, Toh, and Yang (2018) analyzed results from their study with a truly impressive database: 18,200 US children aged 5–7. They also documented the children's socioeconomic status (SES). Like many other studies of cognitive flexibility, the researchers looked at task-shifting abilities of the monolingual and bilingual groups with the *Dimension Card Sort Task* (DCCS) (Zelazo, 2006). The children were asked to sort cards by, first, color, then shape. The third task-shift activity was to sort cards depending if they had a black border or not. The DCCS test can be considered an experimental task, that is, purposely structured and controlled in contrast to an activity that naturally occurs in daily life. Hartanto and colleagues augmented their examination of cognitive flexibility by including a measure that was unique when compared to other research in this area: they collected teacher reports on each child in terms of the children's attention, engagement, and resisting inappropriate responses in the classroom. These skills are often referred to as *self-regulatory behaviors*. Hartanto and colleagues found that two groups of children—the bilingual group and the high SES group—outperformed the other children on both the more experiment-like cognitive flexibility card task (DCCS), and the teachers' reports of children's self-regulatory behaviors in the real-life classroom setting. Very interestingly, even bilingual children who came from low SES backgrounds did as well as the children from high SES backgrounds not only on measures of experimental tasks such as the DCCS, but also from teachers' reports of their classroom behaviors. Put another way, for children coming from a low-income household, bilingualism lessened any possible detrimental effect on attentional focus and self-regulatory skills. We hope that more researchers will follow the lead of Hartanto and colleagues and include measures outside of the laboratory to examine bilingualism and cognitive advantages in real-life settings.

Before looking at one more study in this section, let's consider the theory behind the wide-spread documentation of bilinguals' advantage in cognitive flexibility. Once again, the thinking is that bilinguals have long-time practice with shifting between languages in their life experiences. Neuroscience has documented through imaging that both languages are always active in the brain (DeLuca, Segaert, Mazaheri, & Krott, 2020). Therefore, bilinguals' constant managing of multiple languages seems to confer a generalized skill in focusing on and adapting to changed circumstances (Bialystok & Craik, 2022).

For our last close look at a study in this section, we return to the experimental lab for a very intriguing study. In this research, 4, 5, and 6 year olds who were simply exposed to another language, that is, not fully bilingual, showed surprising perspective-taking skills (Fan, Liberman, Keysar & Kinzler, 2015). Fan and colleagues gathered 72 young children and categorized them into three language groups: (1) English-only speakers; (2) "Exposures," that is, children exposed to another language at home, but primarily English-speaking; and, (3) Bilinguals. The children were asked to participate in what the researchers termed a communication task that required them to take the perspective of their conversational partner to successfully complete the activity. As such, the children were asked to flexibly shift from their own perspective to the other person's perspective.

Each child sat with an adult (the "Director") and looked at a small structure consisting of a grid of 16 small boxes (Figure 1.1). The children could see into all 16 boxes on their side, but on the Director's side, four of the boxes were occluded, that is, blocked so that nothing could be seen in those boxes on the Director's side. Figure 1.1 shows the two different views, the children's (labeled "Participant's"), and the Director's. During practice, the child was able to sit on the Director's side and could observe that some of the boxes on the Director's side were blocked.

After some training, the children listened to the directions of the Director, and moved the objects in the box—toy cars, a spoon, and so on—according to her instructions. At one point the Director said, "I see a small car. Move the small car by the spoon." The children could see all three cars, from their perspective, so the small car for them would be the one on the far left in Figure 1.1, circled in dark gray.

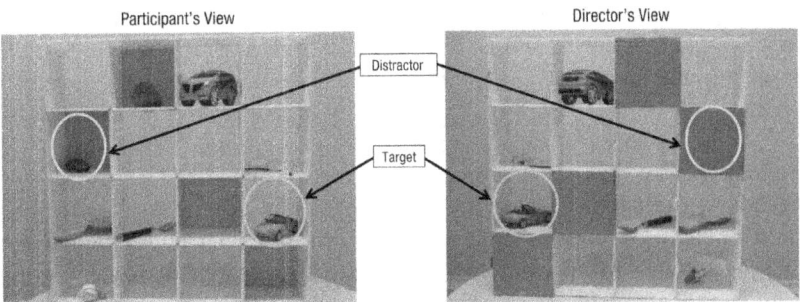

Figure 1.1 Two views of a grid—one blocked and one open—that children ("participants") used to either take the perspective of the adult ("director") or not during the task (Fan et al., 2015).

But two groups of children—the Exposure and Bilingual groups—moved their eyes back and forth between the cars and concluded that the Director could *not* see that smallest car because the adult's view was blocked. These two groups of very young children then took the perspective of the Director, and ignored the smallest car that they could see. Instead, they moved what the Director saw as the small car, even though to them it was the medium size car. In short, simply being exposed to a second language was connected to more successful shifting of perspectives from one's own, to another's. It certainly would be useful in the future to see if these results regarding bilinguals' sensitivity to others' perspectives manifest beyond the experimental setting to natural, real-life social interactions. Fortunately, such exploratory efforts have begun as in the case of researchers comparing bilingual and monolingual middle-schoolers (aged 9–12) on their perspective-taking in essays (Hsin & Snow, 2017). Not surprisingly to readers, the bilingual children outperformed the monolingual children in this study in their ability to acknowledge other's perspective, and to articulate it. In summary, in both experimental settings (e.g., Nguyen et al., 2023) and educational settings (Hantanto et al., 2018), bilingualism has been shown to confer a valuable set of skills related to cognitive flexibility.

Age-Related Cognitive Decline in Executive Functioning

This subheading summarizes the research very aptly: as we become older, our core EFs weaken. Yet we can also find good news in this research when we turn our attention to studies of bilingualism and the aging brain. It turns out that studies with this focus have found that bilingualism often acts as a protective factor against the loss of many cognitive functions (Bialystok, 2021; Costa & Galles, 2014). For us as a society, any delay in the onset of cognitive decline or dementia is beneficial in terms of deferring personal and economic costs. So, it is encouraging that in the face of this natural decline, scientists have identified something they call *cognitive reserve*. Cognitive reserve refers to protective factors that help people conserve cognitive functioning despite structural changes in the brain due to the normal course of aging, or due to illness. Bialystok (2021) has recently compiled studies comparing older monolinguals and bilinguals, and summarizes the results of her review:

> ... bilingualism offered some protection against symptoms of dementia, even if it did not prevent the disease from occurring. Bilingualism has also been cited as a protective factor in other neurological disorders, including cognitive recovery following stroke, intensity of aphasia following similar levels of stroke, and degree of symptoms of Multiple Sclerosis, Parkinson's and Huntington's Disease. Moreover, bilingual AD [Alzheimer's disease] patients with clinical dementia outperformed comparable monolingual patients on tests of memory and attention. Together these results are consistent with a persistent benefit from bilingualism in the context of neurodegenerative disease.
>
> (2021, p. 10)

The theory explaining why bilingualism may be associated with cognitive reserve as we age is familiar territory for us thus far in the chapter: the bilingual experience is related to stronger EF skills, and these are precisely the skills that naturally decline in all of us as we age. The on-going practice of these EF skills through multiple language use can potentially enhance the mental resources for cognitive reserve.

Autism Mitigation

Another exciting area of research exploring the idea of a bilingual advantage is in autism. Autism is a developmental disability that affects how people communicate, interact, learn, and behave. Though the range of symptoms and severity can vary widely, scholars in autism have documented that autistic children and adults have challenges in several EF areas. Of particular concern is attentional/inhibitory control, as well as cognitive flexibility. Given the large number of studies showing a bilingual advantage with certain EF skills, some researchers have begun to investigate whether bilingualism could be a benefit to autistic children. Thus far in this relatively new area, the preponderance of research is documenting that bilingualism seems to lessen the impact of autism related to EF skills.

An example of this emerging research is a study by Peristeri, Baldimsti, Vogelzang, T'Simpli, and Durrleman (2021). These researchers administered a series of tasks with a group of 103 autistic children aged 7–15, approximately half of whom were bilingual and half monolingual. Overall, the researchers indeed found that the bilingual children performed better on behaviors that called on attentional control, working memory, and cognitive flexibility. An especially intriguing finding was related to what cognitive scientists have called *Theory of Mind*. Schroeder (2018) provides a succinct explanation: "Theory of Mind refers to the ability to attribute mental states to other people and to predict and explain other people's behavior on the bases of those attributed mental states" (p. 2). Autism researchers have documented for some time now that autistic individuals tend to underperform on tasks developed to explore Theory of Mind. Consequently, discovering evidence similar to bilingualism's protective factor for aging brains in the area of autism would be helpful.

Understanding Theory of Mind is a bit tricky but worth doing in order to investigate possible cognitive benefits or drawbacks of bilingualism in autistic people. Looking a bit more closely at research using a frequent Theory of Mind task, *false belief*, can help us both comprehend what researchers are studying and then its relationship to bilingualism. False belief (FB) tasks come into play in this area of research because part of knowing others' mental states and predicting their behavior is recognizing that what people believe to be true may not actually fit with the real state of affairs (a false belief). In research with typically developing children, it is not until they reach about age 4 years that they can accurately complete FB tasks. But there is also evidence that autistic children have continued challenges with FB tasks when they are several years older (Schroeder, 2018).

Let's consider an example of a classic experimental FB task used in research comparing both typical-developing and autistic bilingual and monolingual children called the *Sally–Anne Task* (Baron-Cohen, Leslie, & Frith, 1985). In the Sally–Anne Task, children are presented with the sequence of pictures in Figure 1.2. The top panel introduces the figures of Sally and Anne, and shows the figures alongside drawings of a picnic basket and of a plain box. The next pictures in the sequence show Sally putting her ball in the picnic basket, and then leaving, all the while being observed by Anne. After Sally leaves, Anne takes the ball from the picnic basket and relocates the ball into the box. The final panel shows Sally between the two boxes, Anne gone, and poses the question to the child: *Where will Sally look for her ball?*

The Sally–Anne Task and many others assess children's skills in taking into account what a person other than themselves is perceiving or thinking, and then predicting their behavior. Arriving to the correct answer in these tests involves focusing on whether children can "put themselves in the other person's shoes," including when the person is wrong (false belief), and is potentially going to act in a way that is not appropriate or accurate because of that belief.

Returning to the Peristeri et al. (2021) study we mentioned earlier that compared EF skills of bilingual and monolingual children ages 7–15, we see that among the large battery of tests the researchers administered were several scenarios depicting false belief situations similar to the Sally–Anne Task. Piersteri and colleagues found that the bilingual autistic children outperformed the monolingual children at assessing and predicting the video characters' mental state, here, their incorrect belief, at significantly higher rates. This finding was especially noteworthy because the bilingual children on average came from lower income households, and were less proficient in the national language, Greek. The bilingual children better controlled their own perspective and knowledge in service of taking the perspective of the other person. Put another way, the bilingual autistic children were

Figure 1.2 Panels of pictures presented to children in a classic false belief task (Peristeri et al., 2021).

better at figuring out the beliefs of others. Given that autistic children and adults are often challenged to effectively respond and interact with others, this advantage conferred by bilingualism—the skill to take on another's viewpoint—can possibly lead to more positive social interactions. Specifically, if autistic children can better understand or predict others' mental states, their comfort and success in social interactions may be enhanced (Peristeri et al., 2021; Schroeder, 2018).

How do researchers explain these and other similar findings regarding the bilingual advantage in autism studies? Once again, the bilingual experience of the participants is the central part of the theory. Specifically, bilinguals' practice in determining the language of the person they are interacting with, and then mobilizing that particular language while keeping their other language at bay until needed, constitutes on-going perspective-taking of others rather than their own. Put another way, a bilingual's focus on the other person's language seems to generalize to bilinguals more easily attending to others' perspectives.

As in the area of cognitive reserve for aging adults, more research into the area of autism mitigation is needed. However, researchers in the two fields of bilingualism and autism are encouraged by additional studies finding a bilingual benefit (Peristeri et al., 2021; Schroeder, 2018). Certainly, it is very important to get the word out about a bilingual advantage to educators of autistic children so that, if their students or clients come from a bilingual household, they can support and celebrate continued exposure to two languages, not discourage it. As Peristeri and colleagues conclude: "Parents and carers should thus not feel pressured to abandon bilingualism, a decision which moreover may result in detrimental effects on emotional bonding, social, and professional opportunities" (2021, p. 1706).

Test yourself! What did you learn?: Re-consider each statement from the beginning of the chapter. Use your background knowledge *and* new information gained from reading the chapter to decide whether the statements reflect current research on multilingualism (True), or not (False). Answers are in Appendix A at the back of the book.

True or False	Multilingualism
	1. Research has documented that bilingual people as a group have higher earning power.
	2. Employers of professions not requiring a college degree, such as construction, retail, and manufacturing, do not show any notable preference for bilinguals.
	3. Young bilingual children outperform monolingual children in being able to take another person's perspective that may be different from their own.
	4. Both monolinguals and bilinguals seem to experience the same level of cognitive decline as they reach advanced age.
	5. Parents of autistic children should keep to one language only in their homes so as not to further negatively impact their children's language and cognitive development.

Time to Think and Connect

Multilingualism across Professional Settings

1. As you think about your current or future profession, is being bilingual an asset? If so, generate a list of ways that bilingualism would be a benefit. Consider the question from both the perspective of your professional colleagues and of the people/clients you serve.
2. This chapter explores the connection between multilingualism and mental Executive Functions such as attentional/inhibitory control; working memory; and cognitive flexibility. In your daily life, whether in the work, home, or community setting, which executive functions emerge as the ones that you call on regularly? Give examples when possible.
3. Kind-hearted people often think that it is best for people with disabilities, such as autism, Down's Syndrome, or learning disabilities, to be shielded from bilingual environments and concentrate on one language only. They imagine that people with disabilities have a difficult time learning one language well, and bilingual exposure would be confusing or in some way harmful to their development. Given the information in this chapter, and your own experience with people with disabilities, how would you respond to that perspective?

Chapter 2

The Development of Multilingualism

Overview

This chapter explores the answer to the question: How does multilingualism develop? Here we detail the processes at play as people become multilingual, beginning in childhood, and continuing through adulthood. We describe recent research regarding the unique ways that children and adults display and mobilize their multilingual repertoire. We then go into depth on how people acquire additional languages either through their interaction with their families, communities, or solely in educational settings. We also provide information from the research on factors that influence those processes. Those include broad sociocultural considerations such as the status of multiple languages within a country, and also individual factors such as age, personality, motivation, among others.

Test yourself! (Tapping into your background knowledge): Before reading the chapter, consider each statement below and use your current knowledge and experiences to decide whether the statement is true or false.

True or False	Development of Multilingualism
	1. About two-thirds of the world's children are growing up bilingual.
	2. Only those individuals who have equal knowledge of each language, and speak both without an accent, should be labeled "bilingual."
	3. When bilinguals intermix their languages in a single sentence or conversation, it is a sign that they have serious language gaps in one or both of their languages.
	4. The more proficiency immigrant children have in their home language, including some schooling in that language, the faster and better they will learn the new language in their new country.
	5. Though in many ways the earlier one learns a second language is best, adults and older children outperform younger children in certain aspects of language learning.

DOI: 10.4324/9781003216414-5

Bilinguals and Bilingualism

In the introduction to this book, we provided a general way of referring to people who speak more than one language as *multilingual* or *bilingual*. This initial definition allowed us to explore the benefits of bilingualism in the previous chapter, especially when we compared the attributes and performance of bilinguals to monolinguals. As we now delve into ways people develop multilingual skills, we need to revisit who it is we are characterizing as bilinguals.

The first fact to recognize is that about 66% of children in the world are learning two languages at a young age (Lightbown & Spada, 2021; Smith & Meeks, 2018). This acknowledgment may come as a surprise to those of us who live in countries that in many ways project a single, exclusive "national language," such as English in the US and Britain. Most countries throughout the globe, however, assume that their populations will become bilingual through exposure to multiple languages and the functional need to carry out daily life in those languages.

As we mentioned in this book's introduction, scientists, linguists, and everyday bilingual folks have a multitude of conceptions of who is and is not bilingual. Those conceptions range from believing that only people with native-like proficiencies in both languages are bilingual, including those who do not have any detectable accents, to considering that simply having some skills in both languages constitutes bilingualism. Thankfully, François Grosjean, a highly esteemed Swiss scholar in the study of bilingualism, and one whose work we will often refer to in this chapter, recently reviewed a range of sources defining bilingualism, including dictionaries, language scientists, and bilinguals themselves (Grosjean, 2022). To illustrate the wide span of conceptions of bilingualism among these sources, Grosjean offers examples of bilinguals:

> At one end of the range we find the migrant worker who may speak with some difficulty the host country's language and who does not read and write it. At the other end, we have the professional interpreter who is fully fluent in two languages. In between, we find the scientist who reads and writes articles in a second language but who rarely speaks it, the foreign-born spouse who interacts with friends in his first language, the member of a linguistic minority who uses the minority language only at home and the majority language in all other domains of life, the Deaf person who uses sign language with her friends but a spoken language (often in its written form) with a hearing person, and so on. Despite the great diversity among these people, they all share a common feature: They lead their lives with two or more languages.
>
> (2011, p. 11)

Based on this particular inquiry, and decades of research into bilingualism, Grosjean shares the definition of bilingualism that he has come to use in his work and that we will adopt for this chapter: Bilinguals are ... *those who use two or more languages (or dialects) in their everyday lives* (Grosjean, 2022, p. 11).

With this straightforward definition, we need to be careful not to oversimplify what bilingualism is, or the unique ways bilinguals use the languages in their linguistic repertoire. The danger comes from solely focusing on bilinguals' individual languages such as French, Japanese, Chinese, etc., and the separate degree of proficiency in each of those languages. If we limit ourselves to measuring and viewing bilinguals in terms of the degree of proficiency in language X and, separately, in language Y, we miss the unique and dynamic ways that bilinguals leverage their languages across communicative settings. Reacting to this over-emphasis on socially defined languages instead of how bilinguals actually process and use their languages, Grosjean wrote a seminal article with a very telling title: "Neurolinguists Beware! The Bilingual is Not Two Monolinguals in One Person" (Grosjean, 1989). In heeding Grosjean's warning, it turns out that the same cognitive and linguistic sciences we depended on in the previous chapter as we explored the advantages of bilingualism, can help us understand this critical aspect of who bilinguals are: how bilinguals cognitively process and use their multiple languages.

Active Multilingual Processing

There is a central defining characteristic of bilinguals that is important to recognize from the outset of our discussion of how multilingualism develops. That attribute is the unique language processing system of bilinguals within which they are able to manage any and all of their linguistic and cognitive resources to communicate at any one time (Jeddy & Beketova, 2024). For the purpose of this book, we have chosen to call the cognitive processing and use of multiple languages by bilinguals as *active multilingualism* (Cummins, 2017; Grosjean, 2012). The way that bilinguals process and use their linguistic repertoire—active multilingualism—differs from monolinguals' processing and use of their one language. Cognitively, a bilingual's languages connect and intersect in unique ways as they adapt to their communicative needs. For example, research has documented that bilinguals do not compartmentalize their cognitive activity by what we socially define as distinct languages, e.g., "Now I'm thinking and learning a math concept in Spanish; but, now I'm thinking in English, so I need to start over and learn that math concept in English." We will explore what researchers have acknowledged as a unique system of proficiency underlying both of a bilingual's languages in the next section, but for now, it is timely to recall what neurolinguist Grosjean has reminded us since 1989 and through the present (2024), bilinguals are not "two monolinguals."

While the field has documented active multilingualism in many ways, to help us more fully understand the concept we will highlight here one of those behaviors in which multilinguals manifest their active processing in ways that we can easily observe: *Code-switching*. "Code" refers to a socially defined language or dialect, and "switching" means fluid changing or shifting among a bilingual's languages and dialects. No doubt that if readers are themselves bilingual, or interact closely with people who are, you have noticed occasional language mixing among bilinguals, or have yourself combined your languages in a single conversation.

Interestingly, looking at examples of code-switching allows us to witness bilinguals' skills in engaging the languages (or disengaging them when the situation calls for it) in their multilingual repertoire as they respond to the needs of particular communicative settings. And it is important to recall at the onset of our discussion of code-switching information from the previous chapter on the degree to which the cognitive benefits of bilingualism, such attentional control and cognitive flexibility, were precisely linked to bilingual children's and adults' skills in dynamic switching among their languages.

Code-Switching

When socially defined languages are in contact, multilingual speakers in those contexts can choose to move fluidly among their languages and use all of them in dynamic ways. One of the most common ways that people, even monolinguals, bring in more than one language to their speech is language *borrowing* (Poplack, 2018). As English speakers, we have a long record of borrowing words from other languages, such as "rodeo" from Spanish, or "kindergarten" from German, or "entrepreneur" from French. These *loanwords* are often decades if not centuries, old, and widely incorporated into English using English pronunciation.

The loanword "rodeo" from Spanish can illustrate one of the central distinguishing features of a loanword, which is the adaptation of its pronunciation from the original language—the *donor language*—as the pronunciation is integrated into the *recipient language*. In Spanish, the donor language, the word "rodeo" begins with a trilled "r", a rapid series of taps by the tongue on the front roof of the mouth, but in American English, the recipient language, the "r" is more of a rounded sound. Additionally, in Spanish, the "e" vowel of "rodeo" would have the sound of a long "a" as in the first syllable of "bacon," but in English, the "e" in "rodeo" sounds like a long "e," as in the word "see." Finally, in Spanish, the syllable stress—subtly increased loudness and/or length—would be on the next to the last syllable, but in English we place the stress on a different syllable, the first one, "ro-". These borrowed and long-established words like "rodeo" have allowed us to expand the concepts we use when we communicate in English, and thereby have enriched our language expression. Obviously, one does not need to be bilingual at all to use these words donated from other languages long ago. For example, the word "kindergarten" from the donor language of German is now firmly established in the recipient language of English, and non-German speakers in the US use "kindergarten" to talk about schooling all the time. And we do so with a very English, not German, pronunciation.

Relevant to our discussion of active multilingual processing, however, is a very different type of loanword: *spontaneous borrowing* (Grosjean, 2017). Spontaneous borrowing is a communication strategy of bilinguals in which they insert single words from a donor language into a longer stretch of speech in the recipient language. These borrowings are novel loanwords that bilingual speakers use once or twice in conversation. They do not enter wide-spread use by the speech community, nor become part of the community's permanent stock of words as do loanwords.

A useful example of spontaneous borrowing comes from a study by Waltermire and Valtierez (2019). The research was conducted in the US state of southern New Mexico, very near the US–Mexico border, with adult Spanish–English bilinguals. One of the study's participants was recorded saying in conversation the following sentence in Spanish with one English word inserted, "babies": "Ya no puede trabajar con *babies* chiquitos." [He can't work with little babies any more.] The speaker used Spanish grammar for this utterance including putting the adjective "chiquitos" after the noun "babies" in contrast to the usual adjective-first, noun-second placement in English, "little babies." Despite using Spanish grammar for the overall sentence, the speaker elected to use the English word "babies" instead of the Spanish word "bebés."

We take a moment here to address the continuing myth held by many people that when bilinguals borrow words from a donor language, as the speaker did in this example with the word "babies," it is because they have a vocabulary gap in the language they are using at the moment. As readers will rightly assume, the word "bebés" is extremely common in the Spanish language. It was certainly not the case that this highly fluent adult speaker of Spanish did not know the Spanish word for "babies"; instead, the speaker simply *chose* to tap into his repertoire of multiple languages and use the English word. (Later in this section we will examine why the speaker may have elected to use the English term in that moment when he easily could have continued speaking only Spanish and said "bebés.")

Applied linguists, those who study how people use language in the real world, have rebutted for many years the belief that a vocabulary gap among bilinguals is responsible for spontaneous borrowing. What is unique about the research conducted by Waltermire and Valtierrez (2019), however, is that they have added to linguists' argument with documentation. These researchers found that in the overwhelming instances of spontaneous borrowing among their study's bilingual participants, including the speaker who said "babies" in his otherwise Spanish utterance, there was no vocabulary gap; the participants knew the words in both Spanish and English. How did the researchers show that this was true? Waltermire and Valtierrez designed a clever task in which they tested whether these bilinguals could produce equivalents in both Spanish and English for their previously recorded spontaneous borrowing. So, for example, in the case of the speaker who used the English word "babies" in his spontaneous borrowing, they asked if he could supply the Spanish word, "bebés." The researchers gathered all the English loanwords used informally in conversation by the study participants—nearly 500 utterances in total—and then provided the participants with a list of those same loanwords, asking the participants to translate them into Spanish. Results showed that participants were able to provide the Spanish equivalent 85% of the instances of their use of English loanwords. The three participants whose success at translating was below the group average of 85%, hovering around 63%, were people who used less Spanish in their daily lives, and were raised by US-born parents who likely provided less Spanish input in the home. Their relative lower percentages of accurate translations contrasted to the other participants who had more exposure to Spanish and were more successful translators of the loanwords using their multilingual repertoire. This phenomenon of bilinguals who are most proficient in the usage of their languages showing the most skillful multilingual shifts is something we will return to often in this section, and leads us to another illustration of bilinguals' active multilingual processing, *code-switching* of longer stretches of speech.

Though some applied linguists put spontaneous borrowing under the umbrella of code-switching, as we have in this book, they acknowledge that spontaneous loanword borrowing greatly differs from code-switching. Code-switches are longer than single word borrowing, consisting of phrases and sentences. We can define code-switching as the use of more than one language or dialect in either a single utterance, or across multiple utterances, in a conversation. A classic example of a code-switch by a Spanish–English bilingual is from the work of Shana Poplack (1980), one of the leading scholars in borrowing and code-switching: "*I told him that* pa' que lo trajera ligero" [I told him that so he would bring it right away]. This sentence is an example of an *intra-sentential* code-switch, that is, the speaker's language shift occurs *within* a single utterance. Another type of code-switch is when a person uses more than one language *between* utterances in a conversation, and is called *inter-sentential* code-switching. In both intra- and inter-sentential code-switching, bilinguals are alternating their languages. Code-switching, like spontaneous loanword borrowing, occurs across the globe in multilingual communities (Poplack, 2015). Furthermore, code-switching research has a 50-year-plus history in applied linguistics focusing on multilingualism.

The most critical fact to understand about code-switching is that it is very far from random mixing of languages. Instead, research has established for more than half a century that code-switching is highly rule-governed and predictable. It also represents a kind of multiple language expertise that non-code-switchers have difficulty imitating (Gumperz & Hernández-Chávez, 1975.) For example, studies have shown that when bilinguals use a complex intra-sentential code-switch, i.e., two languages within a single utterance, they tend to follow the grammatical rules of both languages. We can immediately glean here that bilinguals who manage multiple language grammars within a single sentence differ from those who simply insert a single, spontaneous loanword into a recipient language, as "babies" was inserted into Spanish in our earlier example.

Poplack's example of an intra-sentential code-switch elucidates that difference for us with the speaker's longer phrases, and fluid and correct use of two language grammars. In this case, the code-switching speaker used English in the first phrase ("I told him that"), and Spanish in the second phrase ("pa' que lo trajera ligero"). The second phrase in Spanish needed the use of a specific verb tense that English would not require. (For those readers who have studied the Spanish language, the speaker here has correctly used the past subjunctive in the switch, a more complex verb structure in this sentence than would be required by its English equivalent.) Clearly, maintaining grammatical structures of defined languages in code-switching is a hallmark of advanced knowledge and application of language skill. In fact, there are numerous studies beginning in 1975 with Lenora Timm's classic article, "Code-switching: El porqué y el how not-to" [The Why and the How-Not-To], and continuing to the present, in which bilinguals can judge a list of code-switches that would naturally occur in real life and would follow a sophisticated series of grammatical and other linguistic norms. They can distinguish these authentic, systematic language shifts from language sequences that they would never produce, such as when the code-switches break grammatical rules of the bilinguals' languages, and veer from established patterns of use.

Why Code-Switch? It is worth looking at one more aspect of borrowing and code-switching before we move on to other evidence of active multilingual processing. We still need to address why the speaker in our first borrowing example spontaneously inserted the English word "babies" into the Spanish utterance, when he could have used the very common Spanish word "bebés." Equally intriguing, why did the fluent bilingual speaker who began with "I told him that …" choose to manage both language grammars instead of simply saying it in one of their languages? Readers will not be surprised that in the long span of research on bilinguals' code-switching, researchers have looked closely at what triggers or motivates code-switching, or what inhibits it (Lanza & Li, 2023). They have also examined the communicative functions that code-switching serves in both informal and formal conversations. In other words, applied linguists have investigated the "why" of code-switching.

In overviewing the findings on why multilinguals code-switch, we are changing from the previous adult examples to code-switching by children. Multilingual children learn to code-switch from other multilinguals in their family and in their communities, and show impressive competence in alternating languages as early as 2 years of age (Smolak, de Anda, Enriquez, Poulin-Dubois, & Friend, 2020). By looking at several examples of children's code-switching, we can call attention once again to an asset view of multilingualism, here the dynamic and systematic use of multiple languages by young bilingual children. In fact, all of the examples of children's code-switching in the next section proceed from earlier studies by our first author, Nadeen, in classrooms for children identified as having specific language learning disabilities (Ruiz, 1988, 1995a, b). To directly confront the misconception that bilingual children or adults with cognitive disabilities should be constrained to only one of their languages, the next section shows impressive, active multilingualism among bilingual children with special needs, and skillful use of their entire multilingual repertoire. We further believe that it is important to hark back to our discussion in the last chapter of children with another disability, autism, and note again how bilingualism served as an enhancement to the communicative and social skills of autistic children. Multilingualism is very egalitarian in this sense: it is of benefit to all!

Code-Switching Functions in Children

Like adult bilinguals, child bilinguals also engage in spontaneous borrowing, as when a primarily Spanish-speaking child schooled primarily in English, says to Spanish-speaking peers in class, "Pásame el chalk!" [Give me the chalk.] In this situation, it may be the case that the child does not have in his Spanish vocabulary the word "gis" or "tiza," given that he has learned and used the word only in the context of schooling, an example of what applied linguists would call a *language domain* or *domain of acquisition*. However, research has offered many examples of bilingual children shifting between languages when it is clear that they have changed languages for a specific purpose or function, not because they have a vocabulary gap in one language. This research illustrates that bilinguals' language shifts are a creative resource and serve a range of functions, e.g., to emphasize, to get attention, to clarify, to make a joke, to change the tone of a conversation, and so on.

One function that highlights bilingual children's multilingual repertoire involves choosing to switch language according to the language proficiencies of the conversational participants. Table 2.1 shows Rosemary (age 11), a student in a special education classroom, switching from English to Spanish with her classmates. The teacher has allowed the children to set up a pretend store and they are busily preparing for this sociodramatic play. Rosemary, like her classmate Nelly (age 8) in the conversation below, speaks Spanish at home with her family, though both girls are fairly proficient in both English and Spanish, as illustrated in the transcript. The

Table 2.1 Switching languages for your friends in a bilingual special education classroom (Ruiz, 1988)

Function	Context	
Language Proficiency of the Addressee	Elementary bilingual special education classroom for children with language learning disabilities. Rosemary, a bilingual, switches from English to Spanish in the conversation when she addresses Spanish-dominant Pilar.	
Speaker	Actual Transcript (verbatim)	Translation to English of Code-switch
Nelly (age 8)	Make the *tiendita aquí*.	Make the store here.
Rosemary (age 11)	No, we're just going to make one.	
Nelly	No, two.	
Pilar (age 8)	Es la misma tienda, oigan. Acá es donde se pagan, okay?	It's the same store, listen. Here is where they pay, okay?
Rosemary	Nooo. Donde pagan no, porque ya tengo mucho dinero aquí.	Nooo. Where they pay, no because I already have a lot of money here.

Table 2.2 Trying to follow your friend's language choice (even though you don't know that language well) (Ruiz, 1988)

Function	Context	
Follow the Leader	Bilingual pre-kindergarten class with children diagnosed as language learning disabled. José Miguel, English dominant, switches to Spanish after Omar's conversational turn.	
Speaker	Actual Transcript (verbatim)	Translation to English of Code-switch
Omar (age 6)	... estaba frío, me pensaya.	It was cold, I was thinking.
José Miguel (age 6)	... mucho *air, windy*.	... a lot of air, windy.

third student in the scene, Pilar (age 8), is dominant in Spanish. In the following excerpt, Rosemary shifts from speaking English with Nelly to Spanish to accommodate Pilar. As readers look at the transcript, it is clear that Rosemary can express her ideas in either language she chooses, but she switches to the language best understood by her addressee, Pilar.

Again, all these children have been diagnosed with language learning disabilities, yet we see a fluid use of their multilingual repertoire. First, Nelly delivers a directive with an intra-sentential code-switch maintaining the integrity of both English and Spanish, "Make the tiendita aquí," and then, second, Rosemary offers Pilar better access to the interaction by her switch to an explanation in Spanish.

The following examples are also from a bilingual classroom for children with special needs (Ruiz, 1988). The particular setting is a bilingual pre-kindergarten special education classroom for children with language learning disabilities. Here, José Miguel, English dominant, follows Spanish-dominant Omar's lead, and uses his very limited knowledge of Spanish to help Omar narrate a story to his teacher. Both José Miguel and Omar have delayed language development.

José Miguel, despite very limited Spanish proficiency, follows Omar's lead and uses what he knows—"mucho" [a lot of]—to help his friend out while speaking in front of the class.

All of the children in Omar's class were instructed solely in English before they entered this bilingual special education classroom where the teacher delivered instruction in both English and Spanish. Consequently, in these transcripts, we do see lingering effects related to the linguistic domain of schooling, which, for these children, was all in English until they began participation in this official bilingual special education classroom. In the transcript below, Omar is speaking with his teacher. Omar has articulation difficulties in both languages and is often difficult to understand. Here Omar attempts to inform his teacher in English about Alberto's infraction of the rules, chewing gum in class. But Omar is unsuccessful until he mobilizes his multilingual repertoire and switches to Spanish. In this context, the function of Omar's switch is a very purposeful *clarification* of his previous conversational turn.

Table 2.3 Choosing the language with the best chance of being understood when you know the word in both English and Spanish and you have articulation difficulties (Ruiz, 1988)

Function	Context	
Clarification	Omar, much more proficient in Spanish than English, struggles first in English to tattle on his buddy's gum chewing, but then is successful in Spanish.	
Speaker	Transcript (verbatim)	Translation of Code-switch to English
Omar (age 6)	**Albert got a /g/ /k/.**	(Two attempts at saying "gum.")
Teacher	**A cut?**	
Omar	**Un chicle.**	A (piece of) gum.

Once again, bilingualism served as a critical resource to Omar with his articulation difficulty: he could mobilize his other language to clarify his intent and get his message across.

Instances of code-switching prove to be continually fascinating as we analyze them for the "why," including in this previous example. If Omar is very dominant in Spanish, why did he first choose to use English to "tell on" Alberto? Was it because of his previous schooling in English, his domain of acquisition, and therefore, for Omar, English is for typical school discourse, like reporting peer misbehavior to your teacher? For the same reason, did Omar choose to call Alberto by his anglicized name from US schooling, Albert, instead of his actual name? Or could it be that Omar's language choice of English to tell on Alberto was influenced by the fact that Omar is Mexican-American, and his teacher is a white woman who learned Spanish as a second language and spoke it with an accent? In other words, did her identity as a teacher, or her ethnicity as a white woman, or both, motivate Omar to begin with his less dominant language, English? As such, was his use of English an enactment of an extremely common function of both adult and child code-switching, *signaling social identity*? Research in code-switching would suggest that all of these reasons to switch are plausible. So, then, how does one arrive at the best explanation for individual instances of code-switching?

These types of questions have been mulled over and answered by applied linguists over the last 50 years. They employ various techniques to methodically analyze code-switching data, such collecting large amounts of code-switched utterances to determine patterns; documenting features of the conversational situations such as the speakers, their background, the setting; and many other factors that research to date has found to trigger code-switching. Compiling information related to all these factors over the course of the study led first author Nadeen to provide documentation that Omar most likely switched from Spanish to English in order to clarify his utterance for his teacher. But most importantly, this example serves to emphasize that though Omar is in the early stages of development in the

English language, and has a documented disability in the Spanish language, he, like other bilinguals, is able to display his active multilingualism at work.

For our purposes, the two most important take-aways from this very large corpus of research on code-switching are: (1) It is a systematic and rule-governed communication strategy used by child and adult bilinguals, with the most sophisticated and complex forms performed by the most fluent bilinguals; and (2) It is a hallmark of active multilingualism, the unique linguistic resource of bilinguals that both persons with typical developmental profiles, and those with atypical development (having special needs), call on to successfully live in their multilingual worlds.

We now have a working definition of who is multilingual—people who use multiple languages in their everyday lives. And after a look at code-switching, we also have a beginning sense of their active multilingual processing, e.g., the unique ways that multilinguals can mobilize any or all of their languages to meet a wide range of communication needs. We will be returning to illustrations of active multilingual processing that have significant educational and other societal impacts. However, it is time to ask, *How do children and adults become multilingual?* (And if some readers do not yet consider themselves multilingual, do not worry. In the next chapter, we will detail the most effective ways to extend your own linguistic repertoire to include more languages and greater proficiency!)

Becoming Multilingual

One way to begin to understand the beginning processes of becoming multilingual is to think about when and how people are first exposed to more than one language. Two terms—*simultaneous bilinguals* and *sequential bilinguals*—are often used for those broad descriptions.

Simultaneous and Sequential Bilingualism

Simultaneous bilinguals are those children who are learning two (or more) languages from a young age in a more or less parallel fashion. Exactly what constitutes a "young age" has not been specifically defined, and therefore ages for the category of simultaneous bilinguals vary in the scientific literature (Gass, Beheney, & Plonsky, 2020). Generally, we can say that simultaneous bilinguals are usually exposed to multiple languages very early on in their lives, often within the first two to three years. This bilingual exposure usually continues on through to when children have reached a basic level of language development, around 6 to 8. An example of a simultaneous bilingual is Libe, almost 4 years old, and the niece of one of the authors of this book, Nadeen. Libe lives in the north of Spain, and since birth has heard and spoken Basque with her parents. At the same time, Libe has heard and spoken Spanish with her grandparents who live nearby and frequently take care of her. (Her grandparents, though ethnically Basque, lived through the years of Spanish dictatorship when the Basque language was severely repressed and consequently did not learn to speak their heritage language of Basque. Later in this chapter we will discuss the significant impact that the wider society has on the development or loss of languages.) Libe has been interacting with her caregivers in Spanish and Basque since birth, and is a simultaneous bilingual.

For almost 100 years, a range of scientists have studied the acquisition of simultaneous bilingualism by babies, toddlers, and young children. We looked at some of that research in Chapter 1 where we cited recent studies, e.g., how babies begin as "citizens of the world" with regard to language sound systems, but if they experience only one language, later become "native language specialists." Earlier research with very young bilingual children often took the form of scientist-parents raising children in a bilingual home, and closely recording and analyzing their children's bilingual language development. Perhaps the most famous of these parent researchers was Werner Leopold, and his four diaries recording daughter Hildegard's path toward multilingualism. Leopold was an early supporter of the one-parent–one-language model of bilingualism in families, that is, one caregiver sticks to one language, and another to a different language, thereby giving the children a somewhat equal distribution of languages. Though the one-parent–one-language stance is currently under some debate (Aronsson, 2018), these older diary studies produced important understandings about early bilingualism that hold up through today: (1) children are fully capable of learning two languages; (2) they do not experience a delay; and (3) around 2 or 3 years of age, bilingual children signal that they have metalinguistic knowledge with two hallmarks documented by many studies. These hallmarks consist of toddlers switching to the appropriate language based on the language proficiency of their conversational partner, and generating two labels for a single referent, e.g., "table" and "mesa" (Spanish).

Following other parent linguists, first author Nadeen documented these two hallmarks of metalinguistic knowledge by her son Roberto, a simultaneous bilingual in Spanish and English. At age 2 and a half, Roberto was dominant in Spanish, but had some exposure to English outside of the home. At a park near a river, Roberto spotted a small boat steered by a man with a mustache, a facial hair feature shared by his Latino father and other Spanish-speaking family members. Roberto shouted out in Spanish, "Hola" [hello] to the man, but then immediately looked doubtfully at Nadeen and asked "Habla español?" [Does he speak Spanish?]. Roberto had already begun to activate his languages according to his assessment of the language dominance of the other person, here, having a mustache like other Spanish-speaking family members. However, in this case, Roberto was aware that he may have been mistaken in his assessment, especially given the lack of reaction of the man in the boat.

A little later in his development as a bilingual, Roberto also gave evidence of the second hallmark of toddler's bilingualism: labels in two languages for a single referent. In this example, Roberto's referent was cheese. While at a family gathering where all were speaking English, Roberto wanted to ask for cheese, but that word in English can be a difficult one for very young children: it starts with the "ch" sound which an affricate, a combination of blowing air and managing a tricky pronunciation stop at the same time. "Cheese" also ends with a /z/ sound, a fricative where both air and vocal cords combine to produce the sound. The word in Spanish, "queso," is easier to articulate, /keso/. Roberto chose to use the Spanish word, but he took the first syllable, the /ke/, and pronounced it in a very English-accented way, blowing out lots of air for the /k/ (in Spanish, that /k/ would not have a burst of air). He also elongated the /e/ sound so that it sounded like "ay" in "play." In a nutshell, Roberto deployed his multilingual repertoire and opted for an easier-to-pronounce word in Spanish, "queso" … but made sure to phonologically adapt the word to make it sound like he was speaking English. Linguistic flexibility and metalinguistic awareness truly begins early in simultaneous bilinguals!

Sequential bilinguals, also known as *successive bilinguals*, differ from simultaneous bilinguals like Libe and Roberto in that they first learn a single language. Grosjean et al. succinctly put it this way: "Sequential bilingual children begin life as monolinguals and later add knowledge of a second [or third] language" (2018, p. 17). Once again, there is some vagueness about when children are considered sequential bilinguals vs. younger simultaneous bilinguals. But using the same general age when children have developed a solid base of their first language, around 6–8 years, we can conceive of sequential bilinguals as individuals who begin to learn a second language anytime around that age, and on through late adulthood.

Whether we are considering the language acquisition process of simultaneous bilinguals, or sequential bilinguals, or bilinguals somewhere in the middle of those rather ambiguous but useful categories, there are several areas that are shared by all emerging bilinguals. As we did in the previous chapter, we will begin our discussion at the broader, societal level and its influence on multilingual acquisition, and then continue narrowing our lens to focus on individual characteristics that interact with language learning.

Social Influences on Bilingualism

One of the most important and wide-spread influences on acquiring multiple languages (or *not* acquiring them) concerns the differing social status of the defined languages within a country/nation state. To examine the relationship between the social status of a language, and the potential of acquiring or maintaining bilingualism, it is helpful to consider whether a language is the *majority language*, as is English in the case of England and the US, and Spanish in Spain; or whether it is a *minority language*, spoken by a smaller ratio of the population, as is the Basque language in Spain. It is almost always the case that the majority language reflects the highest status in a country, at least as projected by state institutions, which in turn exerts many consequences on the patterns of language learning and use for citizens. For example, most government, business, and educational entities require the use of the majority language in their operations, and all citizens are expected to interact in that language, or take steps to learn and use it as quickly as possible. Along with the status of the majority or official language comes a power differential when compared with minority languages (Cummins, 2021). That power often exerts a push away from any substantive, official use of minority languages, except, perhaps, to serve as a temporary or limited scaffold for citizens who do not (yet) speak the majority language, such as translated communications from schools. The power differential between majority and minority languages is increased when minority languages are associated with racial or ethnolinguistic identities of its speakers, identities that do not align with those who identify as majority language speakers (Cummins, 2021). In those cases, which are historically and globally wide-spread, multilingualism in the population is pressured to cede the way to encroaching monolingualism.

An illustration of the power of a national language on future generations of potential bilinguals is contained in the work of researcher Rubén Rumbaut and his colleagues in the Los Angeles, California, area. We first cited the research team's work in Chapter 1 as we reviewed their large-scale studies showing the link between more fluent bilingualism and higher education attainment. However, Rumbaut and colleagues have used these same large data sets to document that, overall, immigrant families who speak a language other than English, lose that language in a generation and a half (Rumbaut, 2014). How can we conceptualize this 1.5 generational path to monolingualism? As an example, Vietnamese-speaking parents who have immigrated to the US will likely use Vietnamese to raise a family in the US. Their children will be bilingual in Vietnamese from the language used in the home and perhaps in the local neighborhood/community, and in English from the wider environment—schools, etc.—which most often require use of the majority language. But results from Rumbaut and team's multiple studies would also predict that among the grandchildren of this family—the second generation—older grandchildren would have greater probability of retaining Vietnamese-English bilingualism over the younger ones. Essentially, after about a generation and a half, grandchildren of immigrants speaking a minority language are likely to lose access to that particular linguistic heritage.

Within schools, researchers have long documented the deleterious impact of a society's negative view of minority languages, especially when associated with ethnic groups. A dramatic illustration of this impact has been documented by several scholars, including first author Nadeen and her colleague, Manuel Barajas, an immigration sociologist (Ruiz & Barajas, 2012). Nadeen and Manuel conducted a study of Mexican immigrant families who were indigenous and had enrolled their children in US schools. The home language of these families was not Spanish, the national language of Mexico, though the adults were born in Mexico and had lived there most of their lives. Instead, the native languages of the families in this study were the indigenous languages of Mixtec and Zapotec. Nadeen and Manuel documented stark cases of language repression and prejudice toward the families, as illustrated by the following quotes from study participants. We first hear from a teacher from Mexico, indigenous himself, from the Mexican state of Oaxaca, also the origin of the families in this study. This teacher was participating in a binational program sponsored by the US Department of Migrant Education as a way to support the education of migrant children. We see in his quote what was in evidence at the time among several school districts in California: the co-opting of the name of a beautiful state in Mexico, Oaxaca, converted to a bullying insult.

Indigenous Teacher from Mexico Working in a Summer Binational Program in the US	English Translation
... [a] padres de Ahuejutla que ya llevan 8 y 10 años en [California] cuando nos invitaron a su casa les pregunté que si ellos siguen enseñando su lengua materna a sus hijos, y la respuesta fue que no. Volví a preguntarles ¿por qué no les enseñan? Los papás dicen que los niños no quieren aprender por la siguiente razón: que los americanos los discriminan. Les dicen "Oaxaquita," "Oaxaca" ...	I asked [indigenous families from Oaxaca] who have been in the US for 8–10 years, when they invited us to their homes, if they were teaching their mother tongue to their children, and the answer was no. I asked them why that was, and they said that their children do not want to learn because of the fact that US children discriminate against them. They call them "Oaxaquita, Oaxaca."

Many study participants echoed this theme of discrimination, including a young Mixtec farmworker laboring in the US.

Young Adult Mixtec Farmworker	English Translation
Ves, que cuando los niños van a la escuela se sienten miedo. Se discriman entre ellos mismos y les da vergüenza hablar el idioma [indígena]. Mejor dicen que no hablan.	You see, when the [indigenous] children get to school, they are afraid. Their peers discriminate against them and they are ashamed to speak the [indigenous] language. So they choose to say that they don't speak it.

In the next quote, a Mixtec mother explains another reason for she and other parents discontinuing the use of the native, indigenous language with their children.

Mixtec Mother	English Translation
Otra de las razones que también como nosotros de padres ya no queremos que nuestra primera lengua siga [es] porque pensamos que esa lengua no nos dio nada y no dejó nada bueno. Y quizás por un mal entendido o por no pensar bien el consejo que les damos a nuestros hijos, les decimos, "¿Para qué quiere el mixteco si el mixteco—fíjate en mí, mírame a mí—si yo hubiera aprendido el español, si yo hubiera sido otra persona? Yo no quiero que eso te pase. Yo no quiero que hables mixteco."	One of the reasons that we as [indigenous] parents don't want our first language to continue is that we think that this language didn't give us anything, it didn't leave us with anything good. So perhaps not understanding, or not really thinking about our advice to our children, we say to them, "Why would you want to speak Mixtec if Mixtec—think about me, look at me—if I would have learned Spanish, if I would have been a different person? I don't want that to happen to you. I don't want you to speak Mixtec."

Another of the Mexican indigenous teachers working in the US summer program expressed some hope for the children now living and going to school in the US in contrast to those remaining in Mexico. However, the teacher implies that there will be a cost to both children's indigenous language and identity.

Indigenous Teacher from Mexico Working in a Summer Binational Program in the US	English Translation
Algo bastante diferente entre alumnos indígenas en México y California es el hecho que en el estado norteamericano éstos tiene la opor- tunidad, si trabajan fuerte, de una vida mejor, de comer aunque sea una vez al día, de imaginar que algún día las cosas cambiarán para ellos y que tal vez en un futuro, sus hijos ya no sufrirán de la manera que ellos lo hacen. Creo que parte del sueño de estas [personas indígenas] es el de imaginar que sus hijos dejarán de ser vistos como indígenas, que se les borrará todo rastro que los identifique como "los otros mexicanos." En cambio, en México, estos indígenas sienten que nunca dejarán de serlo y que todas sus generaciones posteriores cargarán con el estigma de ser eso: indígena.	Something substantially different between indigenous students in Mexico and California is that in the US they have the opportunity, if they work hard enough, of having a better life, of eating, even if it's just once a day, of imagining that someday things will change for them and that maybe in the future their children will not suffer as they have. I believe that part of this dream is that their children will stop being viewed as indigenous, and that every feature that identifies them as "the other Mexicans" will be erased. In contrast, in Mexico the indigenous feel that they will never be viewed as anything else but indigenous, and that all future generations will be burdened with the stigma of being just that: indigenous.

We refer readers to the complete study to see a stark example of what can happen when power, status, and race intersect with minority languages and identities (Ruiz & Barajas, 2012). At the same time, however, readers may detect glimmers of hope. The same Mixtec mother previously quoted is working as an instructional aide and interpreter in her children's US school and has dedicated herself to championing and supporting families in speaking their native indigenous languages to their children. The school where she works has also designed activities such as school assemblies to highlight the assets brought by indigenous families, including their languages, building up a sense of pride among the children. The authors also make sure to cite a marked cultural strength of many Mexican indigenous groups, documented in a wealth of anthropological studies, and that is organizing and helping their community both in Mexico and in the US. Thankfully, this cultural strength is serving a critically important role in working toward the positive integration and success of Mexican indigenous communities in the US.

Language Loss through Subtractive Bilingualism

Both in our hypothetical example of the Vietnamese family losing their heritage language in 1.5 generations and the real-life experiences of Mexican indigenous families in the US, we can clearly see an impact on their languages, and that is what educational researchers and linguists call *language loss*. The definition of language loss is fairly straightforward: diminishing proficiency in the skills of using a particular language. When successive generations of families gradually (or rapidly) lose access to their original home and heritage language, wide-spread language loss occurs.

Helping us understand the societal level of supporting or diminishing multilingualism, and the connection between status and its impact on minority languages, is a long-established concept called *subtractive bilingualism*. The term subtractive bilingualism was first used by researcher Wallace Lambert (1981), a Canadian bilingualism researcher whose work we cited in our discussion of bilinguals' cognitive flexibility. In discussing the situation in much of North America where elementary and secondary education are overwhelmingly conducted in the majority language of English and where many other languages that children bring to school from their homes and communities do not have equal value or status in the eyes of the larger society, Lambert called attention to the gradual loss of children's home languages. He writes, this is

> a "subtractive" form of bilingualism experienced by ethnolinguistic minority groups who, because of national educational policies and social pressures of various sorts, feel forced to put aside or *subtract* out their ethnic languages for a more necessary and prestigious national language.
>
> (1981, p. 12, emphasis added)

Put another way, instead of schools offering instruction that nurtures and further develops the children's home languages in addition to the majority language, a school's sole focus on children reaching high levels of the majority language results in a *subtraction* of one of the children's languages, not an addition. It also leads to a subtraction of the possibility of the children's fluent bilingualism and biliteracy as they grow into adulthood and of the many benefits of those language skills that we have discussed thus far in the book. Finally, subtractive bilingualism also helps explain the findings of Rumbaut and colleagues and their documentation of an overall average loss of minority languages in families in a generation and a half. Disappointingly, conditions for subtractive bilingualism have been identified across many countries and for decades (Cummins, 2021), as we saw in the glaringly harsh experience of Mexican indigenous families in the US.

We hope that we can offer our readers some reason for hope by letting you know that there are ongoing efforts in countering subtractive bilingualism and subtractive education policies that diminish children's home languages and their multilingual potential. Educators and education researchers have identified and detailed educational policies and classroom approaches that develop high levels of proficiency in the majority language while, at the same time, preserving and further developing minority languages. When this type of multilingual instruction can occur, we characterize the result as *additive bilingualism* (Lambert, 1981). Additive bilingualism explicitly recognizes that speaking more than one language is a resource that pays off in many ways (R. Ruiz, 1984). In a nutshell, many educators, scholars, and community organizations are working to reverse subtractive bilingualism with policies and practices that support additive bilingualism. Fortunately, like the research related to subtractive bilingualism, studies on how to promote additive bilingualism also have a decades-long history. Chapter 3 will highlight those additive bilingual principles and practices.

Learning Multiple Languages: Patterns in the Processes

We now come to the question of how people develop multilingualism. Fortunately for us, there is a subfield within applied linguistics known as *second language acquisition*. Researchers in second language acquisition (SLA), that is, the science of how people learn additional languages and develop multilingualism, have a long history of identifying patterns common to building a multilingual repertoire. In this section we identify and explain several of those patterns that are found across all language learners.

As a first step to have that discussion, it is useful to adopt a common short-hand way of referring to first and second languages acquired sequential bilinguals we first introduced in Chapter 1: *L1* for their first language, also called their *home or native language*; and *L2* and *L3* for the sequence of languages learned after the first. These added languages are often referred to in SLA research as the *target language/s*. The use of the term target language is helpful in our discussion both in this chapter of how bilinguals acquire an additional language, and also in the next chapter where we present best practices in teaching and learning with the objective of reaching target language proficiency and the overall goal of becoming multilingual.

Interaction in the Development of Multilingualism: The Need for Input and Output

Absolutely essential to the process of adding on another language are opportunities to interact in the new language with others (Ellis, 2003; Ellis & Shintani, 2014). SLA researchers commonly characterize these opportunities for L2 learners in two main ways: (1) *receiving input* in the new language, that is, the receptive process of listening and reading, and (2) *producing output* in the new language, that is, speaking and writing. Furthermore, researchers have documented the common sense understanding that input in the L2 must be at a level that is appropriate for the learner's current level of L2 comprehension. In writing about learners' needs in terms of their receptive skills for understanding the L2—listening and reading— SLA researcher Stephen Krashen (1985) coined the term *comprehensible input*. He emphasized that learners develop their L2 when input is within the range of their current comprehension, and somewhat beyond, so that continued L2 development occurs. Fortunately, native-speakers of the language still being acquired by L2 learners naturally modify their ways of speaking when they observe that they are interacting with someone newer to the language. For example, just like caregivers adapt their communication for babies and toddlers learning their L1, native-speakers of the language interacting with non-native-speakers may make any number of modifications: they may slow down or shorten their speech; simplify grammar and vocabulary; use gestures; check for comprehension ask for clarification; paraphrase; and so on.

In a fashion similar to comprehensible input, L2 learners need opportunities to generate *comprehensible output*, that is, they need to be able to develop their productive skills of speaking and writing (Swain, 1985). When L2 learners are called upon to produce oral and written language, not only comprehend it, SLA researchers have found that they need to "dig a little deeper" into their knowledge of the L2 in order to generate language that others can understand. In speaking rather than simply listening, L2 learners may vividly notice what features of the L2 they still need to learn. They may also "try out" or hypothesize how the new language works. (We will explain more about L2 hypothesis-testing in the next section when we describe the active and creative way learners add on the L2.) Furthermore, L2 learners may follow-up on a first, unsuccessful attempt at communicating with an expanded version of their first try (Pica, Young, & Doughty, 1987). These conversational moves by native-speakers and L2 learners can help them all negotiate the conversation to attain mutual comprehension (Long, 1983).

In summary, children and adults alike become multilingual when their linguistic environments provide them with opportunities to interact that are sufficient to further develop their languages. We have begun to explain features of that environment here in terms of interaction, and will cover those features in depth in the next chapter when we describe optimal learning conditions for increasing multilingualism.

Creative Construction in Adding a New Language

Whether we are talking about simultaneous bilinguals—those children learning two languages from a very young age—or sequential bilinguals—individuals learning a second language sequentially after their first is well-developed—all share a central learning process: the active and creative construction of their new languages. Learners gradually approximate, through successive steps, greater proficiency in the new language. These approximations—steps to learning but what on the surface look like errors—are actually evidence that the learners are actively analyzing how their new language works.

It may seem like common sense to us that, of course, people move through successive steps of improving their second language skills. But, before the abundance of second language acquisition research in the second half of the past century, it was widely thought that learning a new language was just a matter of enough exposure and/or study to eventually mimic models of the new language. Put another way, before the intensive study in SLA, many believed that learning a new language was simply learning the "new habits." Then came a slew of studies by SLA researchers that have documented for decades and up to the present that something beyond simple memorization and mimicking of the structure and vocabulary of the new language is at work in second language acquisition. Let's look at two of those sources of information that support the idea that learners creatively analyze, approximate, and construct a growing proficiency in their new language.

L2 Approximations Resembling Early First Language Learning

One of the ways that SLA researchers discovered the existence of the creative construction process was by reviewing the actual L2 attempts made by both simultaneous and sequential bilinguals. While we refer to these attempts as *approximations*, that is successive steps toward greater proficiency in the target language, the SLA field has typically called these attempts by budding bilinguals *errors*. As a short-hand in this section we will interchangeably use the terms approximations and errors. But we need to be cautious with the latter term. Recall that before the impressive research base from SLA researchers in the 1970s, language learning was looked at as a matter of habits which included getting rid of the "bad habits" of the first language when learning and using the "new habits" of the target language. This view of language learning would predict, then, that the errors that L2 learners would make would all stem from their previous L1 habits. So, for example, strict proponents of this view would predict that an error for an English speaker learning Spanish who was trying to express that they were 10 years old would be "Soy 10 años," a word-for-word translation of the English way of expressing age, "I am," but nonsensical in Spanish. The correct Spanish expression is to use the "to have" verb to express age, i.e., "Tengo diez años."

While it is true that we can predict some of a language learners' errors by contrasting structures between two languages, SLA researchers have found substantial evidence of a very different set of errors than what would be solely predicted from a person's first language habits. Instead, the errors resembled the usage of very young children acquiring their first language. For both groups of children, L1 and L2 learners, the errors were evidence of their steps toward proficiency in the target language, that is, their approximations. Importantly, adult L2 learners also produced approximations similar to very young L1 learners.

To give readers an illustration of the creative construction process at work in both native English speakers and L2 learners, Table 2.4 provides several examples of errors made by two groups of children. In the middle column are approximations made by toddlers learning their first language of English. In the right-hand column are approximations recorded from older children from Chinese- and Spanish-speaking backgrounds learning English as their second language (Dulay & Burt, 1974). As you scan the approximations made by these two groups, note how similar they are. Also, observe how the differing first languages of the L2 language learners—Spanish and Chinese—do not seem to influence their creative construction in their new language of English, a finding documented in many studies (Lightbown & Spada, 2021).

The type of SLA research represented in Table 2.4, often referred to as *error-analysis*, has long demonstrated that something else other than habit formation is at work while bilinguals develop their new languages. First, there is the overlap in error-analysis research between approximations made by young English speakers learning English as their L1, and children who were acquiring English as their L2.

Table 2.4 Similarities in approximations (errors) between children acquiring English as their first language and children learning English as a second language (Ruiz, 1988)

Error Types	English-speaking children	Chinese- and Spanish-speaking children learning English
Omission		
Article—*The*	__ book drop	__ cat go there
Plural—*s* and *-es*	More cookie__	It's got some flower__
Double Marking		
Repeated Marking of Past Tense	I didn't spilled it	Why didn't you came to school?
Repeated Direct Object	We took it away the hat	Put it down card
Regularization		
Irregular Past tense	I catched it	I runned
Irregular Plural	Foots	Foots
Word Order		
Questions	What that is?	What this is?
Embedded Questions	I know what is that	I know what is that

Both groups had surely not heard the target language spoken with those errors, and therefore were not mimicking what they had heard. Some process other than habit formation was at play. Second, there is the fact that the children came from very different language groups, as did adults in later error-analysis research (Bailey, Madden, & Krashen, 1974). Yet study participants still produced similar approximations, providing evidence that the language "habits" from the participants' first languages (Spanish and Chinese in the child study, and an international mix of languages such as Greek, Turkish, Japanese, Italian, etc., in the adult studies) could only explain part of the language patterns used by L2 learners. SLA researchers have given this process several different names, including *creative construction*. They have also pointed out that learners are generating hypotheses about how the new language works, and, with more additional input, they keep some hypotheses, discard others, and create new ones. Essentially, the conclusion from decades of research is that language learning is a highly active cognitive process whereby learners produce utterances that reflect their understanding of the patterns of the new language at a certain point in time. Then, given sufficient quantity and quality input in the target language, they continue approximating the target language until there is a greater match between their developing language skills and the target language.

Let's look at one more source of evidence for active cognitive processing as the way that learners acquire multiple languages rather than simply changing a set of "language habits" from their L1 to their L2.

Developmental Sequences while Moving Toward the Target Language

Years of SLA research has revealed that budding bilinguals acquire certain grammatical features of a target language in a fairly predictable sequence, regardless of a person's first language background. As an example, here is what research has documented as a general order of using negative forms in English (Gass, Beheney, & Plonsky, 2020; Lightbown & Spada, 2021). The utterances are all from people learning English as a second language.

Stage 1—The "no" or "not" is usually at the front of the utterance or preceding the verb.
No cake.   **I no like it.**   **Not swim today.**

Stage 2—The words "no" and "not" alternate with "don't," sometimes incorrectly.
I don't can sing.   **He don't like it.**   **I will don't go tomorrow.**

Stage 3—Variations of "don't" to include "didn't" and "doesn't."
I didn't went to the store.   **She doesn't walked there by herself.**

Stage 4—Working out that helping verbs (auxiliaries) need to change to reflect the correct tense and person, but not the main verb. So, the examples in Stage 3 eventually become:
I didn't go to the store.   **She didn't walk there by herself.**

SLA researchers have identified a number of general English grammatical sequences in addition to the acquisition of negatives, such as learning to use questions, past tense, possessive nouns, and so on. Such research is fascinating to explore in detail, but, again, our take-away here is that learning a new language requires active processing including analyzing, hypothesis-testing, comparing, and evaluating—not just mimicking phrases from the target language.

Before we leave this first component of the active and creative processes bilinguals use to acquire their multiple languages, we do want to add that, yes, at times, we can find evidence that sequential bilinguals use their L1 structures in their approximations toward the target language. We may observe, for example, that Spanish speakers learning English as their L2 spend a little more time in Stage 1 of acquisition of negatives because negative sentences in Spanish correctly begin with the words "no" and "not" ["no" and "ni" in Spanish] as in "*No* voy al cine hoy," and not after the subject as in English, "I'm *not* going to the movies today." German speakers may remain at Stage 3 a little longer because in German the negative comes after the verb unlike the English placement before the verb. So German-speakers may produce something like "They come not home" in English from the influence of the German grammatical structure, "Sie kommen nicht nach Hause" (Lightbown & Spada, 2021, p. 51). Such L1 influence occurs, but as we have seen, the L1 cannot fully explain the evidence for the creative construction process of L2 learners. When learners do apply language patterns from their L1 to their L2, it is not accurate to view the L1 as a negative influence, or as "negative transfer." To the contrary, when L2 learners add on languages to their L1, they include both the previous learning that comes from their L1, *and* the dynamic L2 cognitive processes that occur across speakers of all language groups. In fact, in the next section we directly examine how the active processing of a new language, especially for sequential bilinguals, owes a large debt to the first language.

The Interconnected Underlying Language Proficiency of Bilinguals

The processing aspect of bilinguals that is perhaps most important to recognize as distinct is the cognitive and linguistic interconnections across their languages, whether they have acquired languages simultaneously or sequentially. Near the beginning of this chapter we saw concrete evidence of the interconnection in the form of spontaneous borrowing and in linguistically complex intra- and inter-sentential code-switching. We reviewed transcripts of very young bilinguals, including those with a range of disabilities, who fluidly and grammatically switched among their languages to creatively fulfill a range of communicative functions. And it turns out that a bilingual's interconnected languages have critical relevance for explaining the school-related aspects of bilingualism. Given that there are such great numbers of young bilinguals across the world, concerning ourselves with their education is extremely worthwhile. Furthermore, these educational examples offer a dramatic and consequential illustration of how bilinguals' languages proficiencies interconnect.

In the 1970s and 1980s, educators across the world began to see a pattern in the language proficiencies as well as the academic performance of large groups of immigrant children, for example, Finnish children immigrating to Sweden (Skutnabb-Kangas & Toukomaa, 1976, cited in Cummins, 2021). These children arrived to their new countries speaking a minority language with their families. In almost all of these countries at the time, the immigrant children went to school where the majority language was used as the sole means of instruction. It is not surprising that the host countries were interested in the immigrant children learning the majority language as quickly as possible, and reaching levels of academic achievement on a par with non-immigrant children. The common sense approach to reaching that goal was to "immerse" or "submerge" the immigrant children in the majority language in their schooling, a process that some people referred to as "sink or swim." The submersion idea was propelled by the thinking that the more time children spent in the majority language, the faster their majority language proficiency and academic achievement would occur.

Many of these efforts were well-meaning and took into account the immigrant children's best interests, as well as the society's goal of their integration into the mainstream. But, if we reflect a bit more on the policy and practice of sustained immersion in the majority language to the exclusion of children's home languages, we can examine core beliefs behind the approach: (1) the majority language takes precedence over children's home (minority) languages, and (2) children's home languages are separate and have little to do with the goal of efficiently and effectively teaching the majority language and academics. However, educators looking at the academic progression of immigrant children began to see some wide-spread and recurring data that significantly called into question "the more, the better" view of the majority language, and the "less is better" view of children's home languages. These emerging data challenged the idea that language proficiency in the children's L1 "did not count" when the goal was majority language proficiency and academic achievement. Instead, the data began to suggest that different language proficiency levels in the children's home languages were significantly correlated with school success in the majority language. And second, despite intensive immersion of immigrant children in majority language schooling, a very substantial number of children were taking longer than a few years to reach the kind of academic language proficiency linked to school success. The more usual timeline for the immigrant children was around 7–8 years, and sometimes longer. Importantly, this last set of statistics also began to suggest that there was something different about everyday language proficiency, and the language skills needed at school.

These intriguing findings came to the attention of researchers and educators as they reviewed studies that had administered a series of language and academic achievement tests in many different countries worldwide (Cummins, 2021). They found a surprising convergence of results related to children's L1 and L2, and their rate and eventual attainment of the majority language and academic proficiency. Those main patterns of findings are listed here:

Pattern 1—Children who immigrated around ages 9–10 (they had passed through a basic level of knowledge of native languages), attained higher and more rapid academic achievement in the majority language than children who immigrated at an earlier age. This effect was especially notable when the older immigrant children came with a few years of formal schooling in their native country and languages.

Pattern 2—Overall, children with higher levels of proficiency of their home languages more efficiently and effectively attained higher levels of proficiency in the majority language.

Pattern 3—On the very rare occasions that immigrant children could participate in bilingual education, that is, when they received academic instruction in *both* their home language and the majority language, these students academically out-performed children who were educated in monolingual, majority-language-only instruction. This increased academic performance held true despite the fact that the bilingually educated children spent *less* academic time in the majority language.

Pattern 4—Though immigrant children submersed in majority-language schooling seemed to acquire basic conversational fluency in that language within two years, they took much longer to learn academic varieties of the majority language, such as those related to the oral, reading, and writing forms typical of schooling, essays, presentations, etc.

These documented patterns emerged from all over the world, e.g., Sweden, Canada, the US, and many others at relatively the same time. Together, they dramatically called into question the approach "more majority language and less home/minority language is better" to attain high levels of majority language proficiency and achievement. Specifically, with regard to Pattern 1, it was "more" of the *home language* proficiency of the older children that helped them succeed faster and better in learning the majority language. In Pattern 2, for any immigrant child of any age, the "more" *home/minority-language proficiency*, the faster they attained higher proficiency in the majority language. In Pattern 3, children in bilingual education programs out-performed children in monolingual, majority-language-only classrooms in language and academic achievement, despite the distributed instructional time between the two languages resulting in *less* overall time in the majority language. And in Pattern 4, "more and more" majority language did not result in immigrant children acquiring academic forms of the majority language until years after the onset of schooling in the majority language, often resulting in depressed academic achievement. Jim Cummins, one of the most influential researchers in bilingualism since these patterns emerged in the 1970s, summed up the findings this way: "Students with a strong foundation in L1 were in a much better position to develop grade-appropriate language and literacy proficiency in L2 in comparison to those who had much less opportunity to develop a strong literacy-related foundation in L1" (2021, p. 24). And right up to the present, research has continued to document the critically important connection of a bilingual's languages in the schooling of minority-language children across the globe (e.g., Daller & Ungun's study with Turkish-speaking children in the UK, 2018, cited in Cummins, 2021). Children's L1 unquestionably supports their learning of the L2. Adults' L1 serves the same function in learning the L2, but when life chances are affected as in the case of children arriving to school with home languages different from the majority language, the stakes are inevitably higher to recognize and to act on the benefits arising from strong home languages.

So, now that we have listed these well-documented patterns identifying the positive outcomes of a well-developed home language in relation to successive languages, we need a way to explain these findings, one that makes clear the critical interrelationship of a bilingual's languages in producing these results. Fortunately, bilingual scholar Jim Cummins proposed a model of bilingual cognitive and language processing around the time of these original studies that, again, up to the present, explains this relationship in both research and schooling outcomes. He named the model *Common Underlying Proficiency*, and it is depicted in Figure 2.1.

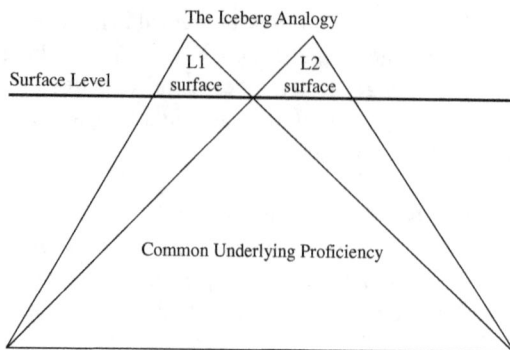

Figure 2.1 Iceberg analogy of surface features and underlying, interdependent language proficiency (Cummins, 2021).

Figure 2.1 depicts a bilingual's dual language proficiency using the metaphor of an iceberg. Above the surface are observable features of a bilingual's languages, including pronunciation, everyday grammar and vocabulary, and fluency. These surface aspects of language can be clearly different in two languages such as Chinese and English. We can group these surface features under the umbrella of *conversational language features*. Studies have shown that children can acquire these conversational language features in both languages relatively quickly on the condition that they receive adequate quantity and quality input in those languages. As we discussed previously, by language input we mean opportunities for language learners to functionally interact with others who use those languages. Given those opportunities, children can acquire L2 conversational language in one to two years.

Underlying the surface aspects of the language in this model is language proficiency that is highly related to academic achievement. Cummins refers to this level of language use as *cognitive academic language proficiency*. Here resides the cognitive and linguistic processing that is highly unified in a bilingual's multilingual repertoire, that is, where a bilingual's languages are fully interdependent and connected. Research over the years has shown this level of linguistic and cognitive processing to include conceptual knowledge and abilities, learning strategies, literacy skills (reading and writing), and oral language forms that are highly related to academics. In Cummins' model of Common Underlying Proficiency, a bilingual's multiple languages share this level of processing. We choose to further stress the interrelatedness of cognitive and linguistic processing of bilinguals and suggest another term in the iceberg model, *Interconnected Underlying Multilingualism*. Whichever the term, we are referring to bilinguals' fusion of conceptual knowledge, abilities, and strategies that they can mobilize in either language, or both. This impressive feat is possible when they have acquired sufficient skills in the more observable components of both languages such as pronunciation, and everyday grammar and vocabulary, the surface features depicted in Figure 2.1.

It should come as little surprise to readers that the length of time children need to to develop cognitive and academic aspects of their new language proficiency is much longer than the time needed to acquire conversational surface features. Specifically, research has repeatedly shown that children arriving at school speaking a minority language can begin to perform as well as majority language speakers on academic achievement tests in the majority language after around 7–8 years (see Cummins, 2021, for a review). Of course, if they have managed to retain their home language either through their family environment, or through participation in a bilingual program with instruction carried out in both the home and majority language, the bilingual children can perform this feat of achievement in not one, but two languages. And we will see in the next chapter that, on average, children in a bilingual education program reach those academic levels faster than those who are in majority-language-only programs, closer to 5–6 years.

Returning to the iceberg analogy, what significance does this interconnected and underlying language proficiency of bilinguals hold in daily life? First and foremost, it continues our theme from the first chapter on the economic, linguistic, and cognitive advantages of multilingualism. We know that bilinguals earn more and are more sought after in a range of professions, so by building on their underlying multilingual proficiency, while retaining surface features of the L1 and adding on the L2, we are fostering high levels of bilingualism (additive bilingualism), and not diminishing languages (subtractive bilingualism). We also know from the research reviewed in Chapter 1 of the consistent bilingual advantage when the performance of bilinguals and monolinguals are compared on a range of executive function tasks. And while those studies are very important to our understanding of the advantages conferred by bilingualism, it is also of major importance to consider the real-life, high-stakes consequences for bilingual children that impact their educational opportunities and achievement. So, in the case of children arriving to school speaking a minority language, we know beyond a doubt that the more skilled they are in that language, the faster they will attain proficiency in the L2. Bottom line, children's well-developed home languages have helped them construct an underlying set of knowledge, skills, and strategies highly related to academic achievement—the base of the iceberg in Figure 2.1—that can immediately be mobilized in the L2 once they begin to learn the surface features of the new language. In addition, it is important to know that the arrow of learning is bi-directional, not only from the L1 to the L2, but the L2 to the L1. So, that is why students in bilingual education classrooms can learn, for example, Newton's Law of Action–Reaction in either language, and only need to do that once; the concept becomes part of their underlying and interconnected stock of knowledge, skills, and procedures that they can express in either language. The same process is true for all of us, even if we are just beginning to add on a new language. Our well-developed L1 means we do not have to re-learn, for example, algebra, or how to write an informational essay, or how to analyze a novel; we have developed those skills and strategies already in our L1. What remains to do is add on the pronunciation, grammar, and vocabulary of the L2 typical of conversational language. In the next chapter we will detail best practices for adding on those features.

Individual Differences that Influence Becoming Bilingual

Now that we have identified several processes that are common for all people becoming bilingual—active multilingualism, societal impact on developing bilingualism, access to interaction in the new language, creative analysis and construction for adding on the L2, and the interaction of languages underlying multilingual proficiency—we turn to characteristics of individuals that can influence the development of their multilingualism.

The Age Factor: It's Complicated

If you casually ask around your friends about the best age to add on a second language, most likely you will hear general agreement that the younger a person begins to add on a second language, the better. In the case of simultaneous bilingual children who are exposed to and interacting in two languages at once before the ages of around 6–8, we can certainly see the advantage of such an early and natural start to bilingualism. We can also applaud that more than 60% of the world's children seem to have that opportunity (Smith & Meeks, 2018). Simultaneous bilinguals get a jump-start toward developing a multilingual repertoire to reap the linguistic and cognitive benefits we discussed in the last chapter. They also have one very distinct advantage over people who begin adding on a second language sometime after puberty: younger bilingual children can often achieve a native-like accent in both of their languages. Though one can find exceptions, for most sequential language learners, there seems to be an optimal period to be able to produce a native-like accent, and that looks to be sometime around or before puberty. So, in terms of accent, young learners of languages have the edge.

But how about learning grammar and vocabulary in the new language? Does the "younger is better" stance hold up? That is where the picture of a child's advantage becomes more complicated. It turns out—and this is good news for those of us starting to add on a new language in our later teens or adulthood—older language learners tend to be faster and better at acquiring certain aspects of the L2, especially when the researchers have administered L2 language proficiency assessments to gauge learners' performance. One explanation for results showing an advantage for older learners of the L2 is that around the ages of 12–13, we become skilled at formal learning in general. Though these may be broad learning skills and strategies, we can apply them to learning the L2, as is the case with conscious rule-learning, memory strategies, and analysis of our successes and gaps in the L2. Overall, older learners can better take advantage of explicit teaching of linguistic forms and rules than young children who are still-developing cognitively. Various studies have actually shown that the rate at which adult learners acquire certain aspects of the L2 is faster than young children (Gass et al., 2020). And in at least one study, the age at which sequential language learners could still attain native-like levels of grammatical correctness was shown to be later than previously thought. The researchers behind this study, Hartshorne, Tenebaum, and Pinker (2018), used an extremely large data set of almost 700,000 native and non-native English speakers. They found that participants starting to learn English as their L2 as late as age 17 could still attain high levels of grammar correctness, though after that age, grammar-learning skills declined fairly rapidly. From this study and others, it looks like different components of a target language, e.g., pronunciation, grammar, markings such as tense and plural, and vocabulary may have different optimal age spans for reaching high levels of L2 skills.

So, besides actual evidence for a pronunciation edge, why does the prevailing belief continue that children are "linguistic sponges" and effortlessly acquire additional languages? There are several explanations, including the unique language learning situations for children. For example, children often receive very simplified input from speakers of their L2 that can help them successively approximate more complex forms. They are also held to lower expectations of language use than adults learning an L2. As an illustration, an adult may say to the child language learner, "Oh, you have a red truck. Can you push the truck?," but turn to the child's parent, also an L2 learner, and ask a question requiring more sophisticated content and form, "What do you think of the government's lowering of interest rates?" It can also be the case that a child's still-developing utterances in the L2 will be praised, but adults held once again to a higher standard of minimal errors in the L2. Another situational factor affecting the "younger is always better" misconception is that in a minority-language family, the children may have many more opportunities to interact with native-speakers of the majority language at school and other settings with peers than would the adults in the home. The much greater amount of input in the L2 to children, and a longer age span within which to interact in those contexts, can certainly be a factor in children reaching high-level skills in the L2. The fact that many adults come up short in terms of attaining skilled proficiency in the L2 may have more to do with a diminished amount of exposure time, with most learning occurring in a separate language class, or as SLA researcher Lourdes Ortega phrases it, under "drip-feed conditions (e.g., 1–3 hours weekly)" (Ortega, 2019, p. 25).

Becoming Multilingual along the Lifespan

On this topic of L2 learning by children and adults, and what is realistic, SLA researcher Ortega warns her colleagues in the field not to emphasize "nativespeakerism" when writing about second language acquisition. If the only target is to reach native-speaker skills in the language we are adding into our repertoire, many of us will fall short. However, many sequential language learners, children and adults alike, can reach very functional levels of L2 language skills that allow them to leverage their bilingual repertoire to accomplish their communicative goals. Again, as we started out this chapter, bilinguals are people who can use multiple languages in their daily lives. They are not two monolingual, native-speakers in one person (Grosjean, 1989); they are unique processors and users of more than one language and can activate them accordingly. Consequently it is worth reading Ortega's own words as she cautions her SLA colleagues:

> As an antidote to the problems of the monolingual bias and nativespeakerism, I proposed (Ortega, 2013) that SLA's object of inquiry be reframed from L2 learning to learning to become bilingual later in life, and that bilingual acquisition across the lifespan, with bilingual learning by children at one extreme and bilingual learning by adults at the other, be taken as two cases of fundamentally the same phenomenon: the development of the capacity to function in more than one language or variety, that is, to become a functioning bilingual or multilingual, along a timing continuum that includes from birth or very early beginnings (for children growing up with more than one language in the family unit) to any time along the lifespan (once the first languages have been consolidated and literacy and schooling have begun).
>
> (2019, p. 26)

In summary, though young children learning the L2 can manage to squeeze within the optimal age span of acquiring an undetectable accent, adults have some advantages in both the rate of acquiring a second language, and applying their general learning skills to make good progress in L2 proficiency, especially in the area of grammar. What we adults can do to enhance our advantage is to seek out opportunities for sustained input and interaction in the L2, as is more often offered to many school-age children. In Chapter 3 we will detail language learning approaches that can help both young children and older learners optimize their L2 learning. In the meantime, we should also heed the reminder of SLA researchers Lightbown & Spada, "Age is only one of the characteristics that determine the way in which an individual approaches L2 learning and the eventual success of that learning" (2021, p. 104). And, echoing Ortega (2019), we would do well to remember that we are acquiring "bilingualism across the lifespan."

Personality Factors

SLA researchers sought for many years to uncover a relationship between an individual's personality, and rate and level of L2 learning. For example, studies investigated whether more socially outgoing learners, i.e, extroverts, might have an advantage over people who are more reserved, i.e., introverts. It certainly makes intuitive sense that extroverts may seek out opportunities to socially interact, thereby gaining interaction time with speakers of the target language to the benefit of their language learning. This position was supported by an influential study of kindergarteners who were adding on English to their repertoire (Wong Fillmore, 1979). Wong Fillmore identified a socially outgoing child, Nora, who used a particular strategy to gain access to conversations with English-speaking peers. Wong Fillmore called these *formulaic phrases*, chunks of sentences that Nora memorized as a whole. One of Nora's original formulaic phrases was "How do you do dese [these]?" The phrase enabled Nora to enact one of the cognitive strategies for learning the L2 that Wong Fillmore identified, "Get some expressions you understand and get talking." As the year progressed, Nora began to "break down" the longer formulaic phrase into movable parts, and use those parts as part of her creative construction of the new language, a process identified in other studies of young bilinguals (Huang & Hatch, 1978). Nora's utterances consisted of the formulaic part, and then the variation slot, such as *How do you do dese **flower power*** and *How did you do dese **little tortillas***. Later, she produced these creative uses of the phrase and slot variations *such as How do you do **cut it***, and at the end of the year, separating out the word *How*, and saying, *How did dese work* and *How does this color is*. (As a side note, pay attention to the effort Nora is putting into learning and using her L2 in contrast to simply being a "linguistic sponge.")

It is true that among the five kindergarteners Wong Fillmore followed in her study, Nora was more out-going. But subsequent studies looking at extroversion and introversion and success at L2 learning have not been replicated sufficiently to identify a clear leg-up for extroverted learners. In some studies, for example, the "quiet observers" were more successful (Lightbown & Spada, 2021). Those studies can help assuage worries about an identified characteristic of some child L2 learners, those who go through a "silent period." Interestingly, there are second language instructional approaches that emphasize the benefits of listening to build up comprehension before requiring learners to speak. So, for some children, experiencing a silent period may be an effective strategy to develop receptive competence in the L2 before venturing out to speaking.

In general, the association between successful L2 learning and a wide variety of personality characteristics such as self-esteem, talkativeness, inhibition, anxiety, empathy, and others have not been definitively established (Lightbown & Spada, 2021). One characteristic—*Willingness to Communicate*—has shown promise in research as a factor that promotes L2 learning, but it, like the previous list of personality characteristics, suffers from effective ways to measure the characteristic and untangle it from confidence in speaking the L2, or lower levels of anxiety, etc. Another personality trait that is receiving some attention in SLA research is *grit* (Wei, Gao & Wang, 2019). Grit, generally conceptualized as perseverance and passion in the pursuit of long-term learning, is whittled down to two main components when focused on language learning: perseverance of effort, and consistency of interest. There does seem to be a convergence of findings so far that grit in L2 learning has a modest association with successful L2 learning. However, even with a recent review of research on grit and L2 learning, there are calls for additional research to justify grit as a personality factor associated with better L2 learning (Zhoa & Wang, 2023). Finally, it is important to recognize that most of this research on personality attributes is related to everyday conversational skills in the L2 that, while important, are not the complete picture of bilingual proficiency. (Re-visit Cummins' iceberg model of Common Underlying Proficiency, Figure 2.1.)

Bottom line, no matter which traits best characterize our personalities, or how those traits change across particular situations or time, there is usually a way that we can leverage them to good effect on our way to becoming bilingual.

Motivation and Attitude in L2 Learning

It may seem to readers a bit repetitive in this section to say that, despite much SLA research into motivation and attitudes toward learning a second language, there is not a clear picture of their association with L2 learning. Again, yes, it makes intuitive sense to suppose that positive language learning attitudes are related to success in learning the L2. However, at the present time, research has been unable to distinguish which way the arrow flows, i.e., Does a positive attitude produce better L2 learning, or does successful L2 learning produce a positive attitude? Or is there an interaction, flowing both ways? Given the uncertainty in the research, for those of us in the position of encouraging bilingualism, it might be more useful to address ways of increasing positive attitudes among L2 learners in our classroom instruction. Chapter 3 will take up ways to optimize student engagement in acquiring the L2.

Aptitude for Learning Languages

Readers may have come across people in their lives that seem like "super language learners." Given the same instruction as others, these people may have jumped ahead in learning the L2. You may have wondered, like SLA researchers, if there is something like an *aptitude* for learning languages. Aptitude in general refers to one's capability or potential for learning new knowledge. Identifying its specific relationship to L2 learning has indeed been of interest in the SLA field. A few studies have identified language aptitude as the individual difference that edges out other learner-internal characteristics for a stronger connection to L2 learning, such as willingness to communicate, high motivation, low anxiety, and so on.

As we would expect in our discussion thus far about individual factors, researchers do not always agree on how to operationalize aptitude or assess it. One early and still-accepted component view of aptitude consists of the ability to: (1) discriminate among foreign sounds and then recall them later; (2) distinguish different grammar elements; (3) infer rules about the L2 from language samples; and, (4) memorize language material (Lightbown & Spada, 2021). While all of us would certainly predict that, yes, abilities in these areas are associated with successful L2 learning, it is interesting to weigh the relevance of this research to people who are intent on becoming bilingual whether they have an aptitude or not, or do not have choice about the matter of acquiring an L2 and must simply get on with it. Furthermore, aptitude components such as these have been found to relate to socioeconomic status. So, with regard to the SLA aptitude research, the question becomes, Are we measuring a valid construct called *language aptitude*, or are we measuring the social and economic opportunities afforded the study participants?

Building on questions like this one, SLA researcher Lourdes Ortega has raised a caution directed to her colleagues. She reminds them that the majority of the participants in many studies of learner-internal factors are what she terms "elite bilinguals" (2019, p. 27). She writes: "Conditions of elite L2 learning ensue when people learn new languages by choice, without any material or symbolic threat to their home languages—and often aided by ample support ... and classroom instruction" (2019, p. 27). Clearly, by Ortega's definition, elite bilinguals do not suffer subtractive bilingualism as we previously discussed in the case of people who speak minority languages, or children who must put their home languages aside when they enter classrooms using only the majority language for instruction. Ortega calls for much more SLA research from what she calls *folk* or *grassroots bilingualism*. She continues: "This kind of multilingual learning is experienced by many people whose languages and/or communities have been minoritized and who must embark—without much choice and often with little support and much hostility—in the learning of a new [majority language] ..." (2019, p. 27). Ortega encourages her fellow SLA researchers to expand their work beyond elite bilinguals and their characteristics and processes. Fortunately for us, it turns out that one area of research on learner-internal factors influencing L2 has had that focus from its very beginning: *identity*.

Identity Matters in L2 Learning

Around 50 years ago, SLA researcher John Schumann (1976) published a case study of Alberto, a Spanish-speaking, adult immigrant from Costa Rica in the US endeavoring to learn English. Of all the participants in Schumann's study, Alberto made the least progress in English acquisition. Analyzing the various explanations for Alberto's lack of progress, Schumann concluded that it was Alberto's perception of social distance from the English language and its speakers that accounted for his struggles. Schumann's early research represented an important step in SLA and its look at individual factors in L2 acquisition: the recognition that an individual's learning path in the L2 was very much influenced by, and in relation to, the broader social context. Later SLA researchers recognized that perceptions such as Alberto's were part of the construct of *identity*, that is, how people view themselves, their roles and values, and how they perceive to be seen by others, including the wider social context. Educators have long-established that identity and learning are deeply connected:

> ... learning settings provide feedback to young people about whether or not they belong. Identity and learning are deeply intertwined, such that when identities are accepted and aligned in learning settings, opportunities to learn open up, and when key identities are rejected, opportunities for learning are shut down.
> (Nasir & Peele-Eady, 2012, p. 1482)

Identity in L2 learning has been defined as "any part of a person's identity that is related to knowledge and use of a second language" (Benson, Barkhuizen, Bodycott, & Brown, 2013, p. 17).

A classic study of identity and second language learning was conducted by Bonny Norton (1995). She followed six immigrant women residing in Canada for a year after they were her students in an English language course. Norton asked the women to keep a journal in which they noted occasions of speaking English, as well as reflections on those experiences, and periodically met with them. Highlighting two immigrants from Poland, Martina and Eva, Norton made the point that they were both very invested in learning English in order to build better lives for themselves and their families. However, both women found that there were situations where they felt uncomfortable with their English proficiencies and how they were viewed as non-Canadians who spoke limited English with very discernable accents. Eventually, both Martina and Eva claimed the right to speak in situations where they first had been silent and ashamed. In the case of Eva, when a customer at her workplace accused her of putting on an accent in order to receive a higher tip, Eva spoke up: "I wish I did not have this accent because then I would not have to listen to such comments" (p. 25). Norton identified Eva's identity shift from outsider, to multicultural citizen of Canada, adding, "Over time, then, Eva's communicative competence developed to include an awareness of how to challenge and transform social practices of marginalization" (p. 25). Norton concludes that it is critical that L2 instruction incorporate the lived experiences of students like Eva and Marina. SLA researchers continue adding to the body of research on what they call in the literature *second language identity* (Miller & Kubota, 2013). We, however, have amended the term to *multilingual identity*. In the next chapters we will present ways to support multilingual identities as part of increasing multilingual competence.

Learning a Third (or Fourth!) Language after the L2

Before we leave this chapter on becoming multilingual, we need to respond to a question that occasionally arises when the topic is learning more than two languages. Essentially, the question regards whether there is an advantage among bilinguals for learning a third language. It turns out that SLA researchers have conducted a number of studies exploring this question. Overall, the studies come down on the side of a small advantage by bilinguals over monolinguals when both groups are engaged in learning the same target language (Cenoz, 2003; Gass et al., 2020). Explaining the advantage, SLA researchers feel that the enhanced metalinguistic awareness of bilinguals—those skills in thinking and talking about language as an object that we discussed in Chapter 1—give bilinguals a leg-up over monolinguals. Enriched Executive Functions skills of bilinguals, such as attentional/inhibitory control and cognitive flexibility, also assist in setting out to learn a new language. Further, bilinguals may have additional very concrete language resources that help them with the third target language. For example, bilinguals may have working knowledge of two grammatical systems, one or both of which may help with the third language, especially if the L3 is linguistically related to the L1 or L2. Reviewing the research on third language acquisition, SLA researchers Gass and colleagues conclude that bilinguals can activate their multiple resources to benefit L3 learning, but caution that other factors can boost or lessen the benefits, for example, age, degree of proficiency in the L1 and L2, linguistic closeness between languages (Gass et al., 2020).

Test yourself! What did you learn?: Re-consider each statement from the beginning of the chapter. Use your background knowledge *and* new information gained from reading the chapter to decide whether the statements reflect current research on multilingualism (True), or not (False). Answers are in Appendix A at the back of the book.

True or False	Development of Multilingualism
	1. About two-thirds of the world's children are growing up bilingual.
	2. Only those individuals who have equal knowledge of each language, and speak both without an accent, should be labeled "bilingual."
	3. When bilinguals intermix their languages in a single sentence or conversation, it is a sign that they have serious language gaps in one or both of their languages.
	4. The more proficiency immigrant children have in their home language, including some schooling in that language, the faster and better they will learn the new language in their new country.
	5. Though in many ways the earlier one learns a second language is best, adults and older children outperform younger children in certain aspects of language learning.

Time to Think and Connect

The Development of Multilingualism

1. Given our working definition of bilingualism—people who use more than one language in their lives—who are the bilinguals you know well, either in your professional, educational, or personal life? If you are bilingual, when and how do you activate your multiple languages?
2. Again, calling to mind those bilinguals closest to you, what factors have influenced either their or your continued development of their multilingual repertoire (increasing proficiency), or their language loss? Have any of them, or you, experienced subtractive or additive bilingualism? What has been the impact on your or their multilingual repertoire?
3. Call to mind these same bilinguals in your work, school, or home life. Are there occasions when they—or you—mix languages in a conversation? If so, what are some examples of spontaneous borrowing and/or code-switching that

you use or hear? How do you think others in your professional, educational, or personal groups currently view spontaneous borrowing and code-switching? How do you now view language mixing, especially as a way that we can observe active multilingualism? Are there times when spontaneous borrowing and code-switching are appropriate, and are there times when they are not? Describe those circumstances.

Chapter 3

Increasing Multilingual Competence in the Home, Community, and Workplace

Applications of the Research on Multilingual Development

Overview

This chapter incorporates the information from the previous chapters and from the fields of bilingual and second language education to provide specific, evidence-based recommendations for developing multilingual proficiency across age span, and educational and professional settings. The authors center their recommendations around six optimal conditions for multilingual development, and share instructional practices that help create those conditions.

Test yourself! (Tapping into your background knowledge): Before reading the chapter, consider each statement below and use your current knowledge and experiences to decide whether the statement is true or false.

True or False	Increasing Multilingual Competence
	1. Research on the effectiveness of bilingual education has only recently begun, and it is too early to determine whether it enhances multilingual development or academic achievement.
	2. Advance work in building up L2 learners' background knowledge before they begin to listen to or read a text greatly enhances their L2 comprehension.
	3. Frequent opportunities to interact in pairs and small groups is one of the best ways to improve second language (L2) learning
	4. Most L2 learners need a strict focus on language forms through drills and worksheets, rather than practice in communicating real messages.
	5. Research-based teaching and learning practices can be integrated into the workplace to support colleagues who are L2 learners.

DOI: 10.4324/9781003216414-6

Two Highly Effective Ways of Developing Multilingualism

We have spent the last two chapters detailing, first, the advantages of being multilingual, and second, how the process of becoming multilingual unfolds. We now come to how it is that we can optimally become bilingual. Those optimal ways center around frequent and sustained opportunities to learn and authentically use our multilingual repertoire in multiple situations. The first path to bilingualism that we highlight here is dependent on the "roll of the dice" for the family context we are given, and that is the opportunity to grow up bilingual in our homes. The second way is still somewhat dependent on the multilingual "luck of the draw": the opportunity to attend a school offering bilingual education. Both of these paths to multilingualism offer us the critical sustained input and high levels of interaction that accelerate the development of multilingual competence.

Family Bilingualism

Being part of a multilingual family unit where we can have access to bilinguals and their multiple languages gives us a tremendous leg-up on becoming bilingual ourselves. Here we use the term "family unit" to incorporate the range of caregivers who raise us, not only parents or biological family members. Such a context gives us natural access to multilingual input—hearing, speaking, reading, and writing those languages—from those people who form part of our socialization process. That input and the opportunities to interact in multiple languages with bilingual caregivers begin to construct our multilingual repertoire. If we experience this multilingual context early on in our lives, then, as we already know, we are simultaneous bilinguals who have two (or more) languages as our "first" or "native" languages. We very much hope that you have had this experience of growing up bilingual, or are in the position to help construct these kinds of early bilingual environments for the younger generation.

We can all agree that growing up multilingual with the people we most care about is a wonderful way to develop our bilingualism. Yet, we know from the last chapter that there are many societal influences that can interfere with continued family bilingualism. Here we recall Rumbaut and colleagues' research regarding the loss of minority languages within a generation and a half (Rumbaut, 2014), and the Ruiz and Barajas study (2012) describing the racial and language discrimination faced by many Mexican indigenous children in US schools. When languages have lower status in the society, and are not truly supported by or integrated into government and educational institutions, they are extremely vulnerable to disappearing from families' generational multilingual repertoire. Consequently, multilingual families need a range of resources to assure them that continuing to provide a multilingual environment for their children and grandchildren is beneficial in a truly broad range of contexts, including those that are social and academic. Families need to know that, far from being detrimental to children, bilingualism opens doors throughout their lifetime, right up to and including old age (cognitive reserve). Specifically, the audiovisual and written resources provided to families should: (1) outline the benefits of bilingualism; (2) acquaint caregivers with normal, early markings of active bilingualism including toddlers' language-mixing and separation of languages; (3) dispel any myths about child bilingualism causing confusion or delay; (4) provide access to materials that support home bilingualism such as bilingual books, television shows, and computer applications; (5) identify local bilingual daycare, preschool, kindergarten through high school bilingual programs, and extracurricular enrichment options; and (6) help bilingual parents join in advocating for all of these resources.

Bilingual Education

What if, however, the caregivers to young children are not bilingual? Or if those caregivers are indeed bilingual, but choose to discontinue speaking their minority language to their children in the understandable attempt to increase their children's life chances by ensuring that they exclusively speak the majority language? Certain caregivers may have experienced ethnolinguistic discrimination and other difficulties as minority-language speakers themselves. As in the case of the Mixtec mother we highlighted in the previous chapter, they may question the benefit of passing on their home language to subsequent generations and ask, "Where has (the minority language) gotten me?" Again, our task as people who now have a good set of facts about the advantages of bilingualism is to consistently share that knowledge with the goal of continuing and expanding home bilingual environments.

This same set of facts can point us to the other efficient and optimal path toward multilingualism: the extremely well-researched educational program called *bilingual education* (Cummins, 2021). As a basic description for discussion purposes, we can say that bilingual education programs incorporate the use of two languages for instruction. (You will also hear the term *dual-language instruction* as a synonym for bilingual education highlighting that there are two instructional languages in the program. See Table 3.1 for a list of common terms associated with bilingual education.) How the languages in bilingual instruction are distributed across content areas (subject matter), and for how many years, and for whom, varies by the type of program, which we will overview here. But linking all bilingual programs, and often, connecting them to the support for family bilingualism, becomes the opportunity for that all-important input and interaction in multiple languages that develops multilingual competence. Bottom line, if the roll of the dice did not place us in bilingual families or communities where we were naturally surrounded by multiple languages, we have a chance at another optimal path toward developing a multilingual repertoire through participation in a bilingual education program.

Bilingual programs in school settings can range from preschool through high school on through to universities. University bilingual programs are especially flourishing in Europe where certain degree programs are taught in a language other than the country's majority language. The US recently caught up to this move at Davenport University, a private university in Grand Rapids, Michigan. The director of the program had this to say about the need for the program, citing both the higher education benefits as well as the economic ones that we discussed in Chapter 1.

> "We need a Latino community that's well-educated ... There's about half a million Latinos in Michigan, but only 2% of us have a college degree ... We have more than 130 companies that are global, that are headquartered here in West Michigan," [Director] Cuevas said. "That tells you that the potential for growth in Latin America is there. With individuals that are coming to get their degree from Davenport, we're able to serve in a very global marketplace." (Frick, 2024)

University classes in this program alternate languages by week, that is, 100% in Spanish for one week, and 100% in English the next. Supporting the students in their university-level development of bilingualism is assistance with admissions, financial aid, counseling, tutoring and library services, all offered in both Spanish and English.

Though university bilingual programs are much less common than kindergarten through high school programs in the US, Davenport University's bilingual degree program highlights a key component of bilingual programs: bilingual instruction integrates academic content, e.g., science or history, with language and literacy instruction in both languages. How this integration happens in preschool through high school varies by program types, and by whether the programs are elementary level (US preschool through Grade 6), or at the less frequent levels of middle school (Grade 7 and 8), and high school (Grade 9 through 12).

At the elementary level, the most highly effective bilingual programs are those that maintain bilingual instruction for 5–7 years, giving all children the time and kind of instruction needed to continue to build up the kind of academic-related language proficiency that was depicted in the deeper level Cummin's iceberg model (Chapter 2, Figure 2.1). A straight-forward way of referring to those types of programs that we will adopt in our discussion here is as *maintenance programs*. In identifying bilingual maintenance programs, we highlight both the goal of students maintaining bilingual proficiency, and the substantial number of years students are provided in order to further develop their knowledge of academic content and the two languages themselves. Given what we know about the time children need to develop their academic language proficiency, explained in Chapter 2, it comes as no surprise that research consistently shows that when children enter a bilingual maintenance program in kindergarten speaking a home language different than the majority language, they catch up academically to their majority-language-speaking peers within that time span, basically, by Grades 5 or 6. And when children in maintenance bilingual programs are given tests in their home language as well as the majority language, results show that they have also reached grade-level performance in that language, too (Cummins, 2021).

It is worthwhile to pause here and directly look at the research on bilingual education, and justify why we have identified it as one of two optimal paths toward multilingualism. Among the many scholars who have conducted studies on the

Table 3.1 Useful terms for understanding bilingual education

Term	Definition
Bilingual education	A school program where instruction is delivered through two languages; includes direct teaching of the oral and written forms of both languages, in addition to content area instruction
Content and Language Integrated Instruction (CLIL)	A term primarily used in Europe to describe a way of teaching minority-language children in the majority language through carefully planned instruction for the content areas, and for oral and written forms of the majority language itself
Content areas/ subject matter	School subjects such as math, science, history, art, and physical education
Dual-language education	A synonym for bilingual education that highlights that two languages are used for instruction
English language development (ELD)	Instruction that focuses on teaching English as a second language, typically with usually less emphasis on content area instruction
Home language/s	The language/s children use within their family unit; for children from immigrant communities, their home language may be a minority language
Immersion program	A bilingual program that is largely conducted in a minority language so as to give students maximum exposure to the target language through the teacher and curriculum materials; the students are often majority-language-speakers whose family supports them learning a second language
Maintenance bilingual program	A bilingual education program with the goal of fully developing both languages through an extended program of 6–7 years, and sometimes continuing through to secondary education
Norming group for achievement tests	The group of children used to establish average performance in the construction of tests assessing students' academic achievement
One-way bilingual program	A bilingual program in which most of the students share a single home language different the target language; typically, few to no native speakers of the target language are present as peer models
Pull-out English as a Second Language (ESL) program	A program for language minority students in which they are pulled out of their general classroom to receive small group instruction through the majority language; focus on L2 language and literacy
Transitional bilingual program	A bilingual program using two languages for instruction for a relatively short period of time, usually three years, e.g., from kindergarten to Grade 2; language minority children transition from bilingual education classrooms to language-majority instruction only
Two-way bilingual program	A bilingual program where approximately half of the students are native speakers of the majority language, and half are native speakers of the minority language; strong peer models for both languages

achievement of minority-language speakers in and out of bilingual programs, two stand-out researchers are Virginia Collier and Wayne Thomas of George Mason University in the US. Collier and Thomas' work is especially useful because their research has spanned over 30 years and has intensely looked into the academic impact of different educational contexts for minority-language speakers. They have analyzed over 7 million student records in cooperation with school districts across several geographical regions in the US (Collier & Thomas, 2017). Their research has encompassed children whose home languages reflected a large number of different languages, for example, Spanish, French, Chinese, Vietnamese, etc. In addition, Collier and Thomas have followed groups of minority-language students for several years in what are called longitudinal studies, and analyzed educational outcomes up to and including the high school years. Furthermore, they have examined bilingual programs that delivered instruction in several minority languages such as Spanish and French, depending on the region.

Based on this exceptionally extensive research base, Collier and Thomas have been able to answer fundamental questions regarding the education of minority-language students. First, we share their response to the question regarding the length of time minority-language learners beginning their schooling new to English need to reach grade-level achievement across the school curriculum in their second language, and to stay at grade level (or above) throughout the remainder of their schooling. (In reading this quote, recall here that in most US bilingual education research, L1 refers to the minority-language speakers' home language, and L2 to the majority language of English.)

> The answer to this question is that it takes a long time—an average of 6 years for those who start in kindergarten and receive quality dual-language schooling in both L1 and L2 for a minimum of 6 years, with at least half of the instructional time in their L1. It takes still longer, 7–10 years or more, if students have not had the opportunity to be schooled in their L1, and many in this situation do not reach grade-level achievement and are often referred to by school personnel as "long-term English learners."
>
> (2017, p. 207)

So, even for children in a maintenance bilingual education program, a significant amount of time is needed for them to perform as well as majority-language-speakers on academic assessments. However, they reach that milestone earlier than those who did not have access to bilingual education. Why is this the case? One significant factor for the higher academic achievement of children in maintenance bilingual programs is that they are provided with instruction in the home and majority languages from the start of their schooling. Bilingual instruction stemming from the onset of their formal education means that minority-language children entering the program do not have to wait a year or two while they work toward having sufficient majority-language proficiency to learn academic content in their L2, depicted as the surface features on the iceberg model in Chapter 2. Instead, they can immediately begin their academic content learning in the home language while they add in the L2. This instantaneous jump-start in both language *and* subject matter content is responsible for the dramatic research convergence about the effectiveness of maintenance bilingual programs.

Before we turn our attention to the actual research showing the positive academic impact of maintenance programs, let's first consider what happens to minority-language children who do *not* have the benefit of instruction in their home language as they learn English. Collier and Thomas and many other researchers have documented a much slower rate of academic progress by minority-language children without access to bilingual education. In the following quote from their work, we can see that Collier and Thomas ground their evidence of the underperformance of language minority children by comparing their achievement scores with those of native English speakers on government-sponsored tests in English. These tests are used to monitor the achievement of all children, but the scores are based solely on the performance of native English speakers; those children make up the norming group on which the tests are based and averages are based on their achievement patterns. Here the researchers explain why it is a challenge for minority-language children to catch up to native English-speaking peers on these assessments if they do not have access to bilingual education. (In reading this quote, note that Collier and Thomas use the term *English learner* to refer to the minority-language learners in their research, and L1 schooling refers to minority-language-speakers' home languages.)

> Why does it take so long—at least 6 years, and longer if English learners do not receive L1 schooling? The norm group for the test is native English speakers. They are a moving target; they make on average 10 months of progress each school year. This performance defines the 50th percentile (grade-level achievement) on standardized tests as the students progress from grade to grade. These tests measure continuous linguistic, cognitive, and academic growth in English. *To eventually close the gap, English learners need to make more progress each year than the native English speakers make, because they start far below the level of native English speakers when they first take the test. The key to accelerated progress is for English learners to receive peer-equivalent, grade-level bilingual schooling, so that they are not falling behind in cognitive and academic development.*
>
> (2017, p. 207, emphasis added)

As a final step in reviewing Collier and Thomas' impressive research base, we will examine a graphic representation of the achievement paths of minority-language speakers in their studies. But before that, let's look at a few terms that are helpful in interpreting the graph (Table 3.1). First, remember that the researchers use the term *English learner* to refer to children whose home language is a minority language, and need to learn the majority language, which in the US is English. Second, the *Two-Way* and *One-Way* program labels distinguish the language profiles of the students who make up the two bilingual programs. Two-Way programs attempt to have equal numbers of children who speak English as their home language, and children whose home language is the minority language. The principle behind matching the group numbers is one that we cited in the previous chapter, and that is the powerful influence of interaction with peer models for L2 learning. Sometimes, however, local communities do not have a sufficient population of minority-language speakers to equalize the two groups of majority and minority-language speakers. In that case, in the US, a One-Way program is created. Most of the children in this type of program are native English speakers, but they are instructed primarily in the target minority language, such as French or Spanish. The term One-Way indicates that the direction of language learning is unidirectional, that is, English-speaking children are learning a new, target language through teacher instruction and through the language and content materials. In contrast, Two-Way programs highlight the emphasis on the bi-directional learning of both groups: English speakers learning the minority language from peers who speak that language as their native language, and minority-language speakers learning English from peers who speak English as their native language.

Figure 3.1 shows the results from Collier and Thomas' national studies of minority language speakers' academic achievement pathways in their L2 of English. The authors used the *National Curve Equivalent* system, NCE, which computes

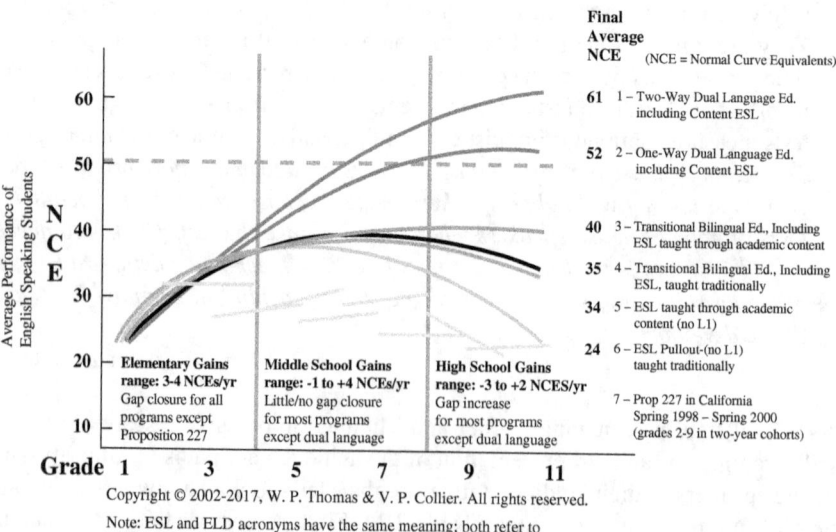

Figure 3.1 Academic achievement patterns of Grades 1–11 students learning English as their L2 and who participate in different types of program models designed to meet their needs as minority-language speakers (Collier and Thomas, 2017)

scores range from 1 to 100, with 100 as the top possible score, to track the success of students participating several models of specialized education for L2 learners. In the NCE system, scores are roughly equivalent to percentiles, e.g., 50 points indicates performance at around the 50th percentile. So, in Figure 3.1, the dotted horizontal line at the 50 point mark shows the average academic achievement level of majority language English speakers. Looking at the right-hand side of the graph labeled "Final Average NCE," we can immediately see that there are only two bilingual education programs in which the L2 English learners have both reached the national average for native English speakers, and surpassed it: (a) the Two-Way program participants performing at an average NCE score of 61, and (b) the One-Way maintenance bilingual programs reaching a 52 point average.

These results should be little surprise given what we have learned about bilinguals' interconnected underlying language proficiency: in bilingual education, minority language children can immediately begin to learn surface features of the new language while actively processing academic content in both languages. Once again, however, it is sobering to consider the pattern of underperformance of minority language children who were *not* afforded the opportunity to participate in the dual language instruction of their minority language and English. Figure 3.1 graphically represents those patterns, from program models producing the highest student performance on achievement tests, to models with increasingly lower success. Accordingly, after the most successful program models—Two-Way and One-Way programs—the next group with a lower level of achievement are those who had a shorter amount of bilingual instruction, usually about three years, in programs called *Transitional Bilingual Education (TBE)*. This group reached the 40 point level, below the national average NCE score of 50 points. The graph further divides this group by whether the TBE children have some specialized minority instruction in content areas such as math and science, or traditional English as a Second Language instruction not specifically linked to grade-level content. This latter group scored slightly lower at 35 points. The remainder of the graph shows the downward trajectory of minority language speakers receiving variations of English-only instruction. Interestingly, the program with the lowest yield in terms of minority language speakers' success is represented by multiple short, horizontal lines hovering around the final average NCE scores of 25–30. Those lines represent a policy reversal in the state of California away from bilingual education to a mandatory imposition of English-only instruction in the year 2000, except in extremely rare cases. Fortunately, the law was repealed in 2017 and California minority-language speakers once again have the choice of bilingual education through the passage of the *Global California 2030 Initiative* (California Department of Education, 2018).

Before we leave the topic of bilingual education as an optimal path to multilingualism, we do want to bring attention to another aspect of Collier and Thomas' work. The researchers have found that even a limited quantity of dual-language instruction, such as typical of the short-term Transitional Bilingual Education programs, had a mild but long-term effect on minority-language speakers' achievement as illustrated in Figure 3.2 below. These data are from Houston, Texas, one of the 37 school districts studied by Collier and Thomas. Note the higher academic

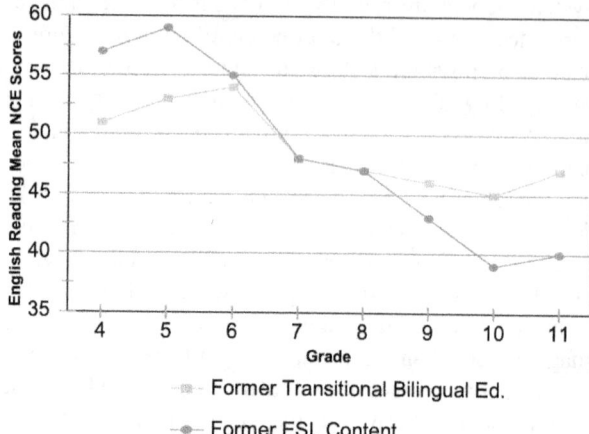

Houston ISD Achievement by Program on the 1999 Stanford 9 in English

- - Former Transitional Bilingual Ed.
—•— Former ESL Content

Figure 3.2 Mild positive effect of short-term (first three years of schooling) Transitional Bilingual Education in Grade 11 compared to English-only instruction (Collier and Thomas, 2017)

performance in Grade 11 by minority-language children who had short-term bilingual instruction.

Though we selected the work of bilingual education researchers Collier and Thomas as our focus, it is important to stress how widely this topic has been studied for decades right up to the present. The convergence of results firmly documenting the academic achievement advantages of bilingual education for all children, minority- and majority-language speakers alike, is striking (e.g., Bialstok, 2018; Cummins, 2021; U.S. Government Accountability Office, 2024; Umansky, Valentino, & Reardon, 2016). Furthermore, in terms of the cognitve benefits of bilingualism that we described in Chapter 1, recent research has found evidence of enhanced attentional and social skills among young, formerly monolingual chidren after only one year of participating in bilingual education (Chamorro & Janke, 2022). In short, bilingual education confers a range of benefits to all on the path to multilingual competence.

It is now time to talk about paths to multilingualism available to us when we have not been afforded the gifts of family bilingualism or participation in a bilingual education program. To drum up enthusiasm (and grit!) before we do, please recall our previous chapter's conclusion that adults can be highly effective L2 learners, and can attain high levels of bilingualism, along with the social, professional, and cognitive benefits we learned about in Chapter 1.

Optimal Teaching and Learning Conditions for Becoming Bilingual

Assured of multilingualism benefits (Chapter 1), and knowledgeable about how multilingualism develops (Chapter 2), we now turn to purposeful teaching and learning of additional languages for the creation and expansion of our multilingual repertoires. We will see that there is a close fit between what the research has said about how languages are learned, and how we should best go about teaching them and supporting them in the workplace.

To help us explain how to optimize L2 learning for multilingual competence, we can rely on the work of a long-time group of researchers, teachers, and teacher researchers who routinely scour the research literature for best language and literacy teaching and learning practices, as well as conduct their own applied research, the *Optimal Learning Environment (OLE) Project*. The OLE Project is grounded on a fusion of evidence from three core fields: (1) Bilingual Education and Biliteracy, (2) Instructed Second Language Acquisition, and (3) Bilingual Special Education (Ruiz, 1989, 1995a, b, 2012, 2023, 2012; Ruiz, García & Figueroa, 1996; Ruiz & Sánchez-Boyce, 2022; Ruiz, Vargas & Beltrán, 2002). The conceptual framework of the OLE Project, built up over years of research with bilingual learners in both general and special education, is the following: Depending on the nature of the instructional context, we can see either the upper or lower range of a person's language abilities; skilled or struggling readers, writers, and speakers; accelerated or slowed language and academic development (Ruiz, 2023). In other words, if we heed the extensive research base of effective instruction for minority-language-speakers, we can construct optimal learning environments (OLE) that in turn lead to optimal language and academic outcomes (Ruiz, 2012, 2023).

Over the years, the OLE Project group has been able to assemble research findings into an easy-to-use tool to explain and to put into practice instructional practices that can accelerate the development of L2 language and literacy. A key term in this tool reflects the work of Australian SLA researchers Cambourne and Turbill (1987) who first used the term *conditions* to identify instructional contexts associated with successful L2 learning (Ruiz et al., 1996). The OLE Project identified 12 optimal conditions from its three core research areas that are linked to accelerated bilingual language and biliteracy development (Ruiz, 2023). And, as we saw in the last section on the bilingual education path to multilingualism, instruction that accelerates language and academic development is especially crucial to young minority-language speaking children who must make more than a year's progress each year to reach (or surpass) grade-level testing standards based on majority-language speakers. But of interest to all are optimal conditions for accelerated multilingual development.

In this book we focus on the first six optimal conditions that are closely tied to the development of multilingualism in both the workplace and formal education settings such as the foreign language classroom. (The remaining optimal *Conditions #7–12* are listed at the end of the chapter with their connections to the professional setting.) For each of *Conditions #1–6*, we first provide an overview. We then connect the condition with key research supporting its identification as one that supports optimal multiple language and literacy development. Some of that research will be familiar as we have previously referred to these studies in the preceding chapter explaining the processes by which people become multilingual, Second Language Acquisition (SLA). Some research will be new as we include information on more formalized instruction for teaching and learning languages, sometimes coming from the field of *Foreign Language Teaching* as well as *Instructed Second Language Acquisition (Instructed SLA)*. Instructed SLA forges a close link between the research on how people acquire a second language, and how best to support and further develop acquisition through a focus on teaching and learning. Whether the research is new or familiar to us, it is important to link what we know about the social and individual learner processes of becoming bilingual (Chapter 2), and how to optimize L2 development through instruction and professional interactions (this chapter). Finally, for each condition, we give examples of optimal instructional practices across the age ranges of young children and adolescents/adults, along with application of the condition to learning and interaction in professional settings. Additional details and procedures for specific instructional practices mentioned in this chapter are located in Appendix B.

Readers will note that some of the optimal conditions overlap, either in their theoretical or applied connections. However, we have found that in terms of guidance for constructing optimal learning environments, these six conditions are fundamental. As we explain them, readers should keep in mind that the conditions can be found not only within formal bilingual and L2 classrooms, but also at the family dinner table, at the corner grocery store, in the conference room at our place of work, and even as we activate a foreign language application on our phones.

Optimal Condition #1: Learner-Centered Instruction and Support

Activities begin with L2 learners' personal experiences, background knowledge, and interests. L2 learners' use of their L1 and full multilingual repertoire are viewed and mobilized as resources to become bilingual and biliterate.

Key Research

We know from years of research that L2 learners' listening and reading comprehension is improved when there is an existing connection between their background knowledge and the oral or written text. Comprehension is also enhanced when the relevant background knowledge is built up through activities before listening or reading (Carrell, 1987; Droop & Verhoeven, 1998; Hudson, 2007; Ruiz, 2012). The same connection is true for the kind of knowledge that is built up in our particular cultures: when there is a match between our own cultural knowledge (often called *cultural schemata*), and when that knowledge is integral to understanding the text, our comprehension improves. Applying this knowledge to teaching and learning contexts, studies have repeatedly shown that L2 learners show enhanced comprehension in a variety of ways when pre-reading or pre-listening activities connect learners' background and cultural knowledge to the texts. For example, L2 learners who have tapped into their background knowledge, or built it up through pre-reading and pre-listening activities can better recall the gist, list the details, summarize

Table 3.2 Optimal conditions for multilingual development #1–6

Optimal Condition #1: Learner-Centered Instruction and Support	Activities begin with L2 learners' personal experiences, background knowledge, and interests. L2 learners' use of their L1 and full multilingual repertoire are viewed and mobilized as resources to become bilingual and biliterate.
Optimal Condition #2: Learner Choice	L2 learners exercise choice in their learning when possible—selecting their own writing topics, books, projects—using their full multilingual repertoire.
Optimal Condition #3: Whole Texts for Maximum Comprehension and Explicit Teaching of Skills and Strategies	Activities center on whole, communicatively functional texts (e.g., books, poems, newspaper articles, professional manuals, etc.) to maximize L2 learners' construction of understanding. Instructors use those texts to explicitly teach the components of language processes, such as: text organization; language forms including phonics; spelling and punctuation; and cross-linguistic connections.
Optimal Condition #4: Active Participation	L2 learners actively engage in activities with long, frequent turns in producing oral and written language. There are high levels of interaction through pair and group work.
Optimal Condition #5: Meaning First, Followed by Form	First, L2 learners construct meaning by speaking and listening, or reading and writing text; and then move to a focus on correct forms of language such as grammar and spelling.
Optimal Condition #6: Authentic Purpose	The end-products of activities have a real-life function that extend beyond the classroom setting to the real world. L2 learners communicate real messages, to real audiences, for real purposes.

important points, and successfully answer test questions. Indeed, research has also shown that less proficient L2 learners can do as well as more advanced L2 learners in reading comprehension tasks when those pre-reading activities have built up the learners' background knowledge relevant to the text (Hudson, 2007).

In addition to highlighting the importance of background knowledge and L2 comprehension, this condition focuses on learners' personal connections with the content. When there are personal connections between the learners and the material to be learned, engagement increases. We know from both L2 (Sulis, 2022; Ruiz, 2012) and general education research (Theobold et al., 2020; Chi & Wylie, 2014) that learner engagement is a crucial factor in active learning.

Examples of Instruction and Support for L2 Learners

Young children. Before beginning to read a story to children, teachers or their caregivers look for the central character's situation, and ask the children if they have ever had that experience. For example, for a book where a girl has asked for a favorite food for her birthday, the adult might say, "This is a story about a girl asking for her favorite food for her birthday dinner. Before we begin reading the story, what is your favorite food?" In a classroom context, the teacher would ask for several children to share their personal connections.

Adolescents and adults. Learners at this age level are often asked to read a variety of subject matter materials, such as a chapter in history or science textbook. Instructors can use the *Survey Text Method* to build up the learners' background knowledge before they begin to read the chapter. (See Appendix B for additional details.) Briefly, in this method, learners are asked to read: (1) the first paragraph, (2) all subsequent subheadings, (3) any captions accompanying photos, and (4) the last paragraph. In pairs or in small groups, they share their predictions for the chapter's main points. (An adaptation of this method is to ask the learners to configure wh- questions—who, what, where, and why—that they believe will be answered by the text.) The instructor can then chart the learners' predictions of the main points. It should be clear how this method allows learners to build up their background knowledge, not only from their own survey of the chapter, but from their peers' work and group discussion. And as we know, the more background knowledge learners have before they begin to read or listen, the better their comprehension.

Professional settings. In many professional settings, new learning and change happen very frequently. When gathering as a work group to present or discuss a new direction, it is possible to optimize minority-language learners' comprehension with a quick, two-step process. Let's consider an example from the business field, and imagine that a new report has been released on a topic very relevant to the company. There is a work meeting called to read and discuss the report and its connections to the group. The first step would be to acknowledge that there is substantial related knowledge distributed among the colleagues in the room. (One should not assume that a person with a still-developing L2 has limited background knowledge; they may have the most conceptual knowledge and expertise in the room!) The second step is to follow with the question, "Given that knowledge, what do we already know about ____ (the general topic)?" In this case, the Survey Text Method just described would be an excellent way for everyone, not only the language learners, to enhance their comprehension of new material (see Appendix B). Another straight-forward approach for tapping into and building background knowledge is to simply ask about colleagues' previous personal experience or expertise with the topic. It is also a good idea to record that distributed knowledge on a chart of some sort that all can see. Bottom line, any up-front work to tap into and build up your colleagues' and your knowledge about a subject enacts the extensive research in this area regarding enhanced comprehension, even among learners relatively new to the target language.

Before closing, a question to readers: Did you notice that at the beginning of each chapter we authors asked you to call up your background knowledge through the "Test Yourself" true and false statements? We have witnessed the power of background knowledge and personal connection when we work with adults, and made sure to integrate it here.

Optimal Condition #2: Learner Choice

L2 learners exercise choice in their learning when possible—selecting their own writing topics, books, projects—using their full multilingual repertoire.

Key Research

Learning sciences have been examining the influence of *agency*. Agency is often operationalized by offering people elements of choice over their learning (Reeve & Tseng, 2011). In Instructed Second Language Acquisition research, agency is a more recent topic, but emerging studies in that field are making clear the link between learner choice and the resulting positive outcomes such as increased motivation and engagement for learning the target language (Larsen-Freeman, 2019). For example, researchers Lambert, Philp, and Nakamura (2017) compared content for L2 classrooms that was pre-selected by the instructor, with content that had been generated by the students. Learner-generated language lessons were those where the students could exercise some choice of topics reflecting their interests and experiences. The researchers found that content chosen by the learners had the most positive impact on engagement and other clear benefits to language learning (Lambert et al., 2017).

The OLE Project team of researchers and teacher researchers have found similar positive effects in their work with bilingual children, including with children who are not yet at grade level and need accelerated language and literacy development to catch up to their peers (Ruiz & Sánchez-Boyce, 2022). The OLE team acts upon the knowledge that even very young language learners carry with them a rich set of lived experiences just as older learners do. The team has documented that when instructors give young learners "space" by offering them agency and choice in their oral language, reading and writing lessons, their biliteracy development is dramatically accelerated (Díaz & Flores, 2001; Flores, 2025; Ruiz, 2023; Ruiz, 2012).

Examples of Instruction and Support for L2 Learners

Young children. One powerful way to create *Condition #2: Learner Choice* when instructing very young language learners is to implement the instructional practice of *Interactive Journals*. Though original research with Interactive Journals (also called *Dialog Journals*) was conducted with college-age and high school students, including Deaf students learning English literacy, researchers have implemented the Interactive Journal approach with even pre-school minority-language learners and found them to effectively promote early literacy development (Ruiz, 1995c; Valero, 2002). The Interactive Journal approach consists of gathering paper with drawing and writing space into a bound journal, such as individual sheets of paper stapled together with a construction paper front and back cover. Teachers first involve children in a discussion where they share what they will choose to draw and write about that day. The next steps occur with every Interactive Journal: (1) children draw and write at their developmental level in the language they choose; (2) teachers/caregivers comment on the child's drawing and writing, and then write a question back to the child based on the journal entry, "sounding out" the message (stretching the letter sounds of the words being written), an especially important step for children not yet independently reading and writing; (3) the child responds to the teacher's question, either orally, or with an attempt at writing a response. (See Appendix B and Ruiz & Sánchez-Boyce, 2022, the latter for an elaboration of these steps and teacher strategies when they do not speak the children's home languages.) The resulting journal is a record of the L2 learners' progress in learning languages, including when they take the risk of communicating through the majority language.

Adolescents and adults. We previously mentioned that the bulk of early research on the benefits of Interactive Journals came from studies with adult minority-language speakers. To name just a few of those benefits, adult language learners began to use a wider range of language functions in their journals, such as describing and recounting; they increased their writing fluency; and, their entries provided instructors with a tangible record of the learners' progress and areas needing more instruction in the L2.

A useful metaphor for Interactive Journals with adolescents and adults is a conversation written down. Steps for this instructional approach are similar to the steps we outlined for younger learners: older students and adults choose the topic to write, and instructors respond to their entries, sometimes with a question. (See Appendix B.) One feature of using *Interactive Journals* with people who are already literate is that the instructor need not write the response with the person present: students will likely be able to read the instructor's response. Also, the instructor, having participated in journal exchanges with the particular student, will be able tailor the written response to the instructional level of the student.

Professional settings. One productive way of implementing *Condition #2: Choice* in the work setting, especially during meetings, is to ask for participants' input in response to a presentation using an approach called *Quick Write*. (See Appendix B.) Let's imagine that nurses have listened to a speaker regarding a new safety procedure when handling certain chemotherapy drugs. Asking participants to write on a half sheet of paper (often less intimidating than a full sheet of paper) their thoughts and reactions to the presentation offers them a choice—agency—in participating as a colleague with the conceptual and professional knowledge they bring to the work setting. A typical next step in *Quick Writes* is to exchange the half sheet with a nearby colleague in the meeting, increasing participant interaction which we know is important for L2 development and we highlight in the next optimal condition. Both participants read each other's *Quick Writes*, and respond to them in writing, returning the papers to the original owner when done. At this time the presenter might then invite those who would like to share their thoughts to the whole group to do so. The experience of choice, as well as rehearsal time with the L2 in the writing exchange, may decrease any anxiety of the L2 speaker for communicating with the whole group, and increase the chances of them taking that risk (Yashima, MacIntyre, & Ikeda, 2018). We know from our discussion of SLA that decreased anxiety about speaking in the L2 is associated with greater willingness to communicate and produce the target language (Ellis & Shintani, 2014; Gass et al., 2020; Lightbown & Spada, 2021).

Optimal Condition #3: Whole Texts for Maximum Comprehension and Explicit Teaching of Skills and Strategies

Activities center on whole, communicatively functional texts (e.g., books, poems, newspaper articles, professional manuals, etc.) to maximize L2 learners' construction of understanding. Instructors use those texts to explicitly teach the components of language processes, such as: text organization; language forms including phonics; spelling and punctuation; and cross-linguistic connections.

Key Research

There are two phrases in *Condition #3* that link to a very large body of effective Instructed SLA research. The first phrase is *communicatively functional texts to maximize the construction of understanding*. This phrase connects to two similar SLA approaches with two different names: *Meaning-Focused Instruction* (Ellis & Shintani, 2014) and *Communicative Language Teaching* (Richards, 2006). For decades, both researchers and instructors have documented the progress that learners make in the L2 with they are asked to transmit and understand messages with an authentic communicative purpose, in contrast to simply imitating a phrase in the L2, or producing a sentence focusing on correct grammar, but not relevant or meaningful to the communication. In essence, when it is important to communicate a message, whether to complete a task for a lesson (*Task-Based Language Teaching*, Ellis, 2003; Ellis, Skehan, Li, Shintani & Lambert, 2020), or to guide a co-worker through a new safety procedure in the construction industry, the emphasis is on effectively conveying or understanding the meaning of the message. And as Instructed SLA researcher Gibbons frames it, such an authentic reason to communicate "puts a press on the speaker's linguistic resources" (Gibbons, 2015, p. 98). In other words, when interacting in real-life communicative exchanges, L2 learners exert extra linguistic effort to successfully reach mutual understanding. And that extra effort is good for continuing multilingual development.

We will revisit this principle of meaningful interactions for optimal L2 development when we discuss *Condition #5: Meaning before Form*. But for *Condition #3* and its promotion of "whole texts," we want to stress how the choice of authentic texts for language learning is key for L2 learners' understanding and meaning-making in the new language. Whole texts, such as those called out in this condition, "books, poems, newspaper articles, professional manuals, etc.," but also, scientific articles, drug fact brochures, and legal briefs, contrast greatly with old-fashioned, traditional language exercises and drills. Those are contrived exercises where, for example, students are given a list of verbs and asked to change them from present tense to past tense. These exercises have little to no relationship with the communicative context of the students, nor do they provide much useful contextual information for students to more easily construct their understanding in the L2. In contrast, whole, authentic texts *do* provide context clues to construct meaning:

picture books contain illustrations for L2 children; short stories follow a narrative structure that adults already carry a conceptual frame for (called *narrative schema*), and an machine-operating manual will have illustrations, captions, and, perhaps most importantly as we noted before, an authentic reason for the L2 machinist to fully understand the material.

But there is a second component to *Condition #3*, highlighted here: ... *Instructors use those texts to explicitly teach the components of language processes, such as: text organization; language forms including phonics; spelling and punctuation; and cross-linguistic connections.* It turns out that a sole focus on conveying and understanding messages—meaning—with no attention dedicated to the more discrete features and forms of language, such as grammar, spelling, and pronunciation, can do a disservice to the L2 learner. Research on effective second language instruction has established a role for attention to the mechanics or correct forms of a language. A familiar term to capture that emphasis is *Form-Focused Instruction* (Ellis & Shintani, 2014; Lightbown & Spada, 2021). There are absolutely times when we do want L2 learners to notice and focus attention on features of the new language, and help them integrate those features into their everyday multilingual repertoire. Let's look at some examples of how these two L2 instructional approaches—Task-Focused (meaning) and Form-Focused (correct forms)—can come together in the educational and professional settings to support L2 learners.

Examples of Instruction and Support for L2 Learners

Young children. Children's picture books are prime examples of whole, authentic texts that facilitate the L2 development of young children. In addition to posing the personal connection question before beginning to read the story that we introduced with *Condition #1, Learner-Centered* ..., teachers/caregivers can look through the illustrations with the children, building up additional background knowledge and vocabulary related to the book. Teachers can also stop periodically through the book and ask for children to predict what will happen next. In the case of a story, children will then rely on their developing narrative schema (mental expectation of hearing about characters, a setting, problem, action, and resolution) to predict events. Furthermore, many picture books for children contain limited amounts of text, and often text that is repeated, allowing for L2 children to focus on the structure and vocabulary of the new language. In these ways, a whole authentic text—a picture book—can support L2 children's comprehension.

Once children have had the opportunity to construct meaning in the second language with a picture book, teachers can then proceed to an emphasis on language forms. For example, emphasizing text structure/genre, they may engage the children in creating a story map, identifying narrative elements such as characters, setting, problem, etc. They may ask the children to collaboratively list new or interesting words and for the children's use in their own writing. Alternatively, teachers may return to the story and list the past tense verbs, dividing them by regular and irregular use. Within an authentic text and its support for comprehension, any and all forms of the new language are up for noticing and integrating into the children's multilingual repertoire.

Adolescents and adults. Poetry lends itself beautifully to *Condition #3, Whole Texts ... For Explicit Teaching of Skills*. The reduced amount of text in poems, but sophisticated concepts and imagery makes it ideal for L2 classrooms with both young and older learners. Once again, instructors can first enhance the L2 students background knowledge by discussing the title, and some of the initial lead-in lines or verses in the poem. Once the poem is read, the instructor may ask the L2 students to choose a verse (there's *Condition #2*—choice!) that especially spoke to them, and then ask them to explain why they chose this verse, either orally, or through a *Quick Write*. Through all of these activities, the emphasis is on maximally comprehending the poem.

Once comprehension of the poem's text is attained, Form-Focused Instruction can then take many directions, e.g., identifying certain parts of speech or verb tenses in the poem. Some instructors reprint the poem but with certain words left out that they want to call attention to in a procedure called *cloze*. (See Appendix B for more detailed steps for using a cloze passage for focus on language forms.) With a cloze activity, students can fill in the passage blanks in pairs, zeroing in on certain language forms. Finally, the instructors may ask students to write a poem of their choice, first as a draft, not stopping to worry whether language forms such as spelling or structure is perfect from the onset. But the critical next step focusing on language forms would be to collaboratively edit the L2 students' draft poems for classroom or wider distribution to families and communities. Drafting, editing, and publishing steps are often referred to as the writing process. (See Appendix B for additional details on implementing the writing process.) The OLE Project team has documented the deep learning of language forms by L2 learners when those forms are embedded in an authentic text that they themselves have written (Ruiz, 2012; Ruiz, 2023).

Professional settings. Professional settings have a leg-up on schools in terms of already having a range of authentic and whole texts that are integral to the professions, whether they are lab reports, legal briefs, instruction manuals, case reports, and so on. L2 learners can bring their previous concepts and experience to aid in the comprehension of these texts, especially when there is an effort to build up background knowledge as a group before reading these texts as we discussed with *Condition #1, Learner-Centered Instruction and Support*. Adult professionals can learn a lot about language forms from the texts themselves. Where supervisors and all of us can support learning L2 forms is by generating ways that L2 learners can be assisted in using correct forms of written language any time the text is going to an audience beyond the professional person and the supervisor. In other words, when L2 learners' writing goes "public," it is an opportunity to help the learners notice correct usage because the stakes are higher, i.e., it will reach a wider audience (See Appendix B for details of implementing the writing process.)

Support for L2 learners' proofing and editing their writing is essential. That support can take the form of editing conferences with the L2 learner, either through a specific service provided by the company itself, or volunteers, helping L2 colleagues develop correct usage. However, these services may be a challenge to establish within a professional organization with its own goals, time-lines, and allocation of resources. Consequently, a significant boost to L2 learners in the workplace are computer-assisted grammar/language applications that provide immediate feedback and assistance with editing of written texts. So far, Instructed SLA research has documented a positive trend in both L2 learners' use of these applications to improve their writing (Marzuki, Widiati, Rusdin, Darwin, & Indrawati, 2023), including L2 learners working in various professional settings, e.g., management (Calma, Cotronei-Baird, & Chia, 2022). Every professional organization should make sure that these resources are made known to colleagues, and that they are encouraged to use them; bilinguals and monolinguals alike can profit from editing help for documents that go public.

Optimal Condition #4: Active Participation

L2 learners actively engage in activities with long, frequent turns in producing oral and written language. There are high levels of interaction through pair and group work.

Key Research

Leading Instructed SLA researchers Ellis and Shintani (2014) succinctly home in on the essence of *Condition #4: Active Participation*. They write: "The opportunity to interact in the L2 is central to developing L2 proficiency" (p. 26). Planning for active participation of all L2 learners opens opportunities for the practice of their current language proficiency and strategies, as well as ongoing language learning from others. Instructed SLA research has further established that the *type of interaction* matters. Traditional interaction in instructional contexts, whether in the general education classroom or in the foreign language classroom, often follows a sequence that is not conducive to language learning. The sequence usually begins with an initiation (I) by the teacher in the form of a question; followed by a response (R) by the learner; and then an evaluation (E) by the instructor, frequently addressing whether the learner response was correct or not. These traditional language interaction patterns, often referred to as *IRE sequences*, usually call for a very short response to the instructor's question. Further, there is often a specific response that the instructor expects to the question, a question referred to as a known-answer or known-information question. Clearly in these situations, there is no room for authentic and extended exchanges of information.

A very different type of communication pattern than IRE leads to better and faster L2 learning, and has been widely and consistently documented in all related fields of multilingualism. In place of the IRE sequence described above, this pattern usually takes the form of participants' two-way talk, that is, alternating initiations and responses by people who are authentically exchanging information with each other. The emphasis is on using language to communicate real messages rather than practicing correct usage for someone to evaluate. L2 learners and their interlocutors in exchanges of information must "negotiate meaning" and they do so in a variety of ways (Long, 1983). Native speakers of the L2 when addressing L2 learners may slow down their language, repeat, paraphrase, simplify—all creating what we brought up earlier, that is, *comprehensible input* for the L2 learner (Krashen, 1985). These same interactive situations require L2 learners to produce *comprehensible output* (Swain, 1985). When producing their L2 in oral and written forms, learners must dig deep in their existing linguistic repertoire, and add on to it by trying out new and more effective ways of reaching mutual understanding with others. For communication to be successful for participants, all—native speakers and L2 learners—must deploy their best strategies to convey and understand information. And when there is a communicative breakdown, all need to collaboratively negotiate back to shared comprehension.

We introduced earlier a method from the Instructed SLA field that necessitates active and extended communication by L2 learners in order to be successful in reaching mutual understanding: *Task-Based Learning*, or *TBL*. We will look at concrete examples of TBL-type activities in the next sub-section, but for now, we can generally describe this approach as calling for the transfer of information that one person or group has, and that the others do not. This situation is sometimes referred to as an "information gap." In TBL activities, success of a task depends on interactively conveying and understanding information across this gap to reach a shared goal. In summarizing the research on TBL, Ellis and Shintani write that there is a: "substantial amount of research in SLA that has shown that task-based teaching is effective and, in fact, more effective for some learners than traditional teaching" (2014, p. 329).

We began this section describing one common component of traditional teaching—Initiation–Response–Evaluation (IRE) sequences. TBL approaches disrupt IRE sequences by requiring authentic communicative exchanges until successful completion of the task, not short replies to known questions. They also require a shared sense of cooperation among the participants to meet their goals. Consequently, a general method of instruction called *cooperative learning*, not limited to language teaching classrooms but rather implemented in general education and professional settings, can also help create *Condition #4, Active Participation* ... Cooperative learning is an approach that organizes participants into small groups or pairs who work together to accomplish shared goals. Reducing the size of the conversational or work group to pairs or a small set of people generally raises the frequency with which all participants must interact, especially in contrast to a large group of 30 or more people. These cooperative learning structures of pairs or small groups offer many opportunities for both comprehensible output and input for L2 learners. In the following examples of optimal instruction and professional contexts for L2 learners, we suggest both TBL and cooperative learning approaches.

Examples of Instruction and Support for L2 Learners

Young children. Earlier in this chapter for *Conditions #1 Learner-Centered Instruction and Support* ... and *#3 Whole Texts for Maximum Comprehension and Explicit Instruction* ... we wrote of young children participating in a read-aloud by an adult. We focused on the children's background knowledge and personal connections to the central situation of the story, their predictions during the read-aloud based on cues from the pictures and narrative sequence, and discrete skills such as creating a story map, and identifying sight words. While these are conditions conducive to multilingual development, the present condition, *Active Participation*, is indispensable. If, during the read-aloud, children have limited turns to talk and interact with their peers, an essential feature of optimal language development is missing. One very efficient way of increasing language interaction is the *Think–Pair–Share* approach, even in the classroom with a large group of children. (Detailed steps of this approach are in Appendix B.) Essentially, with *Think–Pair–Share*, teachers ask the children to interact in pairs before sharing their personal connections or predictions with the larger group. Specifically, they ask the children to stop and *think* of their response before speaking. They then direct the children to talk with a peer in a one-to-one structure, or *pair*, making sure that both children are engaged in speaking and listening. Finally, teachers can offer children the opportunity to *share* their ideas or their partners with the whole group. It should be immediately apparent that this simple, straight-forward approach that does not need any special materials or preparation greatly differs from the teacher selecting only one child among the group to offer a response. Instead, *Think–Pair–Share* engages all of the children and enacts the critical interaction necessary for developing a multilingual repertoire.

Adolescents and adults. The basic principle behind the *Think–Pair–Share* approach is absolutely relevant for working with adolescents and adults. Often when interacting with this age group, we simply call the practice of pairing participants to interact before speaking in a larger group *Turn and Talk*. (Further details are in Appendix B) Interestingly, the whole group can be as large as 100, but *Turn and Talk* allows for 100% participation, and, most germane to our topic, interaction to promote the L2. Again, this approach needs no advance preparation, yet puts into practice the statement we quoted earlier by leading Instructed SLA researchers: "The opportunity to interact in the L2 is central to developing L2 proficiency" (Ellis & Shintanti, 2014, p. 26)

Given the relevance of active participation in multilingual development, we introduce here another approach for heightened interaction, *Home–Expert Groups*. The Home–Expert Groups method hails from cooperative learnings and is sometimes called the *Jigsaw Approach*, the reason for which will become clear as we overview it here. (More detailed steps for Home–Expert Groups/Jigsaw are located in Appendix B.) Basically, Home–Expert Groups divide a text to be read, or a task to be done, into different sections. For this brief explanation, let's assume that there are 25 people in the overall group and they are about to read a rather long article in class. If we divide the article into five different sections to shorten the task for the participants, each Home Group will consist of five people, each of whom will read a different section of the article in order to later put their understandings together ("jigsaw" them) and jointly make sense of the article. Members of the Home Groups then read their assigned section separately. They next move into Expert Groups, that is, all of the people reading the first section will gather together, as will the remaining groups reading the other sections convene. In other words, there will be one Expert Group for each of the five sections of the article. In Expert Groups, participants have the opportunity to clarify misunderstandings, identify the most important points, and so on, with others who have read the same section; they become "experts" in their section of the article.

The final step in our example is for the Home Groups to reconvene. These Home Groups are now composed of five "experts" who have collaborated with others reading and digesting the same section that they did. Going in order, each member of their Home Group now presents their section of the article to collaboratively construct understanding of the entire text. Again, readers can clearly see why this cooperative learning approach is also called Jigsaw: each member has a piece of the puzzle that the others do not have, but they can now gather to assemble the separate pieces to make the whole. Likely, readers will detect the most striking aspect of Home–Expert Groups: the high degree of interaction required to successfully complete the task. And, as a bonus, the chore of reading a long article is now shared with others!

Professional setting. Both approaches discussed in the previous section—*Turn and Talk* and *Home–Expert Groups*—are easily applied to the workplace. When leading a professional work group, periodically asking participants to Turn and Talk with another colleague is easily executed, requires minimal to no advance preparation, and promotes the interaction needed for both enhanced comprehension and further L2 development. We would also suggest that even for native speakers, the opportunity to periodically and actively process information with another colleague is beneficial to the goals of the professional meeting.

Home–Expert Groups function extremely well in the professional setting as the means to share responsibility for new learning. As professionals keeping up with the constant incoming knowledge and changes related to our chosen area of work, we are often called upon to read and digest new information in written form. In addition to written texts, sometimes the new information comes in an audiovisual form, such as a video. Distributing among colleagues the task of reading a section of a text, or taking notes on only a portion of a video, not only reduces the workload on each person, but increases the interaction among them for the authentic purpose of better understanding something related to their work. The result can be increased expertise and progress in the profession for all, but especially for L2 learners. (See Appendix B for additional details on the Home–Expert Group approach.)

Optimal Condition #5: Meaning First, Followed by Form

First, L2 learners construct meaning by speaking and listening, or reading and writing text; and then move to a focus on correct forms of language such as grammar and spelling.

Key Research

Beginning around the last quarter of the twentieth century, Instructed SLA researchers began to observe that the previous emphasis on teaching linguistic forms of the new language such as pronunciation, grammar, and vocabulary, did not seem to result in learners successfully using their L2 in natural communicative situations. It seems that while L2 learners could learn to fill in blanks in language texts, or respond correctly in language drills, they had much more difficulty transferring that knowledge to the interchange of meaningful messages in the classroom and most importantly, in the real world. In the field of language learning, this set of skills and strategies to understand and be understood is known as *communicative competence* (Hymes, 1972)

This widely documented challenge to L2 learners to effectively engage in meaningful communication caused a shift to instructional approaches that can be grouped under the term *Communicative Language Teaching*, but more recently and broadly known in the Instructed SLA field as *Meaning-Focused Instruction*. With Meaning-Focused Instruction (MFI), the goal is successful communication, and learners use language as a tool for the purposes of productive communication. SLA researchers have found that this shift to MFI is connected to a number of benefits to L2 learners, including: (a) increased fluency in the new language (DeKeyser, 1998), (b) motivation and engagement (Hiver & Wu, 2023), (c) increased risk-taking in the L2 and expanded production; (d) decreased anxiety in the L2 in order to accomplish the communicative goal, and (e) overall augmented learning of the L2, much of it through indirect or unconscious means while authentically communicating messages (Ellis & Shintani, 2014). With the support of many studies, then, *Condition #5* forefronts the emphasis on meaningful communication: *First, learners construct meaning by speaking and listening, or reading and writing text ...*

Notice, however, the second part of *Condition #5*: *... and then move to a focus on correct forms of language such as grammar and spelling.* Evidence in the Instructed SLA field has suggested that calling learners' attention to language forms *within* the overall communicative task results in advanced L2 learning. Bottom line, a combination of meaning-based and form-based instruction has been shown to increase fluency and success in exchanging messages (meaning), *and* result in greater accuracy and correct usage (language forms) (Ellis, 2024; Kellem & Halvorsen, 2018; Lightbown & Spada, 2021). Accordingly, below we will see examples of activities that direct L2 learners' attention to specific language forms, but always within the context of authentic communication in which the shared goal depends on effective understanding and expressing of information.

Examples of Instruction and Support for L2 Learners

Young children. One instructional practice that creates a "meaning-then-form" focus is known as *Daily News*. (See Appendix B for detailed steps.) For this activity, the teacher prepares a large paper with an empty space at the top and several lines at the bottom. The instructor gathers the children and informs them that one child will be chosen that day to give his or her news. In order to be ready to share their news, the children are asked to *Think–Pair–Share (Condition #4 Active Participation,* and Appendix B) their own news with a partner in order to be ready to dictate their news if they are selected that day. (Note the language interaction of all children before one child is selected to share, *Condition #4: Active Participation.*) The teacher then selects and scribes the child's message on the large paper while all watch. Once this meaningful message is written and understood by all, the teacher may then focus on linguistic forms. For example, she may engage the children in counting the words to develop their concepts of print, or identifying sight words, underlining capital letters, circling punctuation, etc.

Adolescents and adults. A very useful activity to enact *Condition #3* is to teach L2 learners to use graphic organizers as a way to structure different forms of academic writing, such as a personal narrative, an informational piece, or literary analysis. As an example of the latter, let's say that the group is reading and analyzing a poem. Students would first respond to the meaning of the poem by a group discussion, sharing a line that speaks to them, or free-writing their personal responses in their literature response journal. Once the L2 learners' comprehension is established, the instructor would then move to a focus on linguistic forms. The L2 learners may be asked to identify a theme in the poem, and support the theme with quotes from the text and their explanation of how each quote supports and relates to the theme. The next step to assist the students in writing an organized literary analysis would be for distribute a graphic organizer to help the students organize their thoughts for the essay. (See Appendix B or an example of a graphic organizer for an essay on literary themes.) In the central box, students would write their idea for the theme, i.e., one of the author's central messages about life embedded in the text. In surrounding boxes on the graphic organizer, they would insert a quote from the story in each box, along with a sentence or two explaining why the quote supports their selected theme. The next writing support the instructor could provide is an outline format to assist the actual first writing draft, emphasizing an introductory paragraph, a new paragraph for each selected quote and explanation, and then a concluding paragraph. The instructor may also provide lists of various language forms typical of literary essays, such as topic sentence starters, transition words between paragraphs, and phrases that are typical of conclusions. In sum, the instructor has led the L2 learners from an initial construction of meaning and comprehension, to a focus on the form of a specific genre of academic writing.

Professional setting. Within professional settings, there is a natural emphasis on meaning: communication must be effective and efficient for employees to be successful and the organization to advance. Consequently, in these settings, there is a high priority on implementing various ways to ensure comprehension by L2 colleagues.

In the previous instructional example, we described graphic organizers that aid in writing academic genres. Graphic organizers can also help with listening and reading comprehension in the professional setting. Most of the texts and materials in a professional setting will be informational in nature. As an example, let's imagine that an orthodontic professional group would like to jointly review a recent scientific research article comparing the efficacy of different orthodontic procedures. Before reading the article, discussion leaders can begin by not only tapping into the participants' existing knowledge (*Condition #1: Learner-Centered and Supported Instruction*), but, very importantly, visually mapping that knowledge in some way so as to enhance the ways L2 colleagues can use to best understand the topic. For example, workgroup leaders can create a written web on a screen or chart where the topic is noted in a central circle, and then record the group's knowledge in spokes emanating from the circle. An alternative graphic to support comprehension of reading (or audiovisual materials) is to construct a *KWL Chart* prior to interacting with the topic: a column for what the group already knows about the topic (K), a second column for what they want to know (W), and a third column to be filled out after reading with the important points of what they learned (L). (Additional details of the approach can be found on the website of the *National Highway Institute*, part of the US Department of Transportation, https://www.nhi.fhwa.dot.gov/LearnersFirst/k-w-l-charts.htm) and depicted in Appendix B. Note that the example there is regarding bridge inspections for the construction industries, clear evidence that the KWL activity is not confined to classroom use, but also implemented within professional settings.)

Continuing with our orthodontic practice example and the reading of an article comparing different procedures, we highlight here that first, the group leader for this activity has enhanced L2 learners' comprehension through visual depictions of the group's pooled knowledge. Next, participants read the article, perhaps through the Home–Expert Groups procedure. Then, at a later time, an emphasis on the more discrete aspects of the article can occur, such as a collaborative effort in identifying the L section of the KWL Chart (a list of important learning from the article). Alternatively, the group could create another type of graphic such as a table where participants in groups generate pros and cons of each orthodontic procedure based on information from the article.

Before we leave *Condition #5*, we want to recognize the sensitivity needed in the professional setting when L2 colleagues are asked to produce correct forms of the more micro level of language forms such as grammar and punctuation. Whereas teachers of children and instructors of adult L2 learners in the classroom setting are expected to focus on language forms, and give corrective feedback, that is not the case in the work setting. Public language form corrections or feedback to L2 learners could be responsible for increased anxiety, and consequently, limited engagement or production in the L2. In that case, creating opportunities for one-to-one assistance to L2 colleagues for both formal oral presentations, and written pieces is essential. Equally important is to begin those conferences or offers of assistance, whether personal or through editing technology, affirming that the L2 colleague's knowledge and expertise is by far the most important aspect of their participation, and that assistance with correct language forms is something that can be added on as a way to enhance their growing linguistic competence in the L2. Through mutual respect and trust among colleagues, it may even be possible that L2 colleagues will feel comfortable asking for editing assistance, and others for offering that assistance to them.

Optimal Condition #6: Authentic Purpose

The end-products of activities have a real-life function that extend beyond the classroom setting to the real world. L2 learners communicate real messages, to real audiences, for real purposes.

Key Research

The general shift to Meaning-Focused Instruction has had overall positive effects on L2 learning. One of the central approaches, Task-Based Instruction, put the emphasis on carrying out actions that serve a communicative purpose or outcome (Ellis, 2003). Instructed SLA researchers such as Rod Ellis have further distinguished in this approach tasks that are classroom (pedagogic) tasks, and those that have a real-life function. Many Instructed SLA researchers have indeed documented greater L2 development when there is "situational authenticity" (Ellis et al., 2020). There is also a favoring of learner-generated tasks over teacher-generated activities, as we discussed with *Condition #2: Learners Choice* ... producing L2 learner agency, motivation, and engagement with the resulting growth in the L2. Fortunately, for the professional setting, tasks with real-life consequences are the norm. It is within the classroom that challenges arise in linking tasks with situational authenticity. However, it is possible to create lessons with a real-life function extending beyond the formal classroom as we will see in the following examples.

Examples of Instruction and Support for L2 Learners

Young children. For *Condition #5* consisting of an emphasis on meaning before form, we described the instructional approach of Daily News. One straight-forward adaptation of Daily News to create a real-life purpose with value beyond the classroom is for teachers to "publish" the children's news. (See Appendix B for more detailed steps.) Here the teacher periodically gathers the students' news and binds them into a book. The books can stay in the classroom library until the end of the year, to be raffled to various children, or they can be sent home in a rotating manner for children to share with their caregivers. Another option for older children is for the teachers and students to create a newsletter composed of the students' news as a way to authentically share information with a real-life audience.

Adolescents and adults. One of the best ways to help older L2 learners participate in activities with a real-life function is through the writing process approach. (See Appendix B for additional details.) Whether the L2 learners are writing personal narratives, informational pieces, procedural manuals, fiction, or poetry, the instructor can lead them through the drafting, conferencing, revision, editing, and finally, publishing steps of the writing process.

Professional setting. As noted, the professional settings enact all aspects of this condition by their very nature: *learners communicate real messages to real audiences for real purposes.* Perhaps it is very fitting that in a book dedicated to what professionals need to know about multilingualism, we end with stressing that leg-up that professional settings have in accelerating L2 development with its communicative and high stakes authenticity!

Continuing the Work in Optimizing Professional Settings for Multilingual Development

This chapter focused on the first six optimal conditions for multilingual development both in formal education settings and the workplace. As we alluded to before, there are six remaining conditions which, when present in professional settings, further optimize multilingualism. Table 3.3 lists those conditions with an explanation on how they can be enacted in the workplace.

In the "Time to Think and Connect" section at the end of the chapter, we will ask you to read and reflect upon optimal *Conditions #7–12*, and their role in creating an optimal learning environment in your profession for colleagues on the path to multilingualism.

One more critical piece for understanding multilingualism remains. It is one of its most significant contributions to well-being and productivity in workplace settings, and beyond. We take up that topic in our final chapter: Chapter 4, "Multilingualism and Intercultural Communication: Working toward Intercultural Citizenship."

Test yourself! What did you learn?: Re-consider each statement from the beginning of the chapter. Use your background knowledge *and* new information gained from reading the chapter to decide whether the statements reflect current research on multilingualism (True), or not (False). Answers are in Appendix A at the back of the book.

True or False	Increasing Multilingual Competence
	1. Research on the effectiveness of bilingual education has only recently begun, and it is too early to determine whether it enhances multilingual development or academic achievement.
	2. Advance work in building up L2 learners' background knowledge before they begin to listen to or read a text greatly enhances their L2 comprehension.
	3. Frequent opportunities to interact in pairs and small groups is one of the best ways to improve second language (L2) learning
	4. Most L2 learners need a strict focus on language forms through drills and worksheets, rather than practice in communicating real messages.
	5. Research-based teaching and learning practices can be integrated into the workplace to support colleagues who are L2 learners.

Table 3.3 Optimal conditions for multilingual development #7–12

7. Immersion in Language and Print
L2 learners use a wide variety of print forms and functions, even at the earliest stages of their L2 language development. Print, in addition to oral input, offers critical cues to comprehension for L2 learners, as well as serving as models for L2 writing conventions. All videos created and used in the workplace are captioned to provide access to Deaf L2 learners, and further visual cues for all L2 learners.

8. Demonstrations of Writing for a Range of Purposes
Team leaders and professional colleagues demonstrate their own reading and writing in professional and training settings, and openly share their ongoing efforts with L2 learners. "More expert" L2 learners and native speakers also serve as models for their colleagues, and are encouraged to jointly construct texts (collaboratively write).

9. Approximations
Colleagues of L2 learners know that they will successively approximate L2 language and literacy skills following a developmental course. Colleagues are conscious that what may initially seem like "errors" in the L2 are actually steps toward greater proficiency; they do what they can to lower L2 learners' anxiety in interaction, and to increase risk-taking in using the L2.

10. Response
L2 learners receive timely responses to their oral and written texts that are personalized and thoughtful acknowledgments of their ideas, expertise, and efforts. When appropriate and mutually agreed upon, these responses can take the form of feedback on the learners' use of L2 forms.

11. High Expectations
Colleagues expect that all members of the professional group will increasingly become proficient and independent speakers, readers, and writers in multiple languages. Workgroup leaders and colleagues make sure that scaffolding is in place to help L2 learners meet these expectations.

12. Community of Professional Learning
All colleagues are welcomed into a professional community of speakers, readers, writers, and learners who explore a range of issues relevant to them. Multilingual identities are affirmed by the recognition that those colleagues with the most expertise in the field could be among the L2 learners. The multilingualism of L2 learners is recognized as an asset to the profession, and monolingual colleagues are encouraged to follow their model and extend their own multilingual repertoires.

Time to Think and Connect

Increasing Multilingual Competence in the Home, Community, and Workplace

1. Think about the two optimal paths to multilingualism that we have highlighted here: (a) growing up in a bilingual family and (b) attending a bilingual education program. Have you had either of those experiences? Or, do you know someone who did? What do you see as the advantages of those paths? What disadvantages could there be?
2. Carefully read optimal *Conditions #7–12* in Table 3.3 located in this chapter. Before joining a discussion partner or group, select two of those conditions which seem to you to be the most important to put into action in your specific workplace. Compare your answers with your colleagues' choices.

3. In your current position, either as a working professional or as a college student completing requirements for your future career, what has been your experience with bilingual colleagues/peers? Has their bilingualism been viewed as an asset? In what ways? Or, has it been viewed as a drawback that needs fixing? In what ways? If being bilingual has been viewed as a disadvantage, what facts could you now bring to the conversation from this book and other sources that might open their mind to viewing bilingualism as an asset?

Chapter 4

Multilingualism and Intercultural Communication
Working toward Intercultural Citizenship

Overview

In this final chapter we turn our attention to a critical function of multilingualism not yet addressed in this book: facilitating communication among different linguistic and cultural groups who need to work together. An umbrella term for promoting positive interaction among different groups is *interculturalism*. The two parts of the term itself give us a working idea of its definition: *inter* meaning "between," and *cultural* suggesting that there are some key differences among those groups. These differences can include country of origin, faiths, ethnicities, race, and language. We have selected two components of interculturalism with specific relevance to the work setting: *intercultural citizenship* and *intercultural communication*. We begin by defining both these terms, and then discuss the intersection of linguistic and cultural practices that shape the experiences of professionals. We conclude by presenting promising approaches to promote intercultural communicative competence at work.

Test yourself! (Tapping into your background knowledge): Before reading the chapter, consider each statement below and use your current knowledge and experiences to decide whether the statement is true or false.

True or False	Multilingualism and Intercultural Communication
	1. Despite the growing demand for multilingual skills in today's US workforce, most US workers remain primarily monolingual English speakers.
	2. Language and culture develop separately. You acquire language first and then culture.
	3. Intercultural communication means communication within the same culture.
	4. Self-reflection is an important skill to develop when working with linguistically and culturally diverse families.
	5. Informal interactions with others who are different from you can help reduce prejudice.

DOI: 10.4324/9781003216414-7

Multilingualism and the Workforce

In the previous chapters, we have defined multilingualism, explained how it develops, and discussed its benefits, looking closely at the research that supports the economic and cognitive benefits of bilingualism. Along the way, we have highlighted research findings that explain what we know about the unique ways bilinguals use their linguistic resources to communicate with others within and across languages, and to make sense of their environments. We have also described ways for promoting multilingualism across the lifespan and the optimal conditions that lead to success in developing multilingual competencies at home, school, community, and workspace. In this chapter, we direct our attention to multilingualism in professional communities, and discuss how diverse linguistic skills are shaping the professional landscape in the twenty-first century.

Multilingualism in the workforce can take many different forms. For example, you could be working in an environment, like a hospital or a school, where you have many employees who are bilingual or multilingual. It could be the case that you are part of an organization, like a business or a not-for-profit, that operates in multiple languages across different countries. Or it could be that you are working in an organization, like a community clinic or a state agency, that serves linguistically diverse populations, regardless of whether the employees are bilingual or not. In each of these scenarios, the reality is that you can anticipate that you will encounter individuals who come from cultures different from your own, and who speak languages that you may or may not be familiar with. Each of these scenarios poses opportunities as well as challenges. A major benefit is one that we discussed in Chapter 1, and that is, if you are bilingual, you are highly prized and sought after by employers in many professions. A challenge, however, is that current statistics indicate that not all workers are ready to meet the demand for multilingual competencies in the workforce. Let's look at some numbers with a specific focus on the workplace.

Despite the growing demand for multilingual skills in today's US workforce (New American Economy, 2017), and the increasing number of multilingual homes in the country (as discussed in Chapter 1), most US workers remain primarily monolingual English speakers. Clearly, there is a gap between the growing need to serve a diverse society and the insufficient number of multilingual workers to fulfill this demand. For example, the Center for Workforce Studies (CWS) from the American Psychological Association (APA) projects that by 2030, the need for psychological services tailored to Spanish-speaking US Latinos will increase by 30% (Bailey, 2020). However, only a small percentage of psychologists—5.5%—offer services in Spanish, and just 4.4% identify as Latino. We pinpointed a similar growing demand for bilingual nurses in Chapter 1, but as is the case of many health and allied health professions, there is a shortage of bilingual staff (Meeker, 2022).

What happens, then, when most of the workforce is composed of monolingual individuals serving a majority of multilingual and culturally diverse students, families, and communities across a wide range of professions? The mismatch of linguistic and cultural practices between professionals and diverse individuals is not new and has impacted fields like education and healthcare for decades. Research shows that this mismatch can lead to misinterpretations that can have economic implications, or could lead to poor education or health outcomes for cultural minority individuals or for those who do not speak the majority language. For example, a recent review of research examined studies assessing the healthcare experiences of US Latino families with limited English proficiency over the last 30 years (Escobedo, Cervantes, & Havranek, 2023). Not surprising, the findings confirmed substantial communication barriers, making it difficult for Latino individuals to express their concerns, understand next steps, or build trust with the healthcare providers. The same results have been corroborated in the UK (Zhao, 2023). But the findings also highlight bright spots, as the authors point to some practices identified in the literature that seem to have a positive impact to reduce disparities in healthcare for Latino patients. One key practice was having access to in-person interpreters. In their review, Escobedo, Cervantes, and Havranek found that Latino families preferred interacting with bilingual clinicians or professionals or in-person interpreters, which, the research also indicated, helped reduce errors (2023, p. 1268). However, the authors state:

> Bilingual clinicians and in-person interpretation are not enough to provide equivalent care for Latinx patients. Medical education and workplace education in both *linguistic and cultural fluency* should be provided to all staff caring for Latinx patients who do not speak the dominant language to express their concerns.
>
> (2023, p. 1268, emphasis added)

Education in "linguistic and cultural fluency" in the workplace can mean different things to different people. We understand this as a call for more professionals across a wide range of sectors who can better meet the needs of a range of communities, either by speaking their languages and/or by holding an asset view of people from backgrounds different than their own. Put another way, there is a need for professionals who will be ready to activate their linguistic and intercultural skills in the service of others through promoting and engaging in positive communication and interactions. These characteristics are at the core of being an *intercultural citizen*. We will explore intercultural citizenship and what it specifically means in the workspace a bit later in the chapter, but in the meantime, the *Council of Europe* (2025a) provides us with a helpful working definition:

> [Intercultural] citizenship is about how we engage across cultural differences in our communities and public spaces. *Intercultural citizenship requires understanding that diversity and positive interaction between different cultures can be an advantage* ... In the end intercultural citizenship is about the way we relate to each other on a day-to-day basis to work, learn, and have fun. Most importantly, it is about how we actively change or maintain our communities

taking into account the different points of view we have. There is an aspect of rights, duties, and behaviours that we as both human beings and citizens owe to each other.

(*Council of Europe*, emphasis original)

One of the core components of intercultural citizenship highly relevant to our topic of multilingualism is *intercultural communication*. Before we look at this critical aspect of intercultural citizenship, it is helpful to first understand the connection between language and culture.

Language: What's Culture Got to Do With It?

Thus far in this book we have had a focus on language, as one would expect in a book on multilingualism. In this chapter, however, we have already frequently raised the term "culture" in our discussion. What exactly is the connection between language and culture? To provide an anchor for this discussion, we use Sonia Nieto's definition of culture as "the ever-changing values, traditions, social and political relationships, and worldview created, shared, and transformed by a group of people bound together by a combination of factors that can include a common history, geographic location, language, social class, and religion" (2009, p. 136). That statement contains quite a bit of information about culture! However, in a nutshell, this definition of culture goes beyond thinking about your heritage, or the traditions you hold dear (like holidays, foods, or celebrations). Instead, Nieto calls for a much more dynamic and multilayered understanding of culture. Think about it this way: culture is something that we *do*, rather than something that we *have*. It evolves depending on the social and political contexts where we live and work.

We pause here to give a real-life example from the global business field to illustrate the importance of this deeper understanding of culture. Some readers may have heard about what happened when a very large retail chain from the US, Walmart, set up shop in Germany (Baldwin, González, Brock, Xie, & Chao, 2023). Certainly, Walmart carefully planned for the language shift from English to German in its stores. What Walmart did not take into account, however, were cultural differences between the US and Germany. It turns out that at least three inherent characteristics of Walmart's success in the US were at odds in the German work context. These components required that German Walmart employees do what the US counterparts do, conforming to a sort of "Walmart culture": (a) smile at customers who they did not know; (b) produce group cheers typical of sports games to begin their workday; (c) report on co-workers if they showed what was considered inappropriate behaviors or actions. There was real incongruence, or lack of fit, between this specific and localized retail culture, with its new geographical and cultural context. Walmart eventually folded up its 85 stores and left Germany at a significant financial cost, around 1 billion US dollars (Baldwin et al., 2023). The lesson here? Language *and* cultural awareness matter in the professions!

Whether in the professional setting as illustrated above, or in our communities or personal spaces, culture plays a role in shaping how we perceive and interpret the world around us. As Niza Hidalgo (1993) writes,

> Each of us has been socialized in some culture, and often more than one culture. *Our culture provides a lens through which we view the world and interpret our everyday experiences.* Culture informs what we see and understand, as well as what we omit and misconstrue. Many components make up our view of the world: our ethnic and racial identification, the region of the country we come from, the type of neighborhood we live in, our socioeconomic background, our gender, the language(s) we speak, our disabilities, our past experiences, and our life-style. We need to think about the ways in which these parts of us define our perspectives.
>
> (1993, p. 100, emphasis added)

Notice how Hidalgo calls out different components that shape our understanding of the world that go beyond our ethnicity. For example, where we live (e.g., geographical region, urban, rural, suburban), and how we live (e.g., access to healthcare, education, financial security) influence the *lens* through which we see the world. And, as Hidalgo also points out, one of those components shaping our culture is language.

We know from research that learning language, whether L1 or L2, is a process that is deeply rooted in our cultural experiences. It is through language that we are socialized into the culture we are born into. If you were born in Japan, it is through your learning of Japanese in interactions with your caregivers and others that you acquire Japanese culture. And if you are growing up in a bilingual family, then this process involves negotiating two languages and two cultures (Fogle & King, 2017). Research by Song (2019) offers a clear illustration of this bilingual and bicultural negotiation. Song examined the language socialization of a Korean–English bilingual child growing up in a Korean transnational family in the US. Using qualitative observations and interviews, she documented how the 5-year-old child used language strategically as he learned the cultural expectations of language use in his home. For example, he used Korean when speaking to his elders to show respect and cultural affiliation, while switching to English with siblings in more informal and playful situations. The child then used code-switching as a language strategy to navigate dual cultural expectations: speaking Korean to align with traditional cultural expectations and using English to express a more independent stance. In summarizing the research on socialization in bilingual and multilingual families, Fogle and King (2017) write that through the blending of languages and cultures, children and young adults learn the rules for how each of them works.

Language then allows us to internalize cultural norms, values, and beliefs, and to communicate and reinforce these shared meanings with others in our community. It is through language that we not only convey information but also establish social bonds, express identity, and participate fully in cultural life. As we saw in

Chapter 1, bilingual individuals develop metalinguistic awareness and cognitive flexibility from an early age, which also help shape their perceptions of the world. In other words, language is the tool through which we both interpret and shape our understanding of the world around us. In fact, research has documented over and over that the words we use help us describe and understand our surroundings, while also influencing *how* we form ideas and make sense of what we see (Boroditsky, 2011).

To illustrate the interplay between language and thinking, we offer readers the following examples. The first is research by Winawer et al. (2007) who examined how language influences perception through a color discrimination task with English and Russian speakers. Russian speakers, whose language distinguishes between light blue (*goluboy*) and dark blue (*siniy*), were faster at differentiating shades of blue on a nonverbal task than English speakers, who use "blue" for all shades. In other words, languages with distinct terms for colors, like Russian's two separate words for "blue" (light and dark), enable speakers to differentiate shades of blue faster than those without such distinctions.

The second example has long been reported in linguistic anthropology, but Fantini (2020) nicely summarized as follows. Different cultures across the world use language to match their needs. For example, in regions where snow is a central feature of daily life, such as among the Inuit, speakers have multiple terms to describe different types of snow (i.e., falling snow, hard-packed snow, and so on). We can find a similar phenomenon in Italian, as Italian speakers have many more words for pasta to capture the nuances related to shape, texture, and cooking method, than we do in English or in Spanish. Consequently, when individuals speak more than one language, their linguistic repertoire broadens, *and* their perspective on the world expands along with it.

We know that achieving proficiency in more than one language requires significant time—the lifespan, as Ortega (2019) reminds us—even when becoming bilingual in an optimal learning environment. While we expand our multilingual repertoire, it remains a high priority across professions to interact positively and productively across group differences. Intercultural citizenship, then, can serve as a complementary and inclusive framework to developing professionals prepared to engage effectively with a range of linguistic and cultural groups, regardless of their multilingual status.

Being an Intercultural Citizen in the Workplace

Our initial working definition of intercultural citizenship has provided us with this foundational understanding: it is a way of making our communities stronger through helping to create positive interactions across different groups. But given the increasing linguistic and cultural diversity in the workplace, it is helpful to dig a little deeper into the concept and how we may extend it into our professional spaces.

We frame our discussion of intercultural citizenship from two perspectives. The first one comes from the work of Ricardo Zapata-Barrero (2022) who looks at what intercultural citizenship means to a society as a whole. Zapata-Barrero writes that intercultural citizenship is primarily concerned with "a society that takes advantage of the resource that diversity offers, while also ensuring community cohesion" (2022, p. 17). We interpret social cohesion to mean a sense of connectedness, and solidarity by members of a society, including a willingness to cooperate with each other even when there are differences among them. Zapata-Barrero (2024) further explains intercultural citizenship by identifying it as an active process that requires individuals within a society go beyond passive tolerance to actively engage with people from different cultures. This contact and exchange among different groups—what he describes as "living in diversity"—can build empathy and deeper understanding, which are essential for social cohesion. Emphasizing the importance of interactions across differences to bring people together for society as a whole, Zapata-Barrero writes, "The golden rule of intercultural citizenship is that through contact, people share spaces, socialize in diversity, and develop feelings of membership" (2022, p. 14). In other words, everyday intercultural interactions in communities, the workplace, and public spaces can build up a sense of interconnectedness where all are seen as co-members of their shared society. In this model, Zapata-Barrero emphasizes interculturalism as a social responsibility.

A similar perspective comes from the work of Michael Byram and his colleagues (Byram, 2008; Byram & Golubeva, 2020; Wagner & Byram, 2017). Byram and Golubeva (2020) describe intercultural citizenship as going beyond simply understanding other cultures to acting with social responsibility and promoting dialogue and cooperation between people from various cultural backgrounds and different languages. To accomplish this, Wagner and Byram (2017) contend that intercultural citizenship is engaging "in actions based on an awareness of other perspectives ... where 'other' refers to different cultural groups, normally with different languages." In addition to developing the skills needed for being an engaged citizen at the societal level, these authors stress that intercultural citizenship requires that individuals work on having the needed competencies and dispositions for *intercultural communication* (Byram & Golubeva, 2020). In highlighting intercultural communication, these authors emphasize the dialogue that takes place when people from different groups interact with each other. Further, Byram and colleagues advocate for individuals to develop competencies to foster meaningful communication, understanding, and collaboration across cultural boundaries, all of which are essential for full participation in the twenty-first century workspace.

In summary, acting interculturally involves fostering curiosity and openness while deeply thinking about assumptions about one's own and others' cultural practices. Whether you work in allied health services, education, finance, construction, technology, media, law, or entertainment, it is very likely that you will find yourself in situations that will require you to actively learn and adapt to new cultural practices during interactions with children, youth, families, colleagues, and the public at large.

Intercultural Communication

Imagine a bilingual social worker who immigrated to the US from Guatemala, having learned Spanish at home and English at school. She is working in a public community agency supporting a Latino community that is rapidly becoming more diverse. Her supervisor just added a family to her caseload who recently immigrated from China. Only the mother in the family speaks English, while the rest of her family, including her spouse and two young children, are fluent in Mandarin and in Min, a Chinese dialect spoken mainly in the Fujian province. The social worker and the mother can communicate with one another using English, but there may be some constraints as they are both using their second language or L2. They each have distinct L2 skills emerging from their past experiences and upbringing.

Now imagine another context in which an English-speaking male patient of European descent received health care through a telehealth appointment from a female nurse of Jamaican descent. Both the nurse and the patient were born in the US and speak English as their first language (L1), but the nurse grew up exposed to Jamaican Patois, a creole language used by many Jamaican families. While they are interacting in English, they both have different cultural backgrounds and different expectations for this interaction. The nurse is known for her friendly and informal tone shaped by her Jamaican background, while the patient expects a more formal and straight-forward healthcare interaction.

Finally, readers can envision a third scenario: an English-speaking monolingual occupational therapist meets an older client who has lived in the US for many years but immigrated from Poland as an adult and has very limited English proficiency. The client is struggling to explain the reason for her visit and the source of her pain and discomfort. The therapist is not understanding what the problem is and there are no language assistance services available in the office (e.g., access to a language line to access an interpreter). They end up calling the client's adult daughter to serve as an informal interpreter and help mediate the conversation between them.

Each example shows people from different linguistic and cultural backgrounds, with varying language skills and unique ways of seeing the world, interacting with one another. Though we cited cases from the allied health field, the same holds true for any other profession where successful communication is key, whether in public safety, engineering, entertainment, manufacturing, or administrative support. In every field, professionals have been socialized through different linguistic and cultural practices, with unique identities and worldviews. It is clear why we and the field call these *intercultural communications* (recall how at the beginning of this chapter we identified the parts of the word intercultural as *inter* meaning "between" and *culture* signifying certain differences). Two out of the three previous scenarios involved face-to-face interactions, with one happening in a virtual environment to represent how more and more intercultural interactions use online technology and social media (e.g., Facebook, Instagram, WhatsApp, WeChat, Zoom, and others). And, while not explicitly reflected in the examples, intercultural communication also involves written texts, like emails, letters, or official government notices.

Before we go any further, readers may be asking: What is intercultural communication and why is it relevant? Following Jackson (2024), we understand *"intercultural communication* as the negotiated interpersonal interactions between individuals (or groups) with different identities (e.g., cultural, ethnic, social, linguistic, regional) and varying degrees of power or status who have been socialized in different cultural and/or linguistic environments" (p. 2, emphasis original). We further add to this explanation that, in intercultural communication, we pay special attention when differences impact the nature of the communication in some way (Baldwin et al., 2023). We have already established that, across professional settings, differences in language and culture are the norm. So, as you consider the context where you will be working to serve children, youth, families, and clients, it is highly likely that you will be participating in intercultural communication in your day-to-day work. This is the lens through which we will discuss the construct of intercultural communication in the workplace.

What are the key aspects of intercultural communication? Jackson's (2024) definition provides some insight into this question. First, it explicitly calls for a more complex understanding of the intersection of culture and language in shaping communication. By acknowledging that participants bring their multiple identities (i.e., their sense of who they are in terms of their languages, ethnicity, racial identification, gender orientation, etc.) to any communication encounter, Jackson calls attention to how, through language, cultural identities are activated and negotiated in intercultural contexts. Additionally, these communicative interactions are rooted in sociocultural and socio-political contexts, which may reflect power imbalances (Byram, 2021; Jackson, 2024). We have discussed this earlier in the book (Cummins, 2021), and exemplified it through research with Mexican indigenous students in US schools (Ruiz & Barajas, 2012). Here readers may see a connection with Nieto's (2009) definition of culture previously discussed, which calls for understanding culture as influenced by social, economic, and political factors causing differential access to power, all having a major impact on language status. As a result, Nieto writes that,

> ... the tastes, values, languages, and dialects that have the greatest status are associated with the dominant social class *not because these tastes, values, languages, or dialects are inherently better but because they have higher social prestige as determined by the group with the greatest power.*
>
> (2009, p. 141, original emphasis)

In a nutshell, socio-political contexts and power dynamics can influence who controls the conversation, whose language is used, and whose cultural norms are privileged in any given conversation. All of these aspects of intercultural communication—our languages, our identities, our place in our surrounding society—are at play when we are communicating with others, including and perhaps especially, in professional contexts.

Two Perspectives on a Single Intercultural Communicative Interaction

In a review of intercultural communication in the workplace, Warren and Lee (2020) argue that contemporary views of intercultural communication precisely emphasize a more prominent role for language and a more nuanced understanding of culture as we have described above. This contrasts with historical approaches to intercultural communication (e.g., Hall, 1976 or Hofstede, 1991, cited in Warren & Lee, 2020), which, critics argue, are rooted in very rigid understandings of culture and have failed to value the importance of language. By promoting overly simplistic and fixed ideas about culture, there is the risk that historical approaches can perpetuate cultural stereotypes, and further, reduce possibilities of the successful communication required in all work settings.

Before continuing our discussion of intercultural communication, we think it is helpful to explicitly describe what can happen when we approach intergroup communication with a fixed notion of a culture's style of communication, versus a more dynamic view of how members of different cultural groups can be successful in their communication. We will look at a single scenario of intercultural communication, and interpret it from two different perspectives.

The first perspective comes from anthropologist Edward Hall (1976). Hall proposed a model of understanding different cultures' communication styles along a single dimension and categorized their communication styles as either high-context, or low-context. According to this model, in high-context cultures like those in Japan or China, communication is often subtle and indirect. Meaning is derived from shared experiences, nonverbal cues, and implied messages rather than explicit words. In contrast, Hall contends that there are low-context cultures, like the US, the UK, and Germany, where communication is direct and linguistically explicit. The message in low-context cultures is primarily conveyed through words, with less reliance on nonverbal cues and implicit understanding. We invite readers to pause and consider, what are some of the potential issues that may come up due to this categorization? Then, proceed to read the following scenario.

The scene is a US pre-med class, where a Japanese international student is taking classes with a professor who has only taught university in the US. According to Hall's model, the US professor, coming from a low-context culture, expects students to ask questions explicitly if they need help, as this direct communication approach aligns with typical US classroom norms. The Japanese student, however, comes from a high-context culture and assumes the professor will understand her nonverbal cues (such as attending a study group without asking direct questions), which reflect her need for support without explicitly stating it. The professor may interpret the student's silence as disinterest, while the student may perceive the professor's minimal feedback as unhelpful, leading to communication challenges.

In contrast to the perspective of the High-Context Low-Context Model, Byram's (2021) approach does not assume a fixed, set way of communication by cultural group members. Instead of relying on a pre-established list of cultural characteristics, the focus is on what happens *during* communication. Here, the professor, aware of possible cultural differences in communication, would interpret the student's attendance at study groups as a signal of her need for support, regardless of whether she asks questions or not. Similarly, the student might attempt to clarify her needs by directly observing and recognizing how other US students interact during the study group, and the professor's preference for explicit questions before offering support. In this way, both the student and the professor are dynamically co-constructing understanding through the communication process. And skills like critical cultural awareness, empathy, and adaptability during these intercultural encounters become critical.

What are the key takeaways for readers from the two perspectives regarding this scenario? In summary, using Hall's model alone can lead to misunderstandings if cultural expectations about high–low-context communication styles are rigidly applied. Individuals could then have fixed beliefs that others should conform to *their* cultural communication "type," rather than all participants adapting to each unique interaction. Furthermore, this essentialist view of cultures—"X culture has this list of X characteristics that defines it"—does not take into account that any one member of a cultural group may or may not ascribe to all of the culture's attributes in all contexts. While some general knowledge of cultural patterns can be useful in preparing for intercultural interactions, we should only consider that information as a general outline of possibilities, and be ready to adapt and adjust when we are interacting with an individual.

Interestingly, though we have pointed out some weaknesses in Hall's High-Context Low-Context Model, we can still find evidence of the model's inclusion in current training models, e.g., on the website of a US graduate school of planning and design in relation to the charrette process in architecture (a distinct method of planning in the field). So, readers should not assume that cultural models such as these no longer appear in formal professional development practices. At a minimum, when they do appear, they need to be critically assessed for relevance and utility in the workplace.

Overall, Byram's perspective provides a more dynamic and interactive approach to intercultural communication in contrast to a fixed and overgeneralized notion of cultural styles of communication. In the second characterization of the scenario, both the professor and student could, in the moment of interaction, actively adjust their expectations and communicative approaches, if they are curious and open to understanding each other's perspectives. This flexible, adaptive approach allows individuals to bridge communication gaps, recognizing that each person may communicate differently in various settings. The focus then shifts from "classifying" a culture or person as having a set communication style, to cultivating the ability to dynamically respond to each person's communication needs in the process of interacting with each other. The attitudes, knowledge, and skills we have referred to in this section form part of what we need to develop *intercultural communicative competence*.

Intercultural Communicative Competence

Think about the following scenario as we continue sharpening our focus on understanding intercultural communicative competencies in the workplace. Envision that you're at work, and someone approaches you, and says,

> *Buongiorno, può dirmi da che parte devo andare per raggiungere l'ufficio principale? Credo di essere nell'edificio giusto, ma non riesco a trovare l'ufficio. Grazie.*[1]

If you can understand the speaker, congratulations! You will be able to use your multilingual skills to interact with them. If you do not speak this language, what would be your immediate reaction? Note that your first response in this intercultural encounter will shape your interaction with the speaker. Let's consider your choices. You could make an effort to understand the speaker by asking them to rephrase, or to use nonverbal communication, or even look for a colleague who could help you. Or, you could respond by saying you don't speak the language and cannot understand them. Fantini (2020) asked a similar question to his readers and explained the following. If you choose the first option, he considers that to be the first step toward developing bilingual or multilingual competencies: making an attempt to connect with someone who speaks a different language and may come from a different culture. In this view, Fantini writes, "bilingualism begins with attitude, with a willingness to engage, even when no skill exists. Such a disposition begins the process and allows one to move forward toward gradually developing the needed skills" (2020, p. 273). Essentially, having the *disposition* and willingness to interact with someone who speaks another language, even when you do not speak that language, could be the first step in your journey into bilingualism and successful intercultural communication.

Readers may have already realized that today, with smartphones and internet access, you have additional tools at hand to, as Fantini suggests, begin developing your bilingual competencies. Translation features on search engines (e.g., Google Translate) or dedicated translation apps, could help you engage more meaningfully with others who speak different languages even if you are not (yet) bilingual. There is a lot yet to learn about the benefits and risks of accessing these technological tools in the workplace, particularly in healthcare. But there is some evidence that the use of translation apps could help improve communication between healthcare staff and patients with limited English proficiency (Hwang et al., 2022).

Fantini (2020) also reminds us that when thinking of bilingualism, and for that matter, multilingualism, the goal is to think in terms of "degrees of proficiency along a continuum, not absolutes" (2020, p. 272). But how do you develop the disposition to engage with others from an intercultural communicative stance? We offer readers a framework for understanding the intercultural and communicative competencies needed to participate in the workplace (and beyond) as an intercultural citizen. This work is rooted in the work of Hymes (1972), and his use of the term *communicative competence*. You may recall our introduction of this term in Chapter 3, as the set of skills and strategies speakers use to understand and be understood in the real world.

We begin with Fantini's definition that intercultural communicative competence is a "complex of abilities (including host language proficiency) that are needed to perform effectively and appropriately when interacting with others who are linguistically and culturally different from oneself" (2021, p. 5). As we will describe below, this intentional focus on language helps distinguish intercultural *communicative* competence from other terms commonly used to describe interactions between individuals and cultures. For example, you may have heard of the terms "cultural competence," "cross-cultural competence," or "multicultural competence." Researchers and scholars in various fields, (e.g., education, healthcare, business, counseling), have used these terms for several decades, to explain the ability of individuals or organizations to effectively and respectfully interact with people from diverse cultural backgrounds. Often the focus is on understanding a discrete list of behaviors or cultural characteristics that distinguish each cultural group. But in our previous scenario of the Japanese pre-med student and the US professor, we saw that potential stereotypes can actually impede successful intercultural communication and interaction. Instead, the question becomes, how do we foster mutual understanding through meaningful communication mediated by language(s)?

Intercultural communicative competence recognizes that language skills, the focus of our first three chapters, are integral to effective, respectful communication in intercultural interactions in the workplace and beyond. Drawing from research on intercultural courses in higher education and an analysis of students' experiences in international study programs, Fantini (2020) outlines the following defining characteristics of intercultural communicative competence, summarized in Figure 4.1. Note that "Target Language Proficiency" is one of the five main nodes in the diagram.

Fantini's (2020) model outlines a set of abilities, characteristics, and dispositions (attitudes) that have broad application in communities and professions. The model is also widely applied in international education and professional training to foster greater cultural understanding and effective communication in global contexts (Fantini, 2020). As we preview his framework, we ask that you consider how these components of intercultural communication apply to you and your own linguistic knowledge and experiences. As part of this model, Fantini highlights personal characteristics that can help individuals navigate cultural and linguistic differences, such as openness, curiosity, empathy, and patience. The model also identifies three key skill areas: the ability to build relationships, communicate clearly, and collaborate toward mutual goals. As noted previously, Fantini stresses the importance of target language proficiencies, which he points out enhance understanding and cultural integration. Additionally, the lower part of the model acknowledges that intercultural communicative competence is a dynamic process that develops over time.

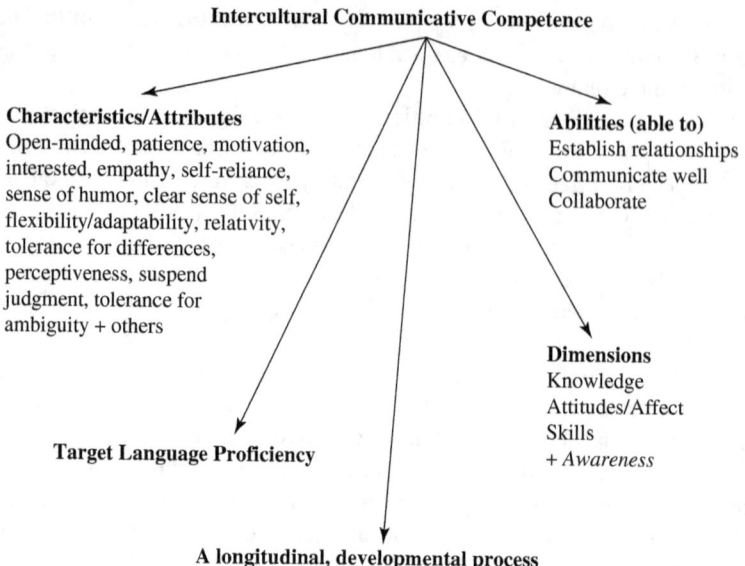

Figure 4.1 Components and aspects of intercultural communicative competence (Fantini, 2020, p. 55).

We want readers to know that it is critical to understand intercultural communicative competence as a developmental process. This is because individuals may begin with very few skills in this area, but can, overtime, develop deeper and more nuanced understandings of diverse cultures, languages, histories, and contexts. Both personal experience and explicit training can foster that development, as we will see in the following section.

Approaches to Promoting Intercultural Communication Across the Professions

Fantini's model of intercultural competence, and other scholarly work reviewed here, has helped us identify and define the necessary knowledge, skills, and dispositions that professionals need to participate in intercultural communications in today's globalized world. Keeping foremost in mind the developmental process in these intercultural competencies, we will describe promising practices to promote further learning and skill acquisition. Given the interconnectedness of language and culture, all the approaches integrate both dimensions, though some focus more on cultural dynamics, while others highlight linguistic aspects.

You may recall in Chapter 3 that we discussed two highly effective paths for achieving bilingualism: family bilingualism and bilingual education. In this section, we follow a parallel structure and present two highly effective approaches to develop intercultural competencies and promote intercultural communication. The first approach involves participating in informal experiences throughout your daily life, where you are exposed to individuals who are different from you in terms of ethnicity, language, and cultural background. The second one is more structured and involves engagement in sustained formal experiences that can take place at any point during your education, or as part of training or professional development once you join the workforce. Both paths intersect and complement one another; both center experiences which require professionals to develop self-awareness, respect for cultural diversity, and the skills to communicate across cultures effectively, adding on to developing multilingual proficiency, our focus in the preceding three chapters.

Informal Intercultural Communication Learning Experiences

Depending on the neighborhood where you grew up, the schools you have attended throughout your schooling, and the places where you have worked before and during your college years, just to name a few, you may have already had substantial exposure to informal intercultural communication experiences. Even if you grew up in a mostly culturally and linguistically homogeneous community, it is more than likely that you have interacted with individuals with different backgrounds from your own in a different informal setting. We are casting a wide net to define informal intercultural experiences to include friendships, relationships with co-workers, sports, and hobbies, as well as other interests, like art or literature. Informal encounters help inform your perceptions of others in both positive and negative ways.

For purposes of this discussion, we will organize informal experiences in two subgroups. One focuses on experiences with people, and the second one focuses on experiences with cultural artifacts and visual texts, like art and literature. Of course, just interacting with others who are different, or being exposed to art and literature is not enough to develop the intercultural attitudes, skills, and attributes identified by Fantini (2020) and by Byram (2021). Such incidental interactions do not necessarily end productively or successfully. The professional development activities we highlight here purposely aim to increase self-reflection, knowledge, and action in promoting positive intercultural interactions.

Experiences in Intergroup Contact

One particularly relevant body of research to explain how intercultural relationships can promote intercultural understandings comes from what is known as the *contact hypothesis*. The contact hypothesis, as outlined by Pettigrew and Tropp (2006), proposes that meaningful interaction between members of different groups can reduce prejudice and foster positive intergroup relations. Originally proposed by Gordon Allport (1954, cited in Pettigrew & Tropp, 2006), the hypothesis suggests that under certain conditions, such as equal status, common goals, intergroup cooperation, and support from those in roles of authority, intergroup contact can help individuals overcome stereotypes, build empathy, and develop more favorable attitudes toward other groups. Results from the authors' meta-analysis of more than 500 studies (yes ... 500!) confirmed that indeed this is the case.

What did the findings of this this large review a research reveal? Pettigrew and Tropp write, "results clearly indicate that intergroup contact typically reduces intergroup prejudice" (2006, p. 766). They further found that Allport's conditions—equal status, common goals, intergroup cooperation, and a supportive context—generally enhanced the positive effects of intergroup contact to reduce prejudice. However, not all conditions were strictly necessary in the same degree for positive outcomes. In other words, while interactions designed around a higher implementation of these conditions yielded stronger effects, meaning they were strong predictors for a reduction of prejudice, studies where interactions had less explicit connection to the conditions still showed reduced prejudice. The authors explain that the "conditions for contact are best conceptualized as functioning together to facilitate positive intergroup outcomes rather than as entirely separate factors" (2006, p. 766).

We were glad to read the results that not all conditions needed to be present in equal degrees, including equal status. As we have cited several times through this book, equal status among different cultural groups is not always initially present due to myriad factors. One body of work, however, within the cooperative learning field has focused on practical ways of equalizing status within a diverse group. Relying mostly on research in educational settings, Elizabeth Cohen and Rachel Lotan (2025) have identified evidence-based and practical ways of raising the status of members of a heterogeneous (mixed) group. Their method of organizing groupwork meets three of the four conditions to reduce prejudice: there is a common goal, a sense of cooperation, and support from the instructor or leaders for the activities. But these scholars also describe concrete steps to create the more difficult condition of equalizing status. Specifically, they include a focus on raising the position of individuals who have lower status. As a brief example, one way Cohen and Lotan recommend to equalize status among a mixed group is for the teacher or leader to look for contributions of the lower status participant and highlight those actions to the larger group. These methods are described in chapters with titles such as "From Lower Status to Intellectual Resource," and "Assigning Competence to Low Status Students." We highly recommend that you read and apply the work of Cohen and Lotan (2025) to your setting. It is applied research that is very relevant to our topic intercultural communication, especially in terms of the contact hypothesis and the more elusive condition of equal status.

Overall, results from the research on the contact hypothesis have direct implications to how we foster relationships with others inside and outside of work. Looking specifically at the workplace, organizations can encourage informal intercultural experiences by ensuring that their staff is comprised of people who bring a range of linguistic and cultural backgrounds. Additionally, hospitals, schools, clinics, and other organizations, should foster opportunities for intercultural collaborative work to achieve a common objective. This can include collaborating on planning presentations, reviewing case notes, or generally problem-solving tasks with others.

These activities would help participants develop key intercultural communicative competencies, such as the ability to collaborate, to be open-minded, and engage in active listening.

Experiences through the Arts

In the case of intercultural experiences with art and literature, we want to first acknowledge that engagement with art and literature are part of our shared human experience; they always have the potential to transform perspectives and broaden our understanding of the world. We will focus our discussion on interactions with literature to promote intercultural understandings, such as participating in book clubs or reading groups. However, Deardorff (2020) also includes watching films and going to the theater as other informal ways of developing intercultural competencies. Deadroff describes literature, film, and theater as forms of storytelling. And we agree, as we believe that "Humans are storytelling organisms who, individually and collectively, lead storied lives," as pointed out by Connelly and Clandinin (1990, p. 2). Through these scholars' work, and others in the field of narrative inquiry, we know that stories—ours and those of others different than us—help us make sense of our diverse world.

In recent years, the power of how stories help frame intercultural encounters gained popularity thanks in part to the now viral TED Talk by Chimamanda Ngozi Adichie (2009). Her talk, entitled, *The Danger of a Single Story*, beautifully captures how narratives and stories shape the way we perceive others, and, in turn, how others perceive us. Adichie uses her transnational experiences growing up in Nigeria, and then, as an international student in the US, to narrate how her life was deeply influenced by the stories she encountered around her. These stories were in the form of British literature, and later African literature; they were in news reports and media, as well as in oral stories told by her family and friends. An underlying thread in her story is how she realized that her perspectives and the perspectives of others were often shaped by a *single story*, which is usually incomplete and is influenced by political and power structures of where the stories take place (recall Nieto's comments earlier in this chapter regarding social prestige and power influences on languages). Without giving away the whole of Adichie's talk, because we would like you to watch it after you finish this chapter if you have not yet seen it, we leave you with one quote:

> Stories matter. Many stories matter. Stories have been used to dispossess and to malign, but stories can also be used to empower and to humanize. Stories can break the dignity of a people, but stories can also repair that broken dignity.
> (Adichie, 2009)

The use of literature to promote intercultural competencies has been well documented in educational research, for example, in K-12 educational settings (Short,

Day, & Schroeder, 2016). There is also a growing body of research focusing on the use of literature in higher education contexts as tools for developing intercultural competencies (González Rodríguez, & Borham Puyal, 2012). There are other informal contexts where books and stories can help us develop specific attributes and abilities and skills of intercultural communication.

Public libraries are one such community setting for intercultural communication. Second author Andrea has written about reclaiming libraries and other community sites as spaces to foster intercultural reading conversations (García & Whitmore, 2011). Andrea helped facilitate a bilingual book club in public libraries in New York that brought together intergenerational readers (parents, grandparents, and children). Through the bilingual reading of culturally relevant stories, participants were able to practice reading, listening, and speaking in two languages in a public space with support from their families and, importantly, library personnel and volunteers. In doing so, they strengthened their ability to communicate in two languages with others beyond their immediate families. Additionally, through the conversations around topics raised in the books (such as immigration and discrimination), participants had an opportunity to practice tolerance for differences in experiences and opinion, along with growing empathy and adaptability, all skills that Fantini (2020) and Bryam (2008) identify as components of intercultural communicative competence.

Actively seeking opportunities to participate in group discussions around books, film, theater in community centers, public libraries, or cultural clubs in your university can offer you a supportive context to practice and strengthen your intercultural communication competencies. Reclaiming spaces for reading conversation can also happen at work. Organizations can incentivize staff members to create a book club that meets during lunch time to discuss a previously selected book. Now that you understand how powerful stories can be in building intercultural communication skills, you might even suggest starting a book club in your organization when you begin working. This activity could help people connect, share experiences, dialogue, and better understand each other's cultures in a simple and meaningful way.

This section has focused on increasing contact between different groups as a way to encourage the development of intercultural communication. Author John Baldwin and colleagues highlight the resulting two-way interaction between both personal growth and intercultural citizenship. They write:

> Communication and contact over time can bring us, in both our face-to-face and socially mediated interactions, from a state of ethnocentrism, where we feel that our way is best, to a state where we see the value in the perspective and ways of living of others. The greatest benefit will come from both education and contact, as these can help us appreciate cultural differences within our own nations and across borders ... making us better world citizens
>
> (Baldwin et al., 2023, p. 6)

The authors add:

> We might, over time, become "intercultural persons," able to move freely between cultures, or at least to understand different cultural perspective more easily.
>
> (p. 7)

Structured Professional Development Approaches to Promote Intercultural Communicative Competence

The research reviewed in the previous section established the many benefits of informal intercultural experiences. However, given the importance of positive intercultural interactions in the workplace, we strongly advise that professional groups purposely plan to implement professional development approaches to foster intercultural communicative competence.

Development of Self-Reflection

Byram (2008) provides us with an initial direction for these approaches, self-reflection. He writes, "[b]ecoming an intercultural citizen involves psychological and behavioral change, including change in self-perception and understanding of one's relationships to others in other social groups" (2008, p. 187). The following professional development activities can promote self-reflection and can help colleagues cultivate curiosity and openness toward their own linguistic profile, along with a deep understanding of their cultural affiliations.

Mapping your linguistic profile. Grab a piece of paper and draw a diagram like the one shown in Figure 4.2 to create your linguistic profile. Then, fill out each circle with the appropriate language(s). You should list the language or languages that you speak, that you understand, that you can read, that you can write, and the language or languages that you encounter. Languages that you encounter refer to all the languages that you would come into contact with, whether at work, at the university, at the grocery store, in your community. One important clarification is that you do not need to be fully proficient in order to list the language on your language map.

Why is creating a linguistic profile helpful? As Byram (2008) describes, developing interpersonal competencies takes time, and requires self-reflection. This approach is intended to be used to broaden your understanding about your linguistic competencies and your contact with multiple languages. It invites you to re-consider your proficiency with languages other than English, by helping you to be expansive in your definition of bilingualism or multilingualism to include those languages that you understand, but perhaps are not able to speak. Alternatively, the languages you list could be ones that you speak but are unable to read or write. The activity also asks you to make explicit the linguistic contexts where you live, play, study, and work by considering the languages that you encounter. Finally, by

Linguistic Profile:
Document the languages that you...

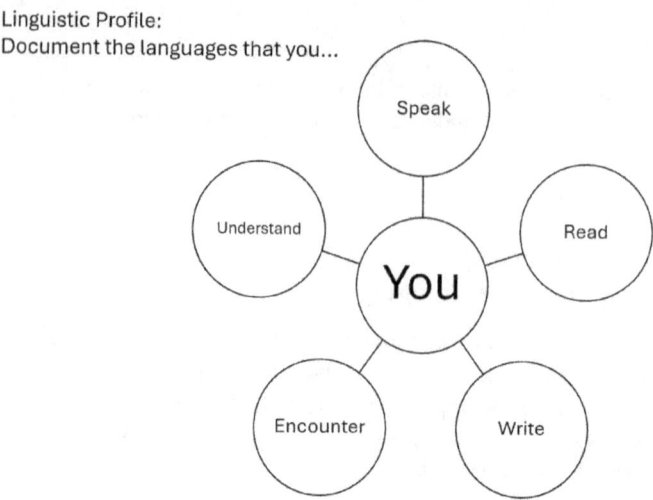

Figure 4.2 Linguistic profile.

documenting the range of languages you come in contact with, you can appreciate first-hand the linguistically diverse world that you live within.

Autobiographies of intercultural encounters. Byram, Barrett, and colleagues (Byram et al., 2009; Barrett et al., 2013) have developed two tools intended to support individuals' critical reflections on their intercultural encounters and on their own cultural identities (Barrett, 2018, p. 99). They are the *Autobiography of Intercultural Encounters (AIE)* and the *Autobiography of Intercultural Encounters through Visual Medial (AIEVM)* (Council of Europe, 2025b). Both tools can be accessed online and are available for use with both adults and children, and in several languages.

The tools are formatted as a structured questionnaire that you can complete independently or in conjunction with colleagues, and are aimed at guiding your analysis of intercultural interactions. The questions encourage reflection and critical examination of your own cultural perspectives. The AIE facilitates critical reflection on direct, face-to-face communication with individuals from different cultural backgrounds. The AIEVM focuses on analyzing and reflecting on your perceptions of others through visual images encountered through television, films, newspapers, and magazines.

To give readers a sense of these tools and their connection to intercultural communicative competence, we describe a few of the questionnaire prompts. For example, respondents are asked to recall an encounter with a person different from themselves, and give it a name that reflects the interaction. In addition to asking about the details of the encoutner (who, what, where), many of the subsequent questions encourage deep self-reflection, like reflecting on their thoughts and feelings to the interaction, and taking on the perspective of the other participants. With regard to intercultural communicative competence, another question asks if they made any changes to how they communicted during the interaction to improve communication.

Why is creating these intercultural biographies helpful? The tools encourage critical reflection starting with your own cultural identities and perception, once again, emphasizing the important and often initial step of self-awareness. But because the activities are designed to be used on numerous occasions over an extended period of time, they are meant to support your continued development of core intercultural communicative attributes and skills. Barrett (2018) indicates that initial studies on the effects of using the AIE and AIEVM with post-secondary students reveal positive effects. Specifically, research has shown that the tools are effectively promoting certain intercultural competencies in participants, such as intercultural awareness, self-awareness, and perspective-taking abilities, and even concrete actions to purposively improve intergroup relationships (Méndez García, 2016). In sum, it is clear that these instruments carefully reflect research on the development of intercultural communicative competence and citizenship. We highly encourage you to explore these tools on your own and to consider their implementation in university and professional development settings.

Formal Intercultural Training Programs

Byram and Wagner (2018) believe that there is a need for formal training programs that focus on developing "interculturally competent service providers" who will be well equipped to respond to diverse needs of clients in a socially responsive way. Formal intercultural communication experiences involve sustained and more structured opportunities to develop the dispositions and skills to act interculturally. It is well-established that learners at a young age can be exposed to engagements and experiences aimed at improving their intercultural competence (Barrett, 2018). But these experiences can continue into your post-secondary studies (Byram et al., 2016), as well as into your professional life once you join the workforce. As we describe them next, please be sure to note any connections you may find between our discussion and your past experiences.

What do these formal experiences look like? Formal intercultural communication experiences have a clear academic outcome and they require sustained engagement. These experiences can also be organized into two groups: the first one includes academic experiences, such as academic courses or webinars for both future and working professionals; and the second encompasses experiential learning opportunities, like study abroad and service-learning projects, or on the job training. We will focus our discussion on the evidence from the literature that supports participation in experiential learning opportunities in this section.

First, however, we pause for a quick look at some of the most common tools used during courses, webinars, virtual seminars, and training that focus on developing intercultural understanding and intercultural communication competencies. Deardorff (2020) conducted a thorough review of these tools and strategies and highlighted the pros and cons of each tool (Table 4.1).

Table 4.1 Pros and cons of intercultural training tools (Deardroff, 2020, p. 8)

Types of Intercultural Training Tools	Pros	Cons
Simulations	Involves experiential learning, allows participants to experience differences and practice intercultural (IC) skills in a safe setting	Usually takes significant time (two to three plus hours); requires extensive debriefing from knowledgeable facilitators; may require particular materials, props, outfits, or space; and may cost money
Role plays	Involves experiential learning, allows participants to practice IC skills in a safe setting, provides a mechanism for generating feedback on communication/behavior	May not be appropriate in some settings, requires participants to "perform" in front of others, requires careful development and selection of scenarios, requires thorough debriefing, requires a trained facilitator
Case studies	Provides concrete examples for discussion, engages participants through exploration of solution(s)	Requires careful development/selection/wording of case studies, focuses primarily on the cognitive level of intercultural competencies (ICC) development
Group activities (games, discussions, structured learning exercises)	Can focus on particular aspects of ICC, engages in face-to-face interaction, allows for guidance and feedback from trained facilitator	Usually found in more formal settings, may require particular materials and space, requires skilled facilitator, needs to match activity with participants' learning styles
Online tools	Does not need to be in a formal learning setting, often utilizes self-directed learning, is available 24/7 with Internet access	There may be limited access to the Internet/computer; some online tools cost money; they have limited face-to-face contact; there is usually no guidance available; they are dependent on individual motivation
Coaching	Allows for tailored feedback on strengths and areas of continued intercultural growth	Requires a trained coach with a strong intercultural background; there are limited availability of such coaches; they often cost money

ICC = intercultural competencies

The training tools include using case studies, role-playing, simulations, and games, all of which can be offered as in-person or online activities. The tools can also be facilitated as individual or group activities. From healthcare and education to business and allied health professions, these tools are essential for engaging learners in developing intercultural competencies. When used effectively, they can significantly impact learner outcomes. And while there is no one tool that can ensure development of intercultural communicative competence, understanding the pros and cons of the different tools available could prepare you to know what to expect when you participate in these types of formal experiences. This knowledge can also come in handy if you ever need to develop similar training programs in the future.

From Deardorff's (2020) analysis of the training tools, we want you to notice two main commonalities among them. Let's start with the pros. All of the tools can provide participants in these trainings with focused, customized scenarios or activities that can enhance learning outcomes. Second, each of the tools requires specialized knowledge not only of the subject matter at hand, but of how to create engaging and meaningful experiences using these tools. Whether facilitated by a trainer or an experienced coach, one thing is clear, incorporating these tools into a formal intercultural experience requires time and careful planning. Otherwise, the potential benefits of these tools may be lost, leaving participants unprepared to effectively apply their learning in real-world intercultural communication interactions.

With the understanding of the available tools used in formal intercultural experiences, we will review two promising approaches for developing the intercultural communication behaviors, skills, and attitudes expected of professionals in your field. These are study abroad programs and service-learning projects.

Study abroad/international education. Perhaps one of the most researched strategies for promoting intercultural communication is having the opportunity to study abroad, also known as participating in an international education program. Through immersion in a host country, students, their parents, and their teachers believe that study abroad is the most effective way to develop an L2 along with intercultural communicative competence. And yes, those beliefs are strongly supported by research. Extensive documentation in this area points to study abroad experiences as positively contributing to increased cultural awareness and sensitivity, improved proficiency in L2, and enhanced adaptability, to name a few outcomes (Fantini, 2020; Jackson, 2020).

Researchers in fields where study abroad opportunities are less common, such as psychology, have been planning and studying such experiences. Findings from these studies align with those in other disciplines, like education, providing similar evidence of the benefits and outcomes associated with study abroad programs. One example of this work comes from Earnest and his colleagues (2016), who designed a short-term study abroad experience for undergraduate students in psychology. The researchers compared student outcomes between two groups enrolled in psychology courses: one group of students participated in a two-week faculty-led study abroad program in Argentina, and the other group took a traditional course in psychology. The goal was to examine the impact of the study abroad experience in the students' ability to understand the perspectives of others who are different from them, which the authors described as the mission of this particular psychology course. Even though the time abroad was short (only two weeks), the authors found that the experiential nature of the international program fostered greater cultural awareness and adaptability among students than participation in a traditional, non-international course.

Recent research on study abroad has provided us with a more nuanced understanding of the circumstances that can support or hinder students pursuing these types of programs. In summarizing the research, Jackson (2020) explains that some of the key factors that can influence the outcome of a study abroad can be categorized into three main groups:

- Features of the program: Including duration of the program, housing arrangements, guided cultural or experiential project work, level of cultural immersion, and the quality and extent of pre-departure orientation, ongoing support, and debriefings.
- Host environment factors: Including host receptivity and the quality and quantity of exposure to the host language and culture.
- Characteristics and choices of the individual participants: Including personality, L2 competence, degree of openness to new experiences, attitudes toward differences, previous intercultural experience, among others.

In the teacher education field, first author Nadeen and colleagues have conducted studies on what they call *Transnational Teacher Education*. Essentially, this kind of teacher education program offers teacher candidates the opportunity to spend extended time, at least six weeks, in an international setting as part of their professional preparation to become a teacher (Ruiz & Baird, 2013; Ruiz, Baird, & Torres, 2016). In Transnational Teacher Education, there is usually a close relationship between the home and host country in terms of immigration's impact on schools, as is the case of the US and Mexico, the primary countries highlighted in these studies. The participants were future bilingual teachers, Spanish-English, studying in either Mexico or Guatemala for part of their teaching credential program. In reviewing the study abroad literature for their research, these authors, too, found evidence that, without careful planning, participants in short-term international programs can actually leave with continuing stereotypical notions about the host country and culture, as illustrated in a study by Talburt (2009), with US undergraduates studying in Spain. With those challenges in mind, Nadeen and colleagues developed an international teacher education program that promoted a sense of interconnectedness between the teacher candidates and people from the host country. One component of the program required participants to teach in host-country schools for a particular period of time, including schools that served Mexican and

Guatemalan indigenous children. (We will more closely examine this type of experience, service learning, in the next section.) The researchers looked for evidence of several components of interconnectedness such as *contact* (instead of social distance); *solidarity* (instead of individualism); *a dynamic view of culture* (instead of an essentialized view); *social action* (instead of observation of others), and *global citizenship* (instead of nation citizen only). Based on data from three cohorts of future bilingual teachers studying in either Mexico or Guatemala, the researchers documented not only increased proficiency in the target language of Spanish, but very importantly, the participants' positive movement toward greater interconnectedness with people and immigrants from the host country. As an example, the four most prevalent themes in participants' outcomes in the Ruiz and Baird (2013) study were:

1. Critical Global Interconnectedness—Recognition of being part of a larger community; emphasis on commonalities despite differences, and connections that transcend nation borders; critical awareness about race, class, gender, politics, and historical relationships between home and target countries.
2. Cultural Proficiency—Acquisition of knowledge about target culture; challenging and dispelling of stereotypes.
3. Bilingual Education and Teaching—The importance of bilingualism, including maintenance of indigenous languages; pride and new understandings about being a bilingual teacher and about bilingual education.
4. Personal Growth—Report of growth in strength, confidence, and self-acceptance.

Clearly, from personal growth to a recognition of becoming a global citizen, well-designed international study and experiential programs, such as the Transnational Teacher Education program in the Ruiz et al. studies, can have a significant positive impact on the attitudes and skills related to intercultural communicative competence. The programs' documented successes certainly warrant a greater expansion within professional settings.

Jackson (2020) and others remain optimistic about the future of study abroad research and the opportunities for students and professionals from various fields to continue participating in these experiential programs. She also points out that the field would benefit from further studies focusing on the students' experiences in other contexts, such as service learning at both the international and local levels. Fortunately for us, that is the next stop in our discussion.

Service-learning projects. We have covered a lot of ground, from exploring how informal intercultural experiences can help reduce prejudice, to discussing factors that make the international education experience a success. And we have seen evidence from research that participating in these experiences has a positive impact on the development of intercultural citizenship and intercultural communication competencies. The last formal intercultural learning experience that we will discuss is service learning. Byram and Golubeva (2020) point out that researchers have long identified structured opportunities to engage in service-learning projects as supporting community involvement, which is one of the key components of intercultural citizenship. Similarly, Fantini (2021) elaborates by stating that civic service programs, like the US Peace Corps, grants participants a "powerful intercultural experience." Contrary to many study abroad programs, the Peace Corps volunteer experience offers sustained long-term commitment grounded in civic service. If you know a former Peace Corps volunteer, you have likely heard stories about their time abroad and been impressed by their intercultural communication skills.

Service learning is an approach that brings together community service with academic learning. It involves using previous academic knowledge to solve problems in the real world. There are many key components, like collaboration with the community as partners, as well as structured time for reflection and introspection. And since the work happens in the community, service learning can provide the ideal backdrop to develop intercultural communication competencies, including L2 skills. Of course, students studying to become social workers, nurses, psychologists, teachers, and other professionals involved in providing services to linguistically and culturally diverse families, can benefit from engaging in service learning, and researchers across these disciplines have documented some interesting examples.

One of these examples comes from the work of Brown (2017), who incorporated a service-learning project into a public health nursing course, as well as international travel. Nursing students from the US participated in a two-week service-learning project within an indigenous community in Belize. They were charged to collaborate with the local communities to identify health-related needs of school age children. The goal of the project was two-fold: first, to address the public health nursing competencies of the nursing students in the course, and second, improve the health and well-being of the local community. The author mapped each of the required nursing competencies to the assignments in the course. Then, he designed the service-learning component to include two key components that we have touched upon throughout the chapter as key aspects of intercultural citizenship: civic engagement and self-reflection. The civic engagement component was directly tied to the nursing students building capacity at the local level for community members to be better equipped to meet their own health needs. The self-reflection component involved open ended questions and group discussions before, during, and after the experience. Through this research, nursing students had the opportunity to practice public health nursing competencies while immersed in a community that was very different than their own. Analyzing the students' self-reflections, the author reports that the students were reflective and revised their initial perceptions of their experiences. For example, the students experienced logistical challenges due to language differences and lack of availability of materials. But findings also revealed that using a service-learning approach allowed the student nurses to work with the community to identify relevant health issues and concrete steps to address them. In addition, the self-reflection component of the work and the immersion in civic engagement demonstrated the potential of service learning to prepare nursing students for intercultural communication contexts in public health practice once back in the US.

Service-learning projects in local communities, without the international experience, can have equally impressive impact on participants' dispositions and skills in intercultural communication. These are approaches that can be implemented by both future and working professionals. For example, in preparation for service learning, it is important for you and your colleagues to explore the linguistic and ethnic composition of the communities you will be serving. Most schools, hospitals, and local clinics track the demographic information of their clients, such as languages spoken, ethnicity, sex, age, economic level, etc. For those professionals in the US, the *American Community Survey* (ACS) comes in very handy to provide you an updated snapshot of the intercultural aspects of the target community.

In this section, we described informal and formal intercultural learning experiences that offer professionals both academic and practical, real-world applications for developing the knowledge, skills, and dispositions of intercultural citizens, including intercultural communication. Both types of experiences approach the development of intercultural competencies not as a once and done experience, but as a life-long process, much like the trajectory of those of us working to add on to our multilingual repertoire. Baldwin and colleagues (2023) remind us of the benefits of engaging in this long-term effort:

> Studying intercultural communication gives us more freedom to make informed choices about how we will or will not follow our culture's expectations, but it also helps us to interact in a more respectful way with the person around the world or the person next door.
>
> (2023, p. 19)

We invite you to consider that perhaps both interactions—with the person around the world and with the person next door—are equally valuable in working toward a broader uptake of intercultural citizenship in the world we live.

Summing Up

We end with a quote from Harold Chorney, a Canadian political scientist, who has often written about economics and multilingualism. Chorney provides a strong rationale for why we should actively cultivate multilingualism, pursue it, and promote it. The quote eloquently captures much of the journey we have made with readers throughout this book, beginning with economic benefits of multilingualism, and ending with ways to work across languages and cultures for the greater good. Chorney writes,

The very act of acquiring knowledge and linguistic competence has a positive disproportional impact on the economic potential of an individual. Furthermore, it contributes to the likelihood that the individual can make a greater contribution to his/her society. Quite literally, their capacity to participate in their society is considerably enhanced. As central Europeans often say, *"the more languages you speak the more times you are a human being."*

(1997, p. 181, emphasis added)

Beyond echoing some of the many benefits of becoming multilingual, which we have covered at length in previous chapters, Chorney connects multilingual competencies with an individual's enhanced ability to engage more fully in society. This connection should resonate with readers from our discussion of intercultural citizenship in this last chapter. Furthermore, Chorney's writing centers multilingualism within our everyday experiences with others to help us reimagine what being human is all about.

Test yourself! What did you learn?: Re-consider each statement from the beginning of the chapter. Use your background knowledge *and* new information gained from reading the chapter to decide whether the statements reflect current research on multilingualism (True), or not (False). Answers are in Appendix A at the back of the book.

True or False	Multilingualism and Intercultural Communication
	1. Despite the growing demand for multilingual skills in today's US workforce, most US workers remain primarily monolingual English speakers.
	2. Language and culture develop separately. You acquire language first and then culture.
	3. Intercultural communication means communication within the same culture.
	4. Self-reflection is an important skill to develop when working with linguistically and culturally diverse families.
	5. Informal interactions with others who are different from you can help reduce prejudice.

Time to Think and Connect

Multilingualism and Intercultural Citizenship

1. Return to Figure 4.1, Fantini's model of Intercultural Communicative Competence (2020). Look closely at the group of Characteristics/Attributes he lists there as effective for carrying out intercultural communication. Which three of those characteristics do you feel best reflect you personally? Is there one characteristic listed there that you would consciously like to work on, in

other words, expand your personal attributes for communicating interculturally? Which one? How do you think you could go about further developing that characteristic?
2. In this chapter, we discuss the term *intercultural communication* to describe interactions between individuals from different cultures. Think of a time when you had to interact with someone who was different from you. What made it easy to communicate with them? What made it difficult? What do you know now that could have made your interaction go smoother? From what you read in this chapter, what do you want to remember for the next time that you need to communicate with someone who may have a different language and culture from yours?
3. Look at the training tools included in Figure 4.3. Have you participated in a class where they have used case studies, simulations, or role-playing? What was the purpose of the lesson? Was there a particular approach that you found most helpful to understand the content? Is there one tool or strategy that you enjoy more?

Note

1 Good morning, can you tell me which way I need to go to get to the main office? I think I'm in the right building, but I can't find the office. Thank you.

Appendix A

True–False Answers to Chapter Anticipation Guides

Chapter 1

True or False	Multilingualism
True	1. Research has documented that bilingual people as a group have higher earning power.
False	2. Employers of professions not requiring a college degree, such as construction, retail, and manufacturing, do not show any notable preference for bilinguals.
True	3. Young bilingual children outperform monolingual children in being able to take another person's perspective that may be different from their own.
False	4. Both monolinguals and bilinguals seem to experience the same level of cognitive decline as they reach advanced age.
False	5. Parents of autistic children should keep to one language only in their homes so as not to further negatively impact their children's language and cognitive development.

Chapter 2

True or False	Development of Multilingualism
T	1. About two-thirds of the world's children are growing up bilingual.
F	2. Only those individuals who have equal knowledge of each language and speak both without an accent should be labeled "bilingual."
F	3. When bilinguals intermix their languages in a single sentence or conversation, it is a sign that they have serious language gaps in one or both of their languages.
T	4. The more proficiency immigrant children have in their home language, including some schooling in that language, the faster and better they will learn the new language in their new country.
T	5. Though in many ways the earlier one learns a second language, the better, adults and older children outperform younger children in certain aspects of language learning.

Appendix

Chapter 3

True or False	Increasing Multilingual Competence
F	1. Research on the effectiveness of bilingual education has only recently begun, and it is too early to determine whether it enhances multilingual development or academic achievement.
T	2. Advance work in building up L2 learners' background knowledge before they begin to listen to or read a text greatly enhances their L2 comprehension.
T	3. Frequent opportunities to interact in pairs and small groups is one of the best ways to improve second language (L2) learning.
F	4. Most L2 learners need a strict focus on language forms through drills and worksheets, rather than practice in communicating real messages.
T	5. Research-based teaching and learning practices can be integrated into the workplace to support colleagues who are L2 learners.

Chapter 4

True or False	Multilingualism and Intercultural Communication
T	1. Despite the growing demand for multilingual skills in today's US workforce, most American workers remain primarily monolingual English speakers.
F	2. Language and culture develop separately. You acquire language first and then culture.
F	3. Intercultural communication means communication within the same culture.
T	4. Self-reflection is an important skill to develop when working with linguistically and culturally diverse families.
T	5. Informal interactions with others who are different from you can help reduce prejudice.

Appendix B

Optimal Instructional and Professional Development Practices to Enhance Multilingual Development

(Instructional practices are listed in alphabetical order)

Appendix B1

Anticipation Guides

Instructions and Example from the US Department of Transportation, National Institute of Highways

(Steps for this approach are located on the U.S. Department of Transportation Website, National Highway Institute, https://www.nhi.fhwa.dot.gov/LearnersFirst/anticipation-guides.htm, and provided below.)

Anticipation guides are an easy way to get participants to think of what they know about a topic and then help them link new information to their prior knowledge. Anticipation guides are a list of statements related to a topic. Participants read the statements and mark whether they agree or disagree. Anticipation guides also help participants set a purpose for learning because they will want to look for information to confirm their initial beliefs or provide reasons to rethink them.

Writing anticipation guide statements takes some thinking. Good anticipation guide statements should:

- Focus on the information you want participants to think about (learning outcomes)
- Be based on information in the course materials that either supports or opposes the statement
- Challenge participants' beliefs
- Be general rather than specific

Instructions

How to use an anticipation guide:

1. Create an anticipation guide using 2–10 statements and provide a way for participants to mark their agreement or disagreement. The statements should relate to the learning outcomes.
2. Ask participants to complete the anticipation guide independently. Then ask participants to discuss their responses with a partner or small group. After the discussion, give participants the opportunity to change their response if they want.
3. Participants read and/or listen and engage with your interactive lecture with the purpose of finding information about the statements. They take notes as to where they found their supporting or disproving information and should be allowed to change their response if they want.
4. At the end of the lesson or unit, conduct a brief class discussion and ask participants if they changed their position about any of the statements. Ask participants to supply specific examples from the course materials.

Example

An example of one statement in an anticipation guide that Abdalla Abdelmoez could have used in his NHI "Instructor Development Course" training presentation, "Impacts under the National Environmental Policy Act (NEPA)", is shown in figure 18.

Statement	Before	Notes	After
National Environmental Policy Act (NEPA) mandates are unreasonable.	T/F		T/F
	T/F		T/F

Connections to L2 learners: Anticipation Guides ask participants to tap into their existing background knowledge on the topic. Research on best instructed second language acquisition has documented for decades that L2 learners' comprehension is significantly enhanced when they participate in activities that activate their existing knowledge before the listening or reading task. Further, tapping into and increasing background knowledge before the task results in those learners with less L2 proficiency performing as well as more fluent L2 speakers.

Appendix B2

Cloze Passages: Focus on Language Forms

(*after* Focus on Comprehension)

General Description

Instructors select texts of interest or importance to the students, such as poems, informational texts, story excerpts, and so on. Once instruction has first focused on comprehension of the text, the instructor then deletes several words from the passage, and engages the students in filling in those blanks with words that retain the meaning, grammar, and spelling of the original text.

Purpose

The purpose is direct students' attention to correct usage of language forms in the new language such as vocabulary, grammar, spelling, and punctuation.

Preparation

Instructor selects a text to read and discuss with the students. The instructor has two options for deleting words from the text to form the cloze passage. The first option is to delete words with a specific function, depending on the students' current instructional needs, such as verbs, adjectives, high frequency words, spelling difficulties, and so on. A second option is to simply delete every seventh word, resulting in a broad look at correct forms and usage of the new language. The passage below is an example of the latter.

Dream Variations

By Langston Hughes (1926)
From the collection, *The Weary Blues* (Public Domain)

Original Poem	Cloze Passage (7th word omitted)
To fling my arms wide	To fling my arms wide
In some place of the sun,	In _____ place of the sun,
To whirl and to dance	To whirl _____ to dance
Till the white day is done.	Till the white day _____ done.
Then rest at cool evening	Then rest at cool evening
Beneath a tall tree	_____ a tall tree

Dream Variations

While night comes on gently,	While night comes ___ gently,
Dark like me—	Dark like me—
That is my dream!	That is ___ dream!
To fling my arms wide	To fling my arms wide
In the face of the sun,	___ the face of the sun,
Dance! Whirl! Whirl!	Dance! ___ ! Whirl!
Till the quick day is done.	Till the quick day is ___.
Rest at pale evening...	Rest at pale evening...
A tall, slim tree...	A tall, ___ tree...
Night coming tenderly	Night coming tenderly
Black like me.	Black like ___.

Steps

1. **Introduce the poem or text excerpt.**

As an example related to this poem, the instructor can begin by asking students a question related to the content such as, "After a long, busy day, what helps you relax or get ready to sleep?" The instructor would also present biographical information on the poet, here, the well-known U.S. poet from the 20th century, Langston Hughes.

2. **Read the poem or text several times.**

The instructor and students read the poem several times, perhaps in different formats such as reading aloud while alternating lines as a class, or in pairs.

3. **Provide opportunities for students to personally react or respond to the meaning of the poem or text content.**

In the case of this poem, examples of students responding to the poem could be selecting their favorite line and explaining why; producing a Quick Write that they share in partners or with the whole group (instructions for a Quick Write are here in Appendix B); or, writing in their poetry/literature journal. For informational text, a Quick Write would also be appropriate.

4. **Collaboratively read and select appropriate words to fill in the cloze passage.**

While facilitating the filling in of the cloze spaces/blanks, engage students in discussion of the language forms, their functions, and correct usage.

> *Connections to L2 learners: Cloze Passages help instructors create the optimal condition for L2 learning of using authentic texts, or their excerpts, for*

maximum comprehension in the new language. Critical to this approach in the next step: a focus on correct L2 usage. As such, this approach puts into place an important component of effective Instructed SLA, Form-Focused Instruction. But rather that focusing on language forms in a decontextualized manner, the explicit instruction on grammar, vocabulary, etc. begins with comprehension of meaningful texts.

Appendix B3

Daily News (Primary Level)
(adapted from Ruiz & Sánchez-Boyce, 2022)

Overview

The teacher and children work together to compose messages that are connected to their lives. The children's news is eventually bound together in a series of monthly books for the classroom library.

Purpose

To explicitly model oral and written languages; to increase the quantity and quality of functional and authentic literacy in the classroom.

Preparation

Gather high-quality paper (white construction paper works well) and draw several horizontal lines in the bottom third or half for the child's news. Leave the top part of the paper without lines so that the child can later accompany the message with a drawing.

Steps

1. Introduction
    a. Ask children to think about something that is happening in their lives.
    b. Children then *Think–Pair–Share* their "news" with a peer. (Instructions for *Think–Pair–Share* are listed in Appendix B.) If children are emergent bilinguals at this point, it is appropriate for this conversation to take place in any language.
    c. Select the child who will share their news for that day's Daily News. (In a classroom, the teacher often selects one child's "name" or "talking" stick from among the others belonging to the whole class.)
2. Modeled Writing
    a. Place on the board or easel a large sheet of paper divided horizontally into two sections, the top part open and the bottom part with several lines for writing the child's news.

b. As the child dictates to you, model how the topic can be taken from an idea to a written representation, scribing the child's message on the bottom lines. Later, the focal child will illustrate his or her message on the top part.
  c. Strive to make this component interactive, engaging the children when possible to assist in writing the text, e.g., "Juan has said that he went to the zoo *el domingo*. Juan knows the days of the week in Spanish! We have learned the days of the week in English. How do we say *domingo* in English?" After the students respond, you can finish the message: Juan went to the zoo on Sunday. Alternatively, you can write the message in both languages, emphasizing the children's expanding multilingual repertoire.
  d. Think aloud the writing process as you write, e.g., "In English, the days of the week begin with an uppercase letter. That's different than in Spanish. Days of the week begin with a lowercase letter."
  e. Depending on the children's level of literacy, you can draw their attention to concepts about print, vocabulary, cross-linguistic transfer, grammar, pronunciation, etc.
  f. When you finish writing the message, you and the students chorally read the daily entry.
3. Illustration
  a. The child who shared the news illustrates the entry on the top half of the large paper. This illustration usually happens after the Daily News time, e.g., during recess or when the child has free time.
  b. Authentic texts for English reading: The "Daily News" charts are stapled together, usually by month. These large, bound books are kept in the classroom as a resource for student reading and conversation. In the OLE Project, we have found that this meaningful and personalized written language resource for the classroom is a favorite reading choice for children.

Connections to L2 learners: In Daily News, the child shares information of her choice. When L2 learners communicate a message that has new or unknown information to others, they are pressed to use language that is as explicit and as effective as they can make it in order to convey that message. In the Instructed Second Language Acquisition (SLA) field, that press on children's productive language is called comprehensible output (Gibbons, 2015). In this instructional practice, there is also an initial focus on meaning, that is, the child effectively communicating, with support from the teacher, the message that she wants to convey to her peers. However, there is also a focus on language forms as the teacher models correct written usage of the message.

Appendix B4

Graphic Organizer Example: Literary Analysis of Theme

(Planning for a Paragraph or Essay)

Name:_____ Date:_____
Title:_____ Author:_____

Theme
(Write here what you believe to be one of the author's messages in the literary piece about how to live our lives.)

Direct quote from the text	➡	How does this quote support the theme you have identified?
Direct quote from the text	➡	How does this quote support the theme you have identified?
Direct quote from the text	➡	How does this quote support the theme you have identified?

*Connection to L2 learners: Graphic organizers support L2 learners by helping them first focus on the quality of their written piece before a concern with language forms (Meaning-Focused Instruction). Graphic organizers also allow for **Optimal Condition #2: L2 Learners exercise choice…** by honoring the good ideas that L2 Learners bring to the instructional or professional setting while they are in the process of further developing their multilingualism. Graphic organizers can support a wide ranges of writing genres such as informative pieces, reports, personal narratives, etc.*

Appendix B5

Home–Expert Groups ("Jigsaw")

General Description

Home–Expert Groups is a cooperative learning strategy that enables each student of a "home" group to specialize in one aspect or component of a learning unit. Students meet with members from other groups who are assigned the same component, usually a written text or a research topic. After mastering the material in the "expert" groups, the students return to the "home" group and teach the material to their group members. Just as in a jigsaw puzzle, every piece—each student's part—is essential for the completion and full understanding of the final learning unit.

Purposes

(a) Learn new material through cooperative learning skills and individual accountability; (b) Develop a depth of knowledge not possible if the students were to try and learn all of the material on their own; (c) Use oral and written language skills to communicate clearly and effectively, given that students are required to present their findings to the "home" group, findings with which they are the "experts" and the other members are not.

Preparation

Divide the text to be read into segments, roughly the number of students who are in the home groups. For example, if there are five students in each home group (five is about the maximum number), divide the text into five parts, and number each segment one through five.

Steps

1. Assign students to "home" teams of four or five students (generally their regular cooperative learning teams). Have students number off within their teams.
2. Assign the text segments to "home" team members, each one with a different segment.

3. Have students move to "expert" groups where everyone in the group has the same segment or topic as themselves.
4. Students work with members of their "expert" group to read about and/or research their topic. They prepare a short presentation and decide how they will teach their topic to their "home" team.

    You may want students to prepare mini-posters while in their "expert" groups. These posters can contain important facts, information, and diagrams related to the study topic.
5. Students return to their "home" teams and take turns teaching their team members the material.

It is helpful to provide or ask the students to create a graphic organizer or chart with the new information.

> *Connection to L2 learners: This instructional approach enacts a fundamental characteristic of Task-Based Teaching: successful completion of the activity depends on successful use of language. In Home–Expert Groups, there is a natural "information gap" in that each member of the group must present their learning to others who do not have that information. As such, the language demands are high and push L2 development. However, the approach integrates these high language demands with group support and many opportunities for language rehearsal among the "experts" before they return to their home groups.*

Appendix B6

Interactive (Dialogue) Journals

General Description

L2 learners engage in a written conversation with others. Children as young as 4 years old hold their own pen and draw and write in their own bound journal. When used with adults, Interactive Journals offer them an opportunity to express sophisticated ideas and convey personal stories, knowing that they will receive an individualized response from an instructor or colleague. This instructional approach honors L2 learners as writers, readers, speakers, listeners, and thinkers, even at the beginning of their L2 development.

There are three general parts in this instructional approach. The table below describes those parts according to the age of the L2 learners: young children, or adolescents and adults (teachers or caregivers wanting additional details on the implementation of this approach for primary age children should refer to Ruiz & Sánchez-Boyce, 2023).

Age Level	Part 1	Part 2	Part 3
Young children	Young children draw and write their journal entry.	Almost immediately after the child finishes drawing and composing, the adult talks with the child about their drawing and writing. The adult generates a question based on their conversation and writes it in the child's journal.	The child responds to the adult's question, either orally or in written form.
Adolescents and adults	Older L2 learners usually opt to write their journal entry.	The instructor responds to the L2 learner's journal at a later time, given that older participants will likely write intelligible messages that can be read and responded to outside of the immediate context.	In the next class session, the participant can respond to the instructor's comment, proceed with a new journal entry, or both.

Purpose

To create an opportunity for L2 instruction to center on the learner; to structure a low-stress interchange of ideas among L2 learners through oral and written expression; to create an authentic reason for communicating information held by one person to another person; to introduce L2 print and writing even at the earliest stages of learning; to create a record of the participants' level of development in writing the L2.

Preparation

Gather paper to make bound journals, as simple as assembling paper stapled together with a construction paper cover, or distribute academic or commercially sold journals.

Steps

1. Before participants write, conduct an oral conversation among the group on what you all think your topic will be for that day's writing.

    We always keep in mind the quote by British literacy scholar James Britton: "Writing floats on a sea of talk." Even children who began the Interactive Journal session not knowing what they were going to draw and write, will gather an idea from their peers, just as adult writers get ideas from other writers. Remember: *NEVER assign topics.* Know that even very young children have rich lived experiences to tell us. Participants always choose what they want to draw and write about.
2. Participants draw and/or write in their bound journal **(e.g., not** simply loose sheets of paper).
3. Instructor responds to the L2 learner.

    For the young child, the teacher composes an oral question and writes it in the immediate context. For older children and adults, the instructor writes a response at a later time.
4. The L2 learner responds to the question posed by the instructor.

    Children may choose to orally respond to the question immediately after the adult has written and vocalized it to them, or they may try to write something back. Older children and adults will continue the written conversation with the instructor.

Connections to L2 learners: When L2 learners communicate a message that has new or unknown information to others, they are pressed to use language that is as explicit and as effective as they can make it in order to convey that message. In the Second Language Acquisition (SLA) field, that press on children's productive language is called comprehensible output (Gibbons, 2015, p. 25).

A critical point to emphasize is that the only type of journal that is associated with accelerated L2 language and literacy is an <u>Interactive</u> Journal, one with an instructor or peer response.

Appendix B7

K-W-L Charts

(Steps for this approach are located on the U.S. Department of Transportation Website, National Highway Institute, https://www.nhi.fhwa.dot.gov/LearnersFirst/k-w-l-charts.htm, and provided below.)

K-W-L chart is a three-column graphic organizer that provides space for participants to record what they **K**now, what they **W**ant to know, and what they have **L**earned. K-W-L charts are an easy way to activate participants' prior knowledge and get them to set an intention for their learning. You can start the activity as a brainstorming session and use the chart to record information gathered or ask participants to fill them out individually. At the end of a lesson or module, participants can reflect and record their new, expanded knowledge in their own words.

One drawback to a K-W-L chart is that participants sometimes recall incorrect information, and it may be a challenge for them to let go of their misconceptions.

Instructions

How to use a K-W-L chart:

1. Create a blank K-W-L chart following the example and make a copy for each participant. Or ask participants to fold a piece of paper into three sections and label them Know, Want to Know, and Learned.
2. Ask participants to brainstorm the words, phrases, or terms they associate with the topic and record them in the Know column.
3. Ask participants to record what they want to learn about the topic, in the form of questions, in the Want to Know column. Ask for a few volunteers to share their learning intentions with the group.
4. As a review activity, ask participants to share the new knowledge they recorded in the Learned column, as well as their "ah ha" moments and unanswered questions.
5. Provide resources to assist participants in locating additional information to answer unresolved questions.

Example

Know	Want to Know	Learned
Basic visual and tactile techniques for underwater bridge inspections	What do I need to do and look for at the different levels of inspections? How are the procedures different for piers and pilings?	Level I: • Detect obvious damage/deterioration of the total exterior surface • Detect undermining or exposure • Limited probing

Source: Cornish (2018)

The above shows a K-W-L chart based on David Cornish's NHI "Instructor Development Course" training presentation, "Diving Inspection Intensity Levels."

Connections to L2 learners: This approach puts its emphasis on comprehension of important material. As such, it is part of what the Instructed SLA field would characterize as Meaning-Focused Instruction, a highly effective approach in optimizing L2 development. KWL also begins with a critical step for L2 learners' comprehension: tapping into and building up participants' background knowledge before reading or listening. Participants can also be encouraged to use their entire multilingual repertoire, including their L1 with other speakers of that language, in an effort to reach the group's goal of increasing their knowledge and expertise with the topic.

Appendix B8

Quick Writes

(Steps for this approach are located on the U.S. Department of Transportation Website, National Highway Institute, https://www.nhi.fhwa.dot.gov/LearnersFirst/quick-writes-entrance-tickets.htm, and provided below.)

Quick Writes/Entrance Tickets

A quick write is a fast and easy way to get participants to collect their ideas and put them into writing. During a quick write, give participants 2 to 10 minutes to write a response to an open-ended prompt or question. Participants can jot their thoughts on a piece of paper or large notecard. Quick writes can be used before a module or lesson (called an entrance ticket), during a module or lesson, or after a module or lesson (called an exit ticket) to encourage participants to think about what they already know about a concept or to reflect on their learning.

If you use a quick write as part of an introduction, you can get a quick measure of participant's past experiences with the topic so you can better tailor your message to their level of understanding. You can also use a quick write as a quick knowledge check to help you and participants monitor their comprehension. Because time is limited and the focus is on content, it is important to stress to participants that grammar and spelling are not graded in a quick write activity.

Writing is a challenge for some participants and adding a time limit can increase the stress they feel to produce something of value. This activity may also be challenging for non-native English writers. Depending on the size of the group, you may find it hard to find enough time to review dozens of quick writes. Also, it is often difficult to read other people's handwriting, especially when it was hastily written.

Instructions

How to use a quick write as an entrance ticket:

1. Write an open-ended question or prompt.
2. Print the prompt and instructions for the activity on a half sheet of paper.

3. Distribute the entrance ticket to participants as they enter the classroom.
4. Explain the activity and set a timer.*
5. Collect the unsigned writing sheets and review them on your next break.

*Note from authors Nadeen and Andrea: To further optimize this activity and integrate additional optimal conditions for L2 development, we recommend the following additional step after participants have completed their quick write. Ask participants to share their writing in one of the following ways: (a) orally share the content of their quick write with a partner and listen to their partner's written points, or (b) exchange their quick write half sheet with a partner; read their partner's quick write, and respond with a written note back to that person; return the half sheets to the original writer. Both additions increase the participants' level of active engagement.

> *Connections to L2 learners: This approach allows participants to emphasize conveying important information to others without an over-focus on correct language forms, a focus that could constrict their expression of ideas related to the topic. As such, implementing Quick Writes is part of what the Instructed SLA field would characterize as Meaning-Focused Instruction, a highly effective approach in optimizing L2 development. In addition, participants are asked to write on a half sheet of paper rather than a full one, and to not worry about spelling or grammar in an effort to encourage them to record as many ideas as possible. These components—a half sheet of paper and emphasis on ideas rather than from-- can further reduce anxiety for participants who are using their L2. Quick Writes also begin with a critical step for L2 learners' comprehension: tapping into participants' background knowledge before they read or listen to content. In Finally, in order to fully optimize this instructional approach, we highly encourage teachers and facilitators to include our additional step above, that is, partners sharing their quick writes in a 1-1 format. This pairing increases each participant's opportunities to listen, speak, read, and write, the kind of active participation and interaction that the Instructed SLA field has found essential to L2 learning.*

Appendix B9

The Survey Text Method

General Description

Participants "survey the text," reading only the title, subheadings, captions, etc., to make predictions before they actually read the text in its entirety.

Purpose

To enhance L2 learners' reading comprehension by: (a) building up their background knowledge *before* they read the text, and (b) engaging them in making predictions about texts, a strategy that good readers use.

Preparation

No specific preparation needed.

Steps

1. Direct participants to scan the title, subheadings, captions, and graphics. Ask them also to read the introductory and concluding paragraphs.
2. From their scanning, ask participants to make predictions about the text. You can ask them to either:
   a. List the main/important ideas that they think will be covered in the text.
   b. List the questions that they think may be answered in the text. (Optional: You can assign each group one of the following question starters: *who, what, where, when, why,* and *how.*)
   (Participants can do these activities individually, in pairs, or in small groups.)
3. Participants read the text.
4. After reading, engage the participants to go back and confirm or modify their predictions, or answer their questions.

Connection to L2 learners: This instructional strategy enables L2 learners to build up background knowledge about a topic **before** they read about it. Increased background knowledge not only enhances reading comprehension, but can help less proficiency L2 learners perform as well as students with more advanced L2 proficiency.

Appendix B10

Think–Pair–Share (Also known as "Turn and Talk")

General Description

A cooperative group structure that pairs L2 learners with a partner to exchange information. Serving as a contrast to typical classroom question–answer routines (i.e., one student responding to a teacher's question or request), *Think–Pair–Share* increases the probability that all students will participate, and consequently, interaction in the L2.

Purpose

To engage all students with the topic at hand; to increase one-to-one interaction; and to promote listening and speaking skills.

Preparation

If you are using this structure with children, demonstrate the process in front of the whole class before you use *Think–Pair–Share* for the first time with your students. Call up a student to be your partner in the information exchange and run through the steps below. Use easy prompts while students are learning this structure, e.g., "Ask your partner to identify their favorite color." You may have to demonstrate and practice with students several times before you use this structure in your content area teaching.

Steps

1. Arrange students or colleagues in pairs.
2. Ask the question or raise the topic to the whole class.
    Examples: "Think about the following: What do you think Harry Potter felt when he saw his parents in the magic mirror?" or "What do you think the impact of this legal case will be on contractual law in the construction industry?"

3. "Think" Phase
     Give participants some quiet time to think.
4. "Pair" Phase
     Ask partners to turn to "elbow partners" (nearby) and take turns sharing the information.
5. "Share" Phase
     You may ask for volunteers to share with the whole group the information exchanged in pairs. Participants can share their own ideas, or you can ask them to share what their partner said in the "Pair" Phase.

Connection to L2 learners: When they are interacting with native English-speakers in this cooperative structure, L2 learners have access to English input (listening to their partner) and English output (speaking to their partner), both critically important for L2 acquisition. Speaking in a one-to-one situation, in contrast to speaking in front of a large group, can help decrease L2 learners' nervousness or reluctance related to their oral performance. Also, when the purpose of the activity is to build knowledge regarding the topic, regardless of the language, teachers can pair L2 learners sharing the same L1, and they can discuss the concept or information in their shared native language.

Appendix B11

The Writing Process (Writing Workshop)

General Description

The Writing Process, often referred to as the Writing Workshop, engages participants in taking the steps that published authors use: (a) generating an idea for a piece of writing; (b) drafting the piece; (c) getting feedback; (d) making revisions accordingly; (e) editing the piece for correct language forms (writing conventions); and, finally, (f) publishing. This is the process followed by authors of a broad range of genres such as academic articles, professional manuals, poetry, novels, informational texts, etc.

Purpose

To make it clear that published writing pieces do not emerge in their final form from authors but are instead the result of sequential steps that real authors use; to put into actual practice the expectation that all participants can be writers and thereby share information with others; to emphasize that writers' ideas are paramount in good writing and are first expressed in drafts that will later be edited for correct language forms before going to a wider audience.

Preparation

No specific preparation needed.

Steps

1. Brainstorming
   Participants generate and talk with colleagues about their topic ideas. They may use a graphic organizer or outline to help visualize the ideas that they will put down on paper.
2. Drafting
   Participants begin to write. The emphasis in this step is to write as complete a draft as possible and convey meaning, without worrying about correct forms of language, such as spelling and punctuation.

3. Conferencing
   Participants take their drafts and share them with a partner or a small group. Feedback to the writer usually first acknowledges the strong elements of the piece. Colleagues giving feedback to the writer should also raise questions for any parts that are unclear or provide suggestions for possibly improving the piece.
4. Revising
   Recognized as the most difficult part of the process, this step is where the writer makes significant changes to improve the piece. These changes most likely stem from conferencing with others and from self-reflection upon re-reading the piece. Revising keeps the focus on the overall meaning of the piece. It involves making changes, sometimes big ones, in order to better convey and showcase the writer's meaning. As examples of revising, a writer may completely rewrite the introduction, change the sequence of events, more fully explain a character, include more dialog, add a new section, and so on.
5. Editing
   Now, the focus is on making all corrections to language forms—punctuation, grammar, spelling, etc.—before the piece goes out to a wider audience. Editing is often collaborative, with peers and colleagues assisting each other, or, in a formal education setting, with the instructor. Writers can also look for computer applications that can help with getting the piece into its final, correct form.
6. Publishing
   The piece is now ready to be "published," in other words, distributed to a wider audience.

Connections to L2 learners: Writing Workshop puts into place both Meaning-Focused and Form-Focused instruction, essential components of effective Instructed Second Language Acquisition. The first steps entirely focus on conveying meaning, which accelerates L2 learning. The latter steps turn to a focus on language forms and their correctness. Given that these lessons in form are imbedded in writing that is highly meaningful to the L2 writer, Instructed Second Language Acquisition research has shown that learners acquire more of those forms to actively and independently use when interacting in the L2.

References

Adichie, C. N. (2009, July). The danger of a single story [Video]. TED Conferences. https://www.ted.com/talks/chimamanda_ngozi_adichie_the_danger_of_a_single_story

Agirdag, O. (2014) The long-term effects of bilingualism on children of immigration: Student bilingualism and future earnings. *International Journal of Bilingual Education and Bilingualism, 17*(4), 449–464. https://doi.org/10.1080/13670050.2013.816264

Aronsson, K. (2018). Myths about bilingual learning in family life settings: Werner Leopold's child language biographies and contemporary work on children's play practices. *Learning, Culture and Social Interaction, 26,* 100226.https://doi.org/10.1016/j.lcsi.2018.03.011

Ayres-Bennett, W., Hafner, M., Dufresne, E., & Yerushalmi, E. (2022). *The economic value to the UK of speaking other languages.* Cambridge, UK: RAND Europe and University of Cambridge.

Bailey, D. (2020, January 1). Answering the demand for services. *Monitor on Psychology, 51*(1). https://www.apa.org/monitor/2020/01/cover-trends-demand-services

Bailey, N. Madden, C., & Krashen, S. (1974). Is there a "natural sequence" in adult second language learning? *Language Learning, 24,* 235–243.

Baldwin, J. R., González, A., Brock, N., Xie, M., & Charo, C. (2023). *Intercultural communication for everyday life* (2nd ed.). Hoboken, NJ: Wiley Blackwell.

Barrett, M. (2018). How schools can promote the intercultural competence of young people. *Youth and Migration: What Promotes and What Challenges Their Integration? European Psychologist, 23*(1), 93–104.

Barrett, M., Byram, M., Ipgrave, J., & Seurrat, A. (2013). *Images of others: An autobiography of intercultural encounters through visual media.* Strasbourg, France: Council of Europe. Retrieved from http://www.coe.int/t/dg4/autobiography/default_en.asp

Benson, P., Barkhuizen, G., Bodycott, P., & Brown, J. (2013). Second language identity. In *Second language identity in narratives of study abroad.* London: Palgrave Macmillan. https://doi.org/10.1057/9781137029423_2

Berko, J. (1958). The child's learning of English morphology. *WORD, 14*(2–3), 150–177. https://doi.org/10.1080/00437956.1958.11659661

Bialystok, E. (2017). The bilingual adaptation: How minds accommodate experience. *Psychol Bull, 143*(3), 233–262. https://doi.org/10.1037/bul0000099

Bialystok, E. (2018). Bilingual education for young children: Review of the effects and consequences. *International Journal of Bilingual Education and Bilingualism, 21*(6), 666–679. https://doi.org/10.1080/13670050.2016.1203859

Bialystok, E. (2021). Bilingualism: Pathway to cognitive reserve. *Trends in Cognitive Science, 25*(5), 355–364. https://doi.org/10.1016/j.tics.2021.02.003

Bialystok, Hawrylewicz, Grundy, & Chung-Fat-Yim. (2022). The Swerve: How childhood bilingualism changed from liability to benefit. *Developmental Psychology, 58*(8), 1429–1440. https://doi.org/10.1037/dev0001376

Bialystok, E., & Craik. (2022). Title. *Psychonomic Bulletin & Review, 29*, 1246–1269. https://doi.org/10.3758/s13423-022-02057-5

Bialystok, E., Peets, K. F., & Moreno, S. (2014). Producing bilinguals through immersion: Development of metalinguistic awareness. *Applied Psycholinguistics, 35*(1), 177–191.

Boroditsky, L. (2011). How language shapes thought. *Scientific American, 304*(2), 62–65. http://www.jstor.org/stable/26002395

Brown, C. L. (2017). Linking public health nursing competencies and service-learning in a global setting. Public Health Nursing, 34(5), 485–492. https://doi.org/10.1111/phn.12330

Byram, M. (2008). *From foreign language education to education for intercultural citizenship: Essays and reflections*. Bristol: Multilingual Matters, UK.

Byram. M. (2021). *Teaching and assessing intercultural communicative competence: Revisited(2nd edi)*. Bristol: Multilingual Matters.

Byram. M., & Golubeva, I. (2020). Conceptualising intercultural (communicative) competence and intercultural citizenship. In J. Jackson (Ed.), *The Routledge handbook of language and intercultural communication* (2nd ed., pp. 70–85). New York: Routledge.

Byram, M., Golubeva, I., Hui, H., & Wagner, M. (Eds.). (2016). *From principles to practice in education for intercultural citizenship*. Bristol: Multilingual Matters.

Byram, M., Barrett, M., Ipgrave, J., Jackson, R., & Méndez García, M. C. (2009). *Autobiography of intercultural encounters*. Strasbourg, France: Council of Europe. Retrieved from http://www.coe.int/t/dg4/autobiography/default_en.asp

Byram, M., & Wagner, M. (2018). Making a difference: Language teaching for intercultural and international dialogue. Foreign Language Annals, 51(1), 140–151. https://doi.org/10.1111/flan.12319

California State Department of Education. (2018). *Global California Initiative 2030*. https://www.cde.ca.gov/sp/ml/documents/globalca2030.pdf

Calma, A., Cotronei-Baird, V., & Chia, A. (2022). Grammarly: An instructional intervention for writing enhancement in management education. *International Journal of Management Education, 20*(3), 100704. https://doi.org/10.1016/j.ijme.2022.100704

Cambourne, B., & Turbill, J. (1987). *Coping with chaos*. (ERIC ERIC Number: ED283209). Portsmouth, NH: Heinemann.

Carrell, P. L. (1987). Content and formal schemata in ESL reading. *TESOL Quarterly, 21*(3), 461–481.

Catts, H. (2022). Rethinking how to promote reading comprehension. *American Educator, 45*(4), 26–40.

Cenoz, J. (2003). The additive effect of bilingualism on third language acquisition: A review. *International Journal of Bilingualism, 7*(1), 71–87.

Chamorro, G., & Janke, V. (2022).Investigating the bilingual advantage: The impact of L2 exposure on the social and cognitive skills of monolingually-raised children in bilingual education. *International Journal of Bilingual Education and Bilingualism, 25*(5): 1765–1781.

Chen, X., & Padilla, A. M. (2019). Role of bilingualism and biculturalism as assets in positive psychology: Conceptual dynamic GEAR model. *Frontiers in Psychology, 26* September. https://doi.org/10.3389.

Chi, M. T. H., & Wylie, R. (2014). The ICAP Framework: Linking cognitive engagement to active learning outcomes. *Educational Psychologist, 49*(4), 219–243.

Chorney, H. (1997). *The economic benefits of linguistic duality and bilingualism: A political economy approach.* In *Official languages and the economy: New Canadian perspectives* (pp. 181–197). Department of Canadian Heritage. Retrieved from https://files.eric.ed.gov/fulltext/ED429447.pdf

Cohen, E. G., & Lotan, R. A. (2025). *Designing groupwork: Strategies for the heterogeneous classroom* (4th ed.). New York: Teachers College Press.

Collier, V.P., & Thomas, W. P. (2017). Validating the power of bilingual schooling: 32 years of large-scale longitudinal research. In *Annual Review of Applied Linguistics, 37*, 203–217.

Connelly, F. M., & Clandinin, D. J. (1990). Stories of experience and narrative inquiry. *Educational Researcher, 19*(5), 2–14.

Costa, A., & Sebastián-Gallers, N. (2014). How does the bilingual experience sculpt the brain? *Nature Reviews Neuroscience, 15*(5), 336–345.

Coulby, D. (2006). Intercultural education: Theory and practice. *Intercultural Education, 17*(30), 245–257.

Council of Europe. (2025a) *Intercultural citizenship.* https://www.coe.int/en/web/interculturalcities/icc-test#:~:text=What%20is%20intercultural%20citizenship%3F,cultures%20can%20be%20an%20advantage

Council of Europe. (2025b). *Autobiography of intercultural encounters.* https://www.coe.int/en/web/autobiography-intercultural-encountershelp_outline

Cowan N. (2014). Working memory underpins cognitive development, learning, and education. *Education Psychology Review, 26*(2), 197–223. https://doi.org/10.1007/s10648-013-9246-y. PMID: 25346585; PMCID: PMC4207727.

Cummins, J. (2017). Teaching minoritized students: Are additive approaches legitimate? *Harvard Educational Review, 87*(300), 404–425.

Cummins, J. (2021). *Rethinking the education of multilingual learners.* Bristol, England: Multilingual Matters.

Deardorff, D. K. (2020). *Manual for developing intercultural competencies: Story circles.* New York: Routledge.

DeKeyser, R. (1998). Beyond focus on form: Cognitive perspectives on learning and practicing second language grammar. In C. Doughty & J. Williams (Eds.), *Focus on form in classroom second language acquisition* (pp. 42–63). Cambridge: Cambridge University Press.

DeLuca, V., Segaert, K, Mazaheri, A., & Krott, A. (2020). Understanding bilingual brain function and structure changes? U bet! A unified bilingual experience trajectory model. *Journal of Neurolinguistics, 56*, https://doi.org/10.1016/j.jneuroling.2020.100930

Diamond, A. (2013). Executive functions. *Annual Review of Psychology, 64*, 135–168.

Díaz, E., & Flores, B. (2001). Teacher as sociocultural, sociohistorical mediator: Teaching to the potential. In M. De la Luz & J. Halcón (Eds.), *The best for our children: Critical perspectives on literacy for Latino students.* Language and Literacy Series. New York: Teachers College Press.

Díaz, V., & Farrar, M. J. (2018). Do bilingual and monolingual preschoolers acquire false belief understanding similarly? The role of executive functioning and language. *First Language, 38*(4), 382–398.

Droop, M., & Verhoeven, L. (1998). Background knowledge, linguistic complexity & second language reading comprehension. *Journal of Literacy Research, 30*(2), 253–271.

Dulay, H., & Burt, M. (1974). Natural sequences in child second language acquisition. *Language Learning, 24,* 37–53.

Dulay, H., & Burt, M. (1980). Second language acquisition. In H. Dulay, M. Burt, & D. McKeon (Eds.), *Testing and teaching communicatively handicapped Hispanic children.* San Francisco: CA: Bloomsbury West.

Earnest, D. R., Rosenbusch, K., Wallace-Williams, D., & Keim, A. C. (2016). Study abroad in psychology: Increasing cultural competencies through experiential learning. *Teaching of Psychology, 43,* 75–79. https://doi.org/10.1177/0098628315620889

Ellis, R. (2003). *Task-based language learning and teaching.* Oxford: Oxford University Press.

Ellis, R. (2024). First person singular; Rod Ellis's essential bookshelf, focus on form. *Language Teaching, 57,* 246–261.

Ellis, R., & Shintani, S. (2014). *Exploring language pedagogy through second language acquisition research.* London and New York: Routledge.

Ellis, R. Skehan, P., Li, S., Shintani, N., & Lambert, C. (2020). *Task-based language teaching: Theory and practice.* Cambridge: Cambridge University Press.

Escobedo, L. E., Cervantes, L., & Havranek, E. (2023). Barriers in healthcare for latinx patients with limited english proficiency-a narrative review. *Journal of General Internal Medicine, 38*(5), 1264–1271. https://doi.org/10.1007/s11606-022-07995-3

Fan, S. P., Liberman, Z., Keysar, B., & Kinzler, K. D. (2015). The exposure advantage: Early exposure to a multilingual environment promotes effective communication. *Psychological Sciences, 26*(7), 1090–1097.

Fantini, A. E. (2020). Reconceptualizing intercultural communicative competence: A multinational perspective. *Research in Comparative & International Education, 15*(1), 52–61.

Fantini, A. E. (2021). Intercultural communicative competence: A necessary ability for all. *World Learning Publications.* 4. https://digitalcollections.sit.edu/worldlearning_publications/4

Flores, B. (2025). Biliteracy con cariño: Using interactive dialogue journals as a bridge to proficient reading while writing in L1 and L2. Walnut, CA: California Association for Bilingual Education.

Fogle L. W., & King, K. A. (2017). Bi- and multilingual family language socialization. In P. A. Duff & S. May (Eds.), *Language socialization, encyclopedia of language and education.* https://doi.org/10.1007/978-3-319-02327-4_7-1

Frick, M. (2024). Michigan university launches first-of-its-kind bilingual program for Spanish speakers. *Michigan Live.* Available at:https://www.mlive.com/news/grand-rapids/2024/03/michigan-university-launches-first-of-its-kind-bilingual-program-for-spanish-speakers.html

Friedman, A. (2015, May 10). *America's lacking language skills.* The Atlantic. Retrieved from.

Gándara, P. (2018). The economic value of bilingualism in the United States. *Bilingual Research Journal, 41*(4), 334–343. https://doi.org/10.1080/15235882.2018.1532469

García, A., & Whitmore, K. (2011). Reclaiming language as a community text. In K. F. Whitmore & R. J. Meyer (Eds.), *Reclaiming reading: Teachers, students and researchers regaining spaces for thinking and action (*pp. 219–223). New York: Routledge.

Gass, S. M., Behebey, J., & Plonsky, L. (2020). *Second language acquisition* (5th ed.) New York: Routledge.

González Rodríguez, L. M., & Borham Puyal, M. (2012). Promoting intercultural competence through literature in CLIL contexts. *ATLANTIS: Journal of the Spanish Association of Anglo-American Studies,* 34(2), 105-124.

Gibbons, P. (2015). *Scaffolding language, scaffolding learning* (2nd ed.). Portsmouth, NH: Heinemann.

Gration, E. (2023). Bilingualism in 2022: The US, UK, and global statistics. Retrieved from https://preply.com/en/blog/bilingualism-statistics/

Grosjean, F. (1989). Neurolinguists, beware! The bilingual is not two monolinguals in one person. *Brain and Language, 36*(1), 3–15. https://doi.org/10.1016/0093-934X(89)90048-5

Grosjean, F. (2010). What bilingualism is NOT. *Harvard University Blog Press.* Cambridge, MA, July 28. https://harvardpress.typepad.com/hup_publicity/2010/07/what-bilingualism-is-not-.html

Grosjean, F. (2012). Bilingualism: A short introduction. In F. Grosjean & P. Li (Eds.), *The psycholinguistics of bilingualism* (pp. 5–25). New York: Wiley & Sons.

Grosjean, F. (2017). Interview of Shana Poplak for life as a Bilingual. *Psychology Today.* Retrieved at: https://www.psychologytoday.com/us/blog/life-bilingual/201711/when-bilinguals-borrow-one-language-another

Grosjean, F. (2022). *Mysteries of bilingualism.* New York: John Wiley & Sons.

Grosjean, F. (2024). *On bilinguals and bilingualism.* Cambridge, England: Cambridge University Press.

Grosjean, F., Byers-Heinlein, K., Antoniou, M., Grüter, T., Hartsuiker, R. J., Peña, E. D., Bedore, L. M. and Shi, L.-F. (2018). *The listening bilingual.* New York: John Wiley and Sons. https://doi.org/10.1002/9781118835722.f

Gumperz, J., & Hernández-Chávez, E. (1975). Cognitive aspects of bilingual communication. In E. Hernandez-Chavez (Ed.), *El lenguaje de los Chicanos.* Arlington, VA: Center for Applied Linguistics.

Hall, E. T. (1976). *Beyond Culture.* New York: Random House.

Hardach, S. (2018). *World Economic Forum,* February. https://www.weforum.org/agenda/2018/02/speaking-more-languages-boost-economic-growth/

Hartanto, S., Toh, W. X., & Yang, H. (2018). Bilingualism narrows socioeconomic disparities in executive functions and self-regulatory behaviors during early childhood: Evidence from the early childhood longitudinal study. *Child Development,* January: 1–21.

Hartshorne, J. K., Tenenbaum, J. B., & Pinker, S. (2018). A critical period for second language acquisition: Evidence from 2/3 million English speakers. *Cognition, (Aug)*177, 263–277.

Hidalgo, N. M. (1993). Multicultural teacher introspection. In T. Perry & J. Fraser (Eds.), *Freedom's plow: Teaching multicultural classroom.* New York: Routledge.

Hiver, P. & Wu, J. (2023). Engagement in task-based language teaching. In C. Lambert, S. Aubrey & G. Bui (Eds.), *The role of the learner in task-based language teaching: Theory and research.* New York: Routledge, 74–90.

Hsin, L., & Snow, C. (2017). Social perspective taking: A benefit of bilingualism in academic writing. *Reading and Writing, 30,* 1193–1214.

Huang, J., & Hatch, E. (1978). A Chinese child's aquisition of English. In E. Hatch (Ed.), *Second language acquisition* (pp. 118–131). Rowley, Ma: Newbury House.

Hudson, T. (2007). *Teaching second language reading.* Oxford: Oxford University Press.

Hwang, K., Williams, S., Zucchi, E., Chong, T. W. H., Mascitti-Meuter, M., LoGiudice, D., Goh, A. M. Y., Panayiotou, A., & Batchelor, F. (2022). Testing the use of translation apps to overcome everyday healthcare communication in Australian aged-care hospital wards-An exploratory study. *Nursing open, 9*(1), 578–585. https://doi.org/10.1002/nop2

Hymes, D. (1972). On communicative competence. In J. B. Pride & J. Holme (Eds.), *Sociolinguistics* (pp. 269–285). Harmondsworth: Penguin.

Irving, D. (2022). RAND Corporation. (2022). *The economic returns of foreign language learning*. July. https://www.rand.org/pubs/articles/2022/the-economic-returns-of-foreign-language-learning.html

Jackson, J. (2020). The language and intercultural dimension of education abroad. In *The Routledge handbook of language and intercultural communication* (2nd ed.). New York: Routledge.

Jackson, J. (2024). Imperatives for intercultural dialogue. In *Introducing language and intercultural communication* (pp. 1–28). New York: Routledge.

Jeddy, U., & Beketova, Z. (2024). The power of language: Myriad of benefits of multilingualism. https://yaledailynews.com/blog/2024/10/09/the-power-of-language-myriad-of-benefits-of-multilingualism/

Johnson, S. (2019). Colleges lose a "stunning" 651 foreign-language programs in 3 years. https://www.chronicle.com/article/Colleges-Lose-a-Stunning-/245526

Kellem, K., & Halvorsen, A. (2018). Understanding and utilizing form-focused instruction in the language classroom. *ORTESOL Journal, 35*, 27–35.

Kellerman, P., & Raisz, A. (2022). *The economic benefits of multilingual learning*. San Francisco, CA: Bay Area Council Economic Institute (October).

Krashen, S. (1985). *The input hypothesis: Issues and implications*. London: Longman.

Kuhl, P. K., Stevens, E., Hayashi, T., Deguschi, S., Kiritani, S., & Iverson, P. (2006). Infants show a facilitation effect for native language phonetic perception between 6a and 12 months. *Developmental Science, 9*(2), F13–F21.

Lambert, C., Philp, J., & Nakamura, S. (2017). Learner-generated content and engagement in second language task performance. *Language Teaching Research, 21*(6), 665–680.

Lambert, W. E. (1981). Bilingualism and language acquisition. In *Annals of the New York Academy of Sciences, 39*(1), 9–22.

Lanza, E., & Wei, Li. (2023). *Code-switching and children in Oxford bibliographies*. Retrieved at: https://www.oxfordbibliographies.com/display/document/obo-9780199791231/obo-9780199791231-0271.xml

Larsen-Freeman, D. (2019). On language learner agency: A complex dynamic systems theory perspective. *The Modern Language Journal, 103*, 61–79. https://doi.org/10.1111/modl.12536

Lezak, M. D. (1983). *Neuropsychological assessment* (2nd ed.). New York: Oxford University Press.

Lightbown, P. M., & Spada, N. (2021). *How languages are learned* (5th ed.).Oxford.

Liu, Q., & Liu, Z. (2021). A review on the relationship between bilingualism and working memory. *Open Journal of Modern Linguistics, 11*, 121–134.

Long, M. H. (1983). Native speaker/non-native speaker conversation and the negotiation of comprehensible input. *Applied LInguistics, 4*(2), 126–141.

Marzuki, Widiati, U., Rusdin, D., Darwin, & Indrawati, I. (2023). The impact of AI writing tools on the content and organization of students' writing: EFL teachers' perspective. *Cogent Education, 10*(2). https://doi.org/10.1080/2331186X.2023.2236469

Meeker, Z. (2022, September). *The demand for bilingual nurses and their impact*. Retrieved at: https://www.nurse.com/blog/demand-bilingual-nurses-their-impact/

Méndez García, M. del C. (2016). Intercultural reflection through the *Autobiography of Intercultural Encounters*: Students' accounts of their images of alterity. *Language and Intercultural Communication, 17*(2), 90–117.

Miller, E. R., & Kubota, R. (2013). Second language identity construction. In J. Herschensohn & M. Young-Scholten (Eds.), *The Cambridge handbook of second language acquisition* (pp. 230–250). Cambridge Handbooks in Language and Linguistics. Cambridge University Press.

Monsrud, M., Rydland, V., Geva, E., Thurmann-Moe, A.C. & Lyster, S.H. (2019). The advantages of jointly considering first and second language vocabulary skills among emergent bilingual children. *International Journal of Bilingual Education and Bilingualism,* DOI: 10.1080/13670050.2019.1624685.

Nasir, N. S., & Peele-Eady, T. B. (2012). Identity and learning. In *Encyclopedia of the Science of learning.* (pp. 1482–1484) Springer.

New America. (2023). www.newamerica.org

New American Economy. (2017). *Not lost in translation: The growing importance of foreign language skills in the U.S. job market.* March. http://research.newamericaneconomy.org/wp-content/uploads/2017/03/NAE_Bilingual_V9.pdf

Nicolay, A. C., & Poncelet, M. (2015). Cognitive benefits in children enrolled in an early bilingual immersion school: A follow up study. *Bilingualism: Language and Cognition, 18*(4), 789–795.

Nieto, S. (2009). Cultural and learning. In *Language, culture, and teaching: Critical perspectives* (pp. 135-159). New York, NY: Routledge.

Nguyen, M. V. H., Hutchison, L. A., Norvell, G. Mead, D. L., & Winsler, A. (2023). Degree of bilingualism and executive function in early childhood. *Language and Cognition,* 1–23. https://doi.org/10.1017/langcog.2023.46.

Norton, B. (1995). Social identity, investment, and language learning. *TESOL Quarterly, 29*(1), 9-31.

Ortega, L. (2019). SLA and the study of equitable multilingualism. *Modern Language Journal, 103* (Suppl), 23–38.

Papp, K. R. (2019). The bilingual advantage debate: quantity and quality of the evidence. In J. Schwieter (Ed.), *Handbook of neuroscience on multilingualism* (pp. 701–735). London: Wiley Blackwell.

Peal, E., & Lambert, W. (1962). The relation of bilingualism to intelligence. *Psychological Monographs, 76*(Whole No. 546), 1–23.

Peristeri, E., Baldimsti, E. Vogelzang, M., T'Simpli, I. M., & Durrleman, S. (2021). The cognitive benefits of bilingualism in autism spectrum disorder: Is theory of mind boosted and by which underlying factors? *Autism Research, 45,* 1695–1705.

Pettigrew, T. F., & Tropp, L. R. (2006). A meta-analytic test of intergroup contact theory. *Journal of Personality and Social Psychology, 90,* 751–783. https://doi.org/10.1037/0022-3514.90.5.751

Pica, T. Young, R., & Doughty, C. (1987). The impact of interaction on comprehension. *TESOL Quarterly, 21*(4), 737–758.

Poplack, S. (1980). Sometimes I'll start a sentence in Spanish Y TERMINO EN ESPAÑOL: Toward a typology of code-switching. *Linguistics, 18*(7–8), 581–618

Poplack, S. (2015). Code switching: Linguistic. In J. D. Wright (Ed.), *International encyclopedia of the social and behavioral sciences* (pp. 918–925). Oxford: Elsevier.

Poplack, S. (2018). *Borrowing. Loanwords in the speech community and in the grammar.* New York: Oxford University Press.

Porras, D., Ee, J., & Gándara, P. (2014). Employer preferences: Do bilingual applicants and employees experience an advantage? In R. Callahan & P. Gándara (Eds.), *The bilingual advantage: language, literacy and the US labor market* (pp. 236–262). Clevedon, UK: Multilingual Matters.

Portes, A., & Rumbaut, R. G. (2005). Introduction: The second generation and the children of immigrants longitudinal study. *Ethnic and Racial Studies, 28*(6), 983–99.

Ramirez, N. F., & Kuhl, P. (2017). The brain science of bilingualism. *Young Children*, May, 38–44.

Reeve, J., & Tseng, C. M. (2011). Agency as a fourth aspect of students' engagement during learning activities. *Contemporary Educational Psychology.* https://doi.org/10.1016/j.cedpsych.2011.05.002

Richards, J. (2006). *Communicative language teaching today.* Cambridge: Cambridge University Press.

Ruiz, N. T. (1988). *The nature of bilingualism: Implications for special education.* Crosscultural Special Education Series, Volume 2. Sacramento, CA: Resources in Special Education.

Ruiz, N. T. (1989). An optimal learning environment for Rosemary. *Exceptional Children, 56,* 29–41.

Ruiz, N. T. (1995a). The social construction of learning abilities and disabilities, I: Profile types of Latino children identified as language learning disabled. *Journal of Learning Disabilities, 28,* 476–490.

Ruiz, N. T. (1995b). The social construction of learning abilities and disabilities, II: Optimal and at-risk lessons in a bilingual special education classroom. *Journal of Learning Disabilities, 28,* 491–502.

Ruiz, N. T. (1995c). A young deaf child learns to write: Implications for literacy development. *Reading Teacher, 49*(3), 206–217.

Ruiz, N. T. (2012). It's different with second language learners: Learning from 40 years of research. In C. Dudley-Marling & S. Michaels (Ed.), *High-expectation curricula: Helping all students succeed with powerful learning* (pp. 145–161). New York: Teachers College Press.

Ruiz, N. T. (2023). Language and literacy at the bilingual special education interface. In D. Nieto, E. Escamilla, E. Almanza, T. Hogan , & Rodríguez (Eds.), *Qué bueno! A history of advocacy and care for culturally and linguistically diverse education.* El Monte, CA: Velázquez Press.

Ruiz, N. T., & Baird, P. J. (2013). Transnational teacher education: Towards theory and practice. *NABE Journal of Research and Practice, 4,* 1–23.

Ruiz, N. T., & Barajas, M. (2012). Multiple perspectives on the schooling of Mexican Indigenous students in the U.S.: Issues for Future Research. *Bilingual Research Journal, 35,* 125–144.

Ruiz, N. T., & Sánchez-Boyce, M. (2022). *ABC-OLE Instructional Resource Guide for foundational biliteracy skills pre-kindergarten through grade 2.* Middletown, DE: Amazon Publishing.

Ruiz, N. T., Baird, P. J., & Torres Hernández, P. (2016). Field practice in La Mixteca: Transnational Teacher Education in the service of Mexican Indigenous students in U.S. schools, *Journal of Latinos and Education,* 1–16.

Ruiz, N. T., García, E., & Figueroa, R. A. (1996). *The OLE curriculum guide.* Sacramento, CA: California Department of Education.

Ruiz, N.T., Vargas, E., & Beltrán, A. (2002). Becoming a reader and writer in a bilingual special education classroom. *Language Arts, 79*(4), 297–309.

Ruiz, R. (1984). Orientations in language planning. *NABE Journal, 8*(2), 14–34.

Rumbaut, R. (2014). English plus: Exploring the socio-economic benefits of bilingualism in Southern California. In R. M. Callahan & P. C. Gandara (Eds.), *The bilingual advantage: Language, literacy, and the labor market* (pp. 182–205). Bristol, England: Multilingual Matters.

Saiz, A., & Zoido, E. (2005). Listening to what the world says: Bilingualism and earnings in the United States. *The Review of Economics and Statistics, 87*(3), 523–538.

Santibañez, L., & Zarate, M. E. (2014). Bilinguals in the U.S. and college enrollment. In R. M. Callahan & P. C. Gandara (Eds.), *The bilingual advantage: Language, literacy, and the labor market* (pp. 211–233). Bristol, England: Multilingual Matters.

Schroeder, S. R. (2018). Do bilinguals have an advantage in Theory of Mind? A meta-analysis. *Frontiers in Communication, 3*(36), 1–36.

Schumann, J. (1976). Social distance as a factor in second language acquisition. *Language Learning, 26*(1), 135–143.

Short, K., Day, D., & Schroeder, J. (Eds.), (2016). *Teaching globally: Reading the world through literature*. Portsmouth, ME: Stenhouse.

Skutnabb-Kangas, T., & Toukomaa, P. (1976). *Teaching migrant children's mother tongue and learning the language of the host country in the context of the socio-cultural situation of the migrant family*. Helsinki: The Finnish National Commission for UNESCO.

Smith, L., & Meek, S. (2018). Society benefits from more bilingual young children. Bipartisan Policy Center (March), https://bipartisanpolicy.org/blog/ society-benefits-from-more-bilingual-young-children/

Smith, R., Snow, P., Serry, T., & Hammond, L. (2021). The role of background knowledge in reading comprehension: A critical review. *Reading Psychology, 42*(3), 214–240. https://doi.org/10.1080/02702711.2021.1888348

Smolak, E., de Anda, S., Enriquez, B., Poulin-Dubois, D., & Friend, M. (2020). Code-switching in young bilingual toddlers: A longitudinal, cross-language investigation. *Bilingual (Camb Engl), 23*(3), 500–518.

Song. (2019). Language socialization and code-switching: A case study of a Korean-English bilingual child in a Korean transnational family. *International Journal of Bilingual Education and Bilingualism, 22*(2), 91–106

Sulis, G. (2022). Engagement in the foreign language classroom: Macro and micro perspectives. *System (110)*. November, accessed at https://doi.org/10.1016/j.system .2022.102902

Swain, M. (1985). The output hypothesis and beyond: Mediating acquisition through collaborative dialogue. In J. P. Lantold (Ed.), *Sociocultural theory and second language learning* (pp. 94–114). Oxford: Oxford University Press.

Talburt, S. (2009). International travel and implication. *Journal of Curriculum Theorizing, 23*(3),104–118.

Theobold, E. et al. (2020). Active learning narrows achievement gaps for underrepresented students in undergraduate science, technology, engineering, and math. Proceedings of the National Academy of Sciences of the United States of America, and *Psychological and Cognitive Sciences 117*(12), 6476–6483 https://doi.org/10.1073/pnas.19169031

Torregrossa, J., Eisenbeiss, S., & Bongartz, C. (2023). Boosting bilingual metalinguistic awareness under dual language activation: Some implications for bilingual education. *Language Learning, 73*(3), 683–722.

Trebits, A. Koch, M. J., Ponto, K., Bruhn, A., Adler, M., & Kersten, K. (2021). Cognitive gains and socioeconomic status in early second language acquisition in immersion and EFL learning settings. *International Journal of Bilingual Education and Bilingualism*. https://doi.org/10.1080/13670050.2021.1943307

Umansky, I. M., Valentino, R. A., & Reardon, S. F. (2016). The promise of two-language education. *Educational Leadership, 73*(5), 10–17.

Valero, A. (2002). *Emergent literacy development among Latino students in a rural preschool classroom.* [Ph.D.] University of California at Davis.

Vygotsky, L. (1968). *Thought and language.* MIT Press.

Wagner & Byram. (2017). Intercultural citizenship. In Y. Yun Kim (Ed.), *The International encyclopedia of intercultural communication.* Kelly L. McKay-Semmler (Associate Editor) JohnWiley & Sons, Inc.

Waltermire, M., & Valterrez, M. (2019). Spontaneo.us loanwords and the question of lexical proficiency among Spanish-English bilinguals. *Hispania 102*(3), 409–422.

Warren, M., & Lee, W. W. L. (2020). Intercultural communication in professional and workplace settings. In J. Jackson (Ed.), *The Routledge handbook of language and intercultural communication* (2nd ed., pp. 473–486). New York: Routledge.

Winawer, J., Witthoft, N., Frank, M., Wu, L., Wade, A., & Boroditsky, L. (2007). Russian blues reveal effects of language on color discrimination (PNAS (Proceedings of the National Academy of Sciences), 104). n.p. *Cognitive Linguistics Bibliography* (CogBib). Retrieved 2024-11-2, from https://www.degruyter.com/database/COGBIB/entry/cogbib.13024/html

Wei, H., Gao, K., & Wang, W. (2019). Understanding the relationship between grit and foreign language performance among middle school students: the roles of foreign language enjoyment and classroom environment. *Frontiers in Psychology, 10,* Article #1508.

Wong Fillmore, L. (1979). Individual differences in second language acquisition. In Ch. J. Fillmore, D. Kempler & W. Wang (Eds.), *Individual differences in language ability and language behavior* (pp. 203–228). Berkeley: Academic Press.

Yashima, T., MacIntyre, P., & Ikeda, M. (2018). Situated willingness to communicate in an L2: Interplay of individual characteristics and context. *Language Teaching Research, 22*(1), 115–137.

Zapata-Barrero, R. (2022). *Intercultural citizenship in the post-multicultural era.* London, UK: SAGE Publications, Limited.

Zapata-Barrero, R. (2024). Intercultural citizenship. In M. García Cabeza & T. Faist (Eds.), *Encyclopedia of citizenship studies* (pp. 425–430). Edward Elgar Publishing.

Zeigler, K., & Camarota, S. A. (2019). 67.3 million in the United States spoke a foreign language at home in 2018. *Center for Immigration Studies,* October. Washington, D.C.

Zelazo, P. D. (2006). The Dimensional Change Card Sort (DCCS): A method of assessing executive function in children. *Nat Protoc. 1*(1), 297–301. https://doi.org/10.1038/nprot.2006.46. PMID: 17406248.

Zhao, X., & Wang, D. (2023). Grit in second language acquisition: A systematic review from 2017 to 2022. *Frontiers in Psychology, 14,* 1238788. https://doi.org/10.3389/fpsyg.2023.1238788

Zhao, X. (2023). Challenges and barriers in intercultural communication between patients with immigration backgrounds and health professionals: A systematic literature review. *Health Communication, 38*(4), 824–833. https://doi.org/10.1080/10410236.2021.1980188.

Index

Note: Page numbers in *italics* indicate figures, and page numbers in **bold** indicate tables in the text

active multilingualism 35–36; code-switching 35–43; spontaneous borrowing 36–37
active participation **81**, 88–91
additive bilingualism 49, 59
Adichie, C. N.115; *The Danger of a Single Story* 115
agency 83
Agirdag, O. 16
Allport, G. 113, 114
American Community Survey (ACS) 125
American Psychological Association (APA) 100
Anticipation Guide 4–5, 132–133
applied linguists 37–40, 42, 50
aptitude, for learning languages 64–65
assets view of linguistic diversity 4
attentional control 21–23
authenticity **81**, 95–96
autism mitigation 28–31
Autobiography of Intercultural Encounters (AIE) 118–119
Autobiography of Intercultural Encounters through Visual Medial (AIEVM) 118–119

Baird, P. J. 123
balanced bilinguals 11, **12**, 15; *see also* bilinguals/bilingualism
Baldimsti, E. 28
Baldwin, J. 116, 125
Barajas, M. 70
Barrett, M. 118, 119
Bay Area Council Economic Institute (2022) 17, 18

Bear/Dragon task 21
Bialystok, E. 28
bilingual education 71, **73**; academic achievement advantages 78; grade-level achievement 74; instruction 71, 72, 74; maintenance programs 72, **73**, 74, 75; minority language 77; National Curve Equivalent (NCE) system *76*, 76–77; Transitional Bilingual Education (TBE) 77, *78*; university 71–72;
bilinguals/bilingualism 10, **12**, 34–35, 49, 56, 59; advantage 19–21, 23; age-related cognitive decline 27–28; attentional control 21–23; autism mitigation 28–31; challenges 14; cognitive benefits of (*see* cognitive benefits); cognitive flexibility 24–27; with dementia 28; economic value of 14–18; employer preference 17–18; family 70–71, 78, 103; in healthcare postings 18; higher earning power 15–17; and higher education 14–15; iceberg analogy *58*, 58–59; income benefit of 16–17; indirect and direct effect 16–17; inhibitory control 21–22; L1 and L2 notation in 11; language proficiency of 55–60, *58*; language switching **40**; linguistic skills 19–20; multilingualism *vs.* 10; one-parent–one-language model 44; one-way *vs.* two-way programs 76; optimal conditions 78–97, **81**, **97**; perspective-taking skills 26–27; proficiency 10–11; social influences on 46–48; special education classroom 39–41, **40**; working memory 22–24; *see also specific entries*

Index

biliterate 11
binational program 46
Bipartisan Policy Center 15, 16
Brown, J. 124
Byram, M. 105, 108, 113, 116–119, 124

Cambourne, B. 79
Center for Workforce Studies (CWS) 100
Cervantes, L. 101
Chorney, H. 125–126
civic service programs 124
Clandinin, D. J. 115
Cloze Passages 87, 134–136
code-switching 35–39, 103; functions in children 40–43; inter-sentential 38; intra-sentential 38, 41
cognitive academic language proficiency 58
cognitive benefits 9, 18–19; executive functioning (*see* executive functions (EFs)); metalinguistic knowledge 19–20
cognitive flexibility 24–27; fluency aspect 24–25; and inflexibility 24–25; task-shifting 25
cognitive reserve 27–28, 31
Cohen, E. 114
Collier, V. 74, 75, 77, 78
Common Underlying Proficiency 57, 58
communication styles 109; high-context and low-context culture 108–109
communicative competence 92, 111
Communicative Language Teaching 92
comprehensible input and output 50–51, 89
conceptual flexibility 24
Connelly, F. M. 115
contact hypothesis 113–114
Content and Language Integrated Instruction (CLIL) **73**
conversational language features 58
cooperative learning 89, 91, 114
Corsi Block Test 23
Coulby, D. 3
Council of Europe 101, 102
creative construction process 51–53, 55
culture: high-context and low-context 108; language and 102–104; Nieto's definition of 102, 107; Walmart 102
Cummins, J. 57, 58, 72

Daily News 93, 95, 137–138
The Danger of a Single Story (Adichie) 115
Davenport University 71–72

Deardorff, D. K. 115, 119, 121
dialects 11, **12**; and language 11
Diamond, A. 20, 21, 23, 25
Díaz, V. 21, 22
Dimension Card Sort Task (DCCS) test 25
distributed knowledge 82
domain of acquisition 40, 42
dominant language **12**
donor language 36
dual-language education **73,** 77
Durrleman, S. 28

Earnest, D. R. 121
economic benefits 9, 14; employer preference 17–18; higher earning power 15–17; higher education 14–15
elite bilinguals 65
Ellis, R. 88, 89, 95
Emergent Bilinguals 11, **12**
English language development (ELD) **73**
English Learner 11, **12**
Enriched Executive Functions 66
error-analysis 52–53, **53**
Escobedo, L. E. 101
executive functions (EFs) 18, 20–21; age-related cognitive decline in 27–28; attentional control 21–23; autism mitigation 28–31; cognitive flexibility 24–27; cognitive reserve 27–28, 31; inhibitory control 21–22; working memory 22–24

false belief (FB) task 29, *30*
family bilingualism 70–71, 78, 103
Fan, S. P. 26
Fantini, A. E. 104, 110–113, 116, 124
Farrar, M. J. 21, 22
Fillmore, W. 62, 63
first language (L1) **12**; sequential bilinguals 54; well-developed 59; *see also* second language acquisition (SLA)
First National Bank of Dallas 16
fluency, cognitive flexibility 24–25
fluent bilinguals 11, **12, 15**
Fogle, L. W. 103
folk bilingualism 65
formal intercultural training programs 119–125; pros and cons of training tools 119–121, **120**; service-learning projects 123–125; study abroad/international education 121–123
Form-Focused Instruction 86, 87

Gándara, P. 16, 17
Gass, S. M. 67
Gibbons, P. 85
Global California 2030 Initiative 77
Golubeva, I. 105, 124
graphic organizer 93, 139
grassroots bilingualism 65
Grosjean, F. 34–35, 45

Hall, E. 108–109
Hardach, S. 15, 16
Hartanto, S. 25, 26
Hartshorne, J. K. 61
Havranek, E. 101
Hidalgo, N. 103
high-context culture 108–109
higher education, bilingualism and 14–15
Home–Expert Groups method 90, 91, 94, 140–141
home languages **12,** 46, 50, 59, 72, **73**; children's 49, 56; content learning in 75; proficiency 57
Hymes, D. 110

identity 65–66
immersion program **73**
inertial tendencies 25
informal intercultural communication experiences 113, 114
information gap 89
inhibitory control 21–22
Initiation–Response–Evaluation (IRE) sequences 88, 89
Instructed Second Language Acquisition (Instructed SLA) 80, 83, 85, 90, 92; interaction patterns 88; Meaning-Focused Instruction (MFI) 92; situational authenticity 95; Task-Based Learning (TBL) 89
Interactive Journal approach 83, 84, 142–143
Interconnected Underlying Multilingualism 58
intercultural citizenship 99, 101, 104; aspects of 124; civic engagement 124; components of 124; personal growth and 116; perspectives 105; self-reflection 124; in workplace 104–105
intercultural communication 99, 102, 106–107, 125; aspects of 107; community setting for 116; contemporary views of 108; dynamic and interactive approach 109; experiences with art and literature 115–117; informal 113; in workplace 108
intercultural communicative competence 109–112, 115; components and aspects of *112*; formal training programs 119–125; pros and cons of training tools 119, **120**; self-reflection 117–119, *118*
interculturalism 99
intergroup contact, experiences in 113–115
Irving, D. 16

Jackson, J. 107, 122, 123
Jamaican Patois 106
Jigsaw Approach 90, 91

Kellerman, P. 18
King, K. A. 103
Krashen, S. 50
Kuhl, P. K. 19
KWL Chart 94, 144–145

Lambert, C. 83
Lambert W. E. 24, 49
language acquisition process 45; second language acquisition (SLA) 50, 51, 61, 67, 79, 80, 83
language loss 14, 48; through subtractive bilingualism 48–49
language proficiency 11, **12,** 44, 55–60, *58*; academic achievement and 56; immigrant children 55
language variety **12**
learner-centered instruction and support 80–82, **81**
learner choice **81,** 82–84
Lee, W. W. L. 108
Limited English Proficient 11
linguistic profile *118*; self-reflection 117–119
loanwords 36–38
Lotan, R. 114
low-context culture 108–109

maintenance bilingual program 72, **73,** 74, 75
majority language 11, **12,** 45–46, 55; academic varieties of 57; high levels of proficiency 49, 56, 57; native-speakers 61
meaning before form **81,** 92–95
Meaning-Focused Instruction (MFI) 92–95

metalinguistic awareness 18–20
minority language 11, **12**, 45, 49, 55, 59, 74, 84; academic achievement patterns 76, *76*; challenge 75; with ethnic groups 46; optional learning environments (OLE) Project 79; proficiency 57
Modern Language Association 14
monolingual 11, **12**, 20, 29, 100
multilingual **13**
multilingual competence 3, 14, 66, 71, 78, 79
multilingual identity 66
multilingualism 3–4, **13**; across lifespan 61–62; active participation 88–91; authenticity 95–96; benefits of 4, 9; *vs.* bilingualism 10; comprehensible input and output 50–51; demographics 13–14; development 33; economic advantage of 14–18; individual characteristics 60; learner-centered instruction and support 80–82; learner choice 82–84; native-speaker 61; optimal conditions 80–97, **81, 97**; whole texts 85–88; workforce 100–102
multilingual repertoire 10, **12**, 38, 40, 41, 60, 79, 104

Nakamura, S. 83
Nasir, N. S. 65
National Curve Equivalent (NCE) system 76
native English-speaking 75–77
native speaker **13**, 50, 51; comprehensible input and output 89; in second language acquisition (SLA) 61
Nieto, S. 102, 107
non-native speaker **13**, 50
norming group for achievement tests **73**
Norton, B. 66

one-way bilingual program **73**, 76
optimal learning environment (OLE) Project 79; active participation 88–91; authenticity 95–96; conceptual framework 79; conditions 79–80, **81, 97**; learner-centered instruction and support 80–82; learner choice 82–84; pre-reading and pre-listening activities 80; whole texts 85–88
Ortega, L. 61, 62, 65, 104

Peace Corps 124
Peele-Eady, T. B. 24, 65

Peristeri, E. 28–29
personal growth 123; and intercultural citizenship 116
personality factors 62–64
Pettigrew, T. F. 113–114
Philp, J. 83
Pinker, S. 61
Poplack, S. 38
Porras, D. 17
primary language **13**
professional settings: active participation 91; authentic purpose 96; learner-centered instruction and support 82; learner choice 84; meaning before form 93–95; whole texts 87–88
Pull-out English as a Second Language (ESL) program **73**

Quick Writes 84, 87, 146–147

Raisz, A. 18
Ramirez, N. F. 19
RAND Corporation 16
recipient language 36, 38
Ruiz, N. T. 46, 70, 122–123
Rumbaut, R. 15, 16, 46, 49, 70

Saiz, A. 15
Sally–Anne Task 29
Santibáñez, L. 15
Schroeder, S. R. 28
Schumann, John 65
second language (L2) **12**; *see also* second language acquisition (SLA)
second language acquisition (SLA) 51, 67, 79; across lifespan 61–62; age factor 60–61; aptitude 64; grit and 63; identity matters 65–66; individual's personality 62; motivation and attitude in 64; native-speaker skills in 61; OLE Project (*see* optimal learning environment (OLE) Project); receiving input and producing output 50; third/fourth language after 66–67
self-reflection 117–119; Autobiography of Intercultural Encounters (AIE) 118–119; linguistic profile 117–119, *118*
self-regulatory behaviors 26
sequential bilinguals **13**, 43–45, 51, 54
service-learning projects 123–125
Shintani, S. 88, 89
Simon Says game 21

simultaneous bilinguals **13,** 43–45, 51, 60, 70
situational authenticity 95
social cohesion 105
Song, J. 103
spontaneous borrowing 36–37
subtractive bilingualism 65; language loss through 48–49
successive bilinguals *see* sequential bilinguals
Survey Text Method 82, 148–149
symbolic flexibility 24

Talburt, S. 122
target language **13,** 50, 52–53; grammatical features of 54
Task-Based Instruction 95
Task-Based Learning (TBL) 89
task-shifting 25
Tenebaum, J. 61
Theory of Mind 28–29
Think–Pair–Share approach 90, 93, 150–151
Thomas, Wayne 74, 75, 77, 78
Timm, L. 39
Toh, W. X. 25
Transitional Bilingual Education (TBE) program **73,** 77, *78*
Transnational Teacher Education program 122, 123
Tropp, L. R. 113, 114
T'Simpli, I. M. 28

Turbill, J. 79
Turn and Talk 90, 91
two-way bilingual program **73,** 76

US Department of Migrant Education 46
US Peace Corps 124

Valtierrez, M. 37
Vogelzang, M. 28

Wagner, M. 105, 119
Walmart culture 102
Waltermire, M. 37
Warren, M. 108
Weinreich, M. 11, 13
whole texts, OLE Project **81,** 85–88
Willingness to Communicate 63
Winawer, J. 104
working memory 22–24; verbal and nonverbal 23–24
workplace: intercultural citizen in 104–105; intercultural communication in 108; multilingualism 100–102
World Economic Forum 15
Writing Process approach 87, 96, 152–153
Wug Test 19

Yang, H. 25

Zapata-Barrero, R. 105
Zarate, M. E. 15
Zoido, E. 15

For Product Safety Concerns and Information please contact our EU
representative GPSR@taylorandfrancis.com
Taylor & Francis Verlag GmbH, Kaufingerstraße 24, 80331 München, Germany

www.ingramcontent.com/pod-product-compliance
Lightning Source LLC
Chambersburg PA
CBHW061716300426
44115CB00014B/2715